The Silver Book of
COCKTAILS

The Silver Book of
COCKTAILS

1,001 cocktails for every occasion

M^cRAE BOOKS

© 2007 McRae Books S.r.l.
Revised edition @ 2009 McRae Books S.r.l.
Via del Salviatino, 1 - 50016 Fiesole, (Florence), Italy
www.mcraebooks.com

Project Director Anne McRae
Art Director Marco Nardi
Photography Alan Benson
Introduction Mariarosa Schiaffino
Texts Carla Bardi, Lorenzo Bigongiaro
Food Styling Claire Pietersen

Project Editor Gabriella Greco
Layouts Los Tudio
Repro RAF

ISBN 978-88-6098-060-1

Printed in China

CONTENTS

1001 COCKTAILS

It has been claimed, clearly by someone more interested in drinking than the silver screen, that cocktails are the greatest contribution that America has made to world culture. Whether you agree with that or not, one thing is sure: the art of mixing alcoholic beverages to create new ones was invented and perfected in the United States, although many other countries, from Europe to the Caribbean, have also contributed to the evolution and spread of the cocktail. Americans have always traveled, both for business and pleasure, and wherever they went they brought their thirst and their passion with them. Hemingway's name will be forever linked with the Ritz Bar in Paris and Harry's Bar in Venice, just as F. Scott Fitzgerald's is linked to the bars and nightclubs of the French Riviera.

In 1943, at the Teheran summit, President Roosevelt prepared a Martini for Stalin. «Not bad» said the Soviet leader, «although it rather chills the stomach». His successor, Nikita Khrushchev, having drunk a fairly strong cocktail, declared it to be «the United States' deadliest weapon». Folklore perhaps, associated with historic meetings, but these quips have stayed on record. It is strange that these drinkers, perhaps more used to that quintessentially Russian drink—vodka (which certainly doesn't muck about when it comes to alcohol content)—should be so struck by the cocktail. But then it is in the mixing that the full effects, pleasures, and possibilities of alcohol are fully revealed. The slender martini glass or the solid collins hold more than just spirits, flavors, aromas, light, and color; they embrace the essence a way of life, made up of balance, harmony, elegance, imagination, as well as history, literature, fashion, and custom.

ART, KNOW HOW, AND SKILL: PREPARING THE PERFECT COCKTAIL

Making the perfect cocktail is not as straightforward as it may seem, which is why we talk of the "art" of cocktail making. According to a few purists, the job should be left entirely to the professionals. And, in truth, the skills and feats of top barmen and women—the ones who work at places like the Palace Bar in Saint Moritz or Raffles in Singapore—are beyond the reach of most normal mortals like ourselves. However, this doesn't mean that those who enjoy mixing drinks should deny themselves the pleasure of trying their hand: the difficulties should urge us on so that our successes are even more rewarding. Cocktail-making is a fascinating subject because it requires both respect for the rules and creativity. With perseverance, attention to detail, and the honest desire to learn, you will obtain some great results and also have a lot of fun, both in the learning and by entertaining friends and family with your experiments.

A word of advice: before setting out to make original drinks and trying daring combinations, it is a good idea to follow a few basic recipes and learn by heart some of the classics that have been developed by international experts. To establish some method in a subject area that lends itself to interpretation and personal variations (often to disastrous effect, as the many improbable "house cocktails" in some bars show), many years ago the International Bartenders Association (IBA) established and certified first 50,

and then 60 cocktails, that have since become standard the world over. This means that these 60 drinks are made in exactly the same way, from Chicago and London to Rome, Hong Kong, and Sydney. If you order «A Negroni, please» you can be sure that you will get red vermouth, gin, and Campari in the prescribed doses, finished with a slice of orange. Of course, this depends on how good your barman is and whether he knows and follows the standard recipes. Unfortunately, this is not always the case and it takes very little to transform a splendid Negroni, Martini, or Manhattan into a tasteless or even undrinkable concoction.

THE COCKTAIL IS BORN:
A LITTLE BIT OF HISTORY

The origins of the art of mixing different more or less alcoholic beverages are lost in time, although they were probably linked to the need to conserve liquids and also to improve the flavor of those that had gone off. But the distant past is of little interest because the cocktail is a modern invention. What's more, despite the name, cocktails have nothing to do with roosters or their tails. No one knows exactly where or when the first cocktail was poured, although there are dozens of theories and legends. Long before the great flood of August 2005, the city fathers of New Orleans had already torn down one of the most commonly cited cradles of the cocktail. A humble 19th-century house at 437 Royal Street bore a simple sign that read «*The cocktail is born.*» According to legend, at the beginning of the 19th century, a refugee from Santo Domingo named Antoine Amédée Peychaud, opened a chemist shop here where his friends and countrymen liked to gather. Peychaud began to offer his guests Dominican drinks, based on a herbal liqueur made from various herbs, sugar, and aromas.

He used a special measuring device, known in French as a *coquetier*. His English-speaking customers came to call it a *cocktei*, which gradually became the English word cocktail.

But other places in New Orleans also lay claim to having invented both the word and the drink, such as the barber's shop that was once the bar of an importer of Sazerac cognac. Here, a drink made by mixing absinthe, cognac, sugar, and lemon peel became very popular. As time went by, the French cognac was replaced by rye whisky, making the cocktail a more American drink.

There are so many stories about the origins of the cocktail and we could go on, and on! Let's just finish with one particularly imaginative story that is said to date from the American Revolution at the end of the 18th century when the original Thirteen Colonies were fighting for independence from their English overlords. According to this story, a buxom landlady called Betsy Foloyagan decorated the glasses of the American army leaders with the feathers of a cockerel during a celebratory lunch.

The golden age of the cocktail

The basic mixed drinks made at the end of the 19th century and beginning of the 20th century were gradually refined by practice and technique into standardized recipes. And the cocktail spread, reaching its zenith in the 1920s, the age of jazz, when it entered into every aspect of American life, from the crime pages to high society events, to literature, advertising, the visual arts, music and, above all, the movies. The cocktail became a part of the American way of life and a part of its legend, with its beautiful and damned heroes and heroines, and their adventurous lives, and its nightspots and bars glittering with bottles, ice, and plunging necklines. Humphrey Bogart and Clark Gable

17

M. Friedlander, a cafè in the 1920s, in Berlin.

were the most handsome of the movie star drinkers, while Walter Pidgeon, in a series of wildly popular films, was the most elegant, and the detective Philip Marlowe, the most fascinating in a series of whodunnits and society films. The cocktail also figured largely in the novels of the time, where they flowed in river-like quantities, and famous American writers such as Hemingway and Fitzgerald became known for their drinking habits as well as their literature. And then came Prohibition: from 1920 to 1933 Americans were forced to drink furtively, out of the public eye. They invented every kind of trick to evade the ban, as many

Clark Gable and Bette Davies in *After Office Hours*, 1935

Opposite:
Douglas Fairbanks Jr. and Rita Hayworth in *Angels over Broadway*, 1940

movies have shown. People drank in hotel rooms, in private homes, and in clandestine bars known as speakeasies. Long Island Iced Tea was a famous cocktail from this era: its innocent-sounding name and the mug in which it was served were both meant to camouflage the alcoholic mixture from the police when the raided the speakeasies. The resulting publicity gave an enormous boost to the popularity of spirits and cocktails that carried over into the time after Prohibition ended and was made official when the newly elected President Roosevelt prepared a Martini dry in the White House, which became known as the Martini FDR.

The 21st century: new cocktails and trends

After the Second World War, American sailors and marines brought home fruit and nut-flavored cocktails from the South Pacific, but it wasn't until the 1970s that tequila and piña colada became widespread, entering into the world of cocktails and long drinks with a certain clamor.

More recently, after a time when cocktails ceded a lot of ground to the growing popularity of wine, especially champagne, and spirits were regarded with suspicion by health and fitness fanatics, there has been a resurgence of interest in mixing drinks (with and without alcohol), governed by moderation and a measure of freedom unknown in earlier times. Fruit juice and fresh fruit are common ingredients in many modern cocktails. The Martini, the most classic of all the cocktails (gin with a splash of vermouth), invented around 1910, has spearheaded a revival which has given it more than 100 variations, almost all of which make it less potent and sweeter, giving rise to the so-called Neo-Martinis. If Vodka Martini, which substituted gin with vodka, was the preferred drink of the great cocktail expert James Bond, many other variations with fruit, anise, rum, and every type of flavored vodka have found favor with modern drinkers. The purists, of course, are not convinced, and the classic mix of gin and vermouth with an olive in an iced glass remains the height of fashion. Perhaps the most difficult thing nowadays is to find someone who really knows how to make a perfect Martini.

Speaking of Martinis, it is interesting to note that this legendary name, the best known in the world of cocktails, probably derives from a Mr. Martini, from Arma di Taggia in Liguria, Italy, who, emigrating to the United States, became head barman at the famous Knickerbocker Club in New York. This was in the fabulous first decade of the 20th century, when clients included bankers, actors, and VIPs of every

sort, who spread the word of the Italian barman's ability, especially with gin and vermouth. According to another urban legend, the Martini was invented by a certain señor Martinez, who worked in a bar in Boston at the end of the 19th century. Whatever the case, the legendary cocktail seems to have Latin blood in its veins. Or perhaps it has something to do with the famous brand of vermouth and other Martini & Rossi bitters, invented in Turin in 1860 and linked to the history of vermouth?

One thing is certain: Martini & Rossi, founded by Alessandro Martini and Teofilo Sala, later joined by Luigi Rossi, was exporting its products to the United States long before the Martini was invented. The name undoubtedly helped spread the cocktail's fame. Even today, vermouth and Martini are virtually synonymous and Martini (& Rossi) continue to sell their product well the world over.

A COOL PLEASURE

But what exactly is a cocktail? The fine art of mixing drinks consists in the search for and the development of perfect balance even among an array of quite diverse ingredients. With the exception of non-alcoholic drinks, usually referred to as mocktails (an appropriate name that indicates the nature of their relationship with a true cocktail), the basis of a cocktail is usually a robust spirit—whisky, gin, vodka, rum, tequila, cognac—which normally makes up at least fifty percent of the entire volume. Complementary flavors, such as vermouth or bitters, are then added which make the drink sweeter, sourer, spicier, more aromatic, or whatever else is desired according to personal taste and when the drink will be served. These ingredients are then shaken or mixed with ice using a shaker, mixing glass, or blender, depending on the drink. Cocktails are almost always served cold, and on some rare occasions hot; but never tepid or warm. When should you serve a cocktail? The ideal time is the hour before a meal, usually before dinner in the evening. A pre-dinner cocktail should not only be pleasant to drink but should also stimulate the appetite. There are also cocktails that can be served after dinner, and they should help digestion (although not everyone would agree that this is the effect they have). Mocktails can be served any time, and they are a perfect way to cool down on long hot summer afternoons at the beach, on the tennis court, or anywhere else for that matter.

SHORT AND LONG DRINKS

We normally distinguish between real cocktails, or short drinks, and the more thirst-quenching long drinks. The former, with about 2–4 fluid ounces (60–120 ml) of liquid in all, require perfect harmony

and balance, like a mathematical equation. As the actor Lionel Barrymore used to say with a malicious smile at cocktail time «I'm off to see my maths teacher». And he stood next to his barman, admiring every move, as he shook, mixed, and served with a flourish.

Long drinks are usually less strong drinks and are less rigorous in their doses and more open to experiment and fantasy in the making. Nowadays the distinction between short and long drinks is less rigid than it was since the tendency is almost always to lengthen with water, soda, fruit juices, or other liquids.

Even the various types of cocktails, usually grouped on the basis of the main ingredient (normally a spirit), have been simplified and drinks are often now classified according to other criteria, such as when they can be served. There are many different types, and we're not even sure that most barmen would know them all.

Here are the most common ones:

• cobbler	• daisy	• grog	• rickey
• collins	• eggnog	• highball	• shrub
• cooler	• fix	• julep	• smash
• cup	• fizz	• mull	• sour
• crusta	• flip	• punch	

In this book we have divided cocktails into chapters according to the best time to serve them: so we have Apéritifs, Long drinks, Classics, Frozen cocktails, Special occasion cocktails, Punches, Shooters, After dinner cocktails, and Mocktails.

EQUIPMENT FOR THE HOME BAR

Here is a list of basic tools for simple and successful cocktail making. Don't skimp on this equipment as it will serve you well over a long period of time:

- barspoon or mixing spoon: a long-handled spoon for mixing drinks in tall glasses or in a mixing glass
- blender
- can and bottle openers
- citrus reamers and juice squeezers (electric or manual)
- corkscrew and/or corkpuller
- glassware: you will need at least two different types. Classic martini or cocktail glasses are a must. You will also need at least one tumbler-shaped glass, such as an old-fashioned or the taller highball or collins glasses.
- ice bucket and tongs and an ice scoop
- ice crusher
- knives: two or three different types, including a sharp paring knife and a serrated knife (for slicing fruit)
- measuring spoons
- mixing glass: should hold at least 16 oz (500 ml)
- pitchers (jugs) in glass or crystal
- shaker
- strainer
- wooden muddler: for muddling citrus fruit

Optional extras:

- coasters
- champagne and other stoppers to conserve drinks in the bottle
- napkins
- picks (for garnishes)
- towels
- trays
- small glass or crystal bowls for serving snacks
- straws: straight and bent
- swizzle sticks
- wine cork retrievers

TOOLS OF THE TRADE

Good tools are essential for good results, so stock up on high quality equipment.

Shakers

The shaker is an essential and almost symbolic tool of the trade; we have all seen showman bartenders shaking them with both arms raised above their heads in a spectacular sound and motion show that ends with an elegant pouring of the drink into the waiting glasses. By definition, the shaker is meant to mix different ingredients; but not all cocktails require shaking, only the ones where the ingredients are hard to combine because of differences in density and alcohol content. There are two basic styles of shaker. The first is a standard "cocktail" shaker made up of a container, a lid with a built-in strainer, and a cap for the lid. The second—and in our opinion, the best—type is the Boston shaker, which has two cone-shaped components that fit together end to end. The lower part is filled with ice while the various liquids and other ingredients go in the top that has a filter and a cap which, during vigorous shaking enables the ingredients to mix thoroughly and emulsify. Never fill the shaker more than three-quarters full with ice to leave enough space for mixing.

When using a shaker the ingredients should be added in the following order (unless otherwise specified in the recipe): first the ice, then the denser ingredients such as syrups and cordials, followed by the alcoholic substances, and finally the fruit juices. Shake the drink vigorously, but not for more than 6–8 seconds, then pour it straight into the glasses (which should already be set out and waiting). If mixing more than one drink at a time, fill the glasses half full then top up with the remaining drink so that they are

more or less even. All this should be done quickly, without missing a beat. This may be a little difficult at first, but practice makes perfect. One final tip: never put champagne or sparkling wine in a shaker.

Mixing glasses

When ingredients are easy to combine, cocktails can be prepared in a mixing glass. The cocktail will stay clear and not turn cloudy or opaque as it will after being shaken. Mixing glasses are large and often have a built-in beak, or spout, to make pouring easier.

The liquids are mixed using a long barspoon or mixing spoon, some of which have a special tip that can be used to crush the ice. Mixing glasses are used together with stainless steel strainers that fit over the glass to filter the drink from the ice and other ingredients.

When preparing large quantities, for example when making a champagne cocktail for several guests, you may prefer to use a large glass or crystal bowl or a stout pitcher (jug) which, filled with ice and the ingredients for the drink, can be held from below and swished rapidly to mix. This will cool the drink without making it cloudy.

Jiggers

Precise measurements are required when making cocktails and you should always use the exact amounts given in the recipes. An experienced barman can often get by without a jigger or measuring device, his or her trained eye and hand instantly recognizing the right dosage. But as an apprentice barman it is wise to start out using a jigger and measuring spoons and cups. Jiggers are small metal devices that come in all sizes. The most common type is a double-ended jigger, with a 1-ounce (30-ml) measure on one end and a $1\frac{1}{2}$-ounce (45 ml) measure on the other. Measuring spoons are important because many drinks call for $\frac{1}{2}$ ounce (15 ml) or even smaller

amounts of an ingredient. A normal set of nested measuring spoons ranges from $1/8$ teaspoon to 1 tablespoon (which is equal to $1/2$ ounce or 15 ml).

Ice tips

Fresh, clean ice is an essential ingredient in almost every cocktail and you will need plenty of it. As American food scientist Charkles A. Becker put it «a tepid drink makes a guest tepid» whereas the bracing chill of ice in a strong drink heats up the mood and the party.

32

Ice made at home in a domestic freezer is not always suitable for cocktails. Sometimes the water used to make it is heavily chlorinated or otherwise "off" in flavor and this spoils the flavor of the drink. Taste homemade ice first before putting it in your drink; even if you made it using fresh, clean water the ice may still have absorbed the flavors of other foods in the freezer. The other problem with ice made in domestic freezers is that it is often cloudy and unattractive and it melts very quickly, making cocktails watery. Crystal clear ice blocks, as hard as diamonds, can be made in an ice-maker or bought at your local supermarket.

Ice is usually made or bought in the form of ice cubes. To turn ice cubes into crushed ice for frozen cocktails you may want to buy a special ice crusher. Manual or electric, these machines are handy and not very expensive. If you don't have an ice crusher, just place the ice cubes in a heavy-duty plastic bag, close it, and whack it with a mallet or rolling pin. Don't try to chop ice in a blender or food processor unless you have the appropriate blade; chopping ice cubes without it may ruin your machine. Remember that crushed ice melts faster than ice cubes and should be kept in a plastic bag in the freezer until just before you use it.

If you have a good freezer or ice maker at home you may like to prepare flavored ice cubes. The flavor you use will depend on the drink you intend to add them to: freeze tomato juice for addition to Bloody Marys, orange, lemon, or lime juice (dilute lemon and lime juice with fifty percent water) for long drinks, and coffee cubes for iced coffee drinks. Don't try to make booze cubes by freezing rum, tequila, whisky, etc. because it can't be done. Alcohol freezes at a much lower temperature than water and won't turn solid in your freezer. For party ice cubes, you may like to add well-washed small or diced fruit or edible flowers to the ice cube tray or freeze whole pieces of fruit in larger containers that can be placed in punch bowls.

Ice buckets and tongs

To have really cold ice always on hand in your home bar it may pay to invest in a small thermic ice container so that ice can be kept on the bar without it becoming watery. Watery ice will spoil a drink by making it too weak. A pair of ice tongs are a must for moving ice cubes around (hands are not allowed!). You may also want to invest in a good ice bucket for keeping wines and champagne cool in the bar or at the table. Ice buckets should be half filled with cold water and ice.

Pitcher (Jug)

Hurricane glass

Old-fashioned or rocks glass

A cocktail, by definition, is served in a classic cocktail or martini glass. But there are many different types of cocktails and each one is best served in the right glass. There are also many different types of glasses, some of which have been made especially for a certain type of wine or other alcoholic drink. Other glasses are more generic and can be used interchangeably.

Collins glass

Highball glass

Shot glass

Heatproof glass mug

Champagne flute

Martini or cocktail glass

Invest in some high-quality glassware for your bar. Sparkling crystal looks superb, but good quality glass can be just as good. Glasses should be transparent, without any decoration, and not too heavily ornamented, as this will draw attention away from the drink in the glass which should always be the main attraction.

Wine glass or goblet

Margarita glass

Punch bowl

Martini or cocktail glass: this is the most common and easily recognizable glass and it takes its name from the most classic cocktail of them all. Triangular in shape, there are two sizes: small-medium for a classic Martini Dry and a slightly larger one that can hold longer apéritifs.

Wine glass or goblet: a classic white wine glass can be used on many occasions. A goblet is usually a little larger, with a rounder cup.

Collins: the tallest of the glasses, a collins is used to serve long drinks that are often topped up with water, soda, tonic, or fruit juices.

Champagne flute: a tall slender glass for serving champagne and other sparkling wines to best advantage. The top is often a little wider than the base. Perfect for champagne or other bubbly cocktails.

Heatproof glass mug: designed for hot drinks such as grog or after dinner cocktails with milk, cream, and liqueurs. These mugs come in a range of sizes and often have a metal handle to protect your hands from the heat of the drink.

Highball: a tall tumbler-shaped glass, perfect for long drinks and juices.

Hurricane: a highly recognizable balloon shape. It is most often used for frozen and blended cocktails.

Margarita: with its large cup, much narrower at the base, this is another easily recognizable glass. It is sometimes known as a Marie Antoinette.

Old-fashioned: this medium-sized tumbler is also known as a rocks glass. Round and with a solid base, it is used for many drinks that are prepared directly in the glass, or for drinks that are served on the rocks (with ice cubes).

Punch bowl: these bowls come in many different sizes. They are perfect for parties where large quanities of drink can be made available to guests all at once. Some crystal punch bowls are very attractive.

Shot: a small glass that comes in many different shapes, it is used to serve small amounts of usually quite alcoholic drink. It is often also used as a measuring tool. Sometimes banged down on the bar or table to mix the drink before drinking it down in one gulp.

Brandy or cognac snifter: short stemmed with a large bowl that is made to be cupped in the hand to warm the brandy or cognac inside.

BOTTLES AND MORE

Clearly, the larger the number of wines, spirits, liqueurs, cordials, and so on in your bar, the larger the range of drinks you will be able to make. But, to get started, you won't need absolutely everything. Here is a basic list of spirits, liqueurs, and other beverages that will suffice to serve elegant and suitable drinks to guests on almost every occasion. As you will see in the pages that follow, some spirits and liqueurs are used often and must be present in every home bar.

Distilled from wine: Cognac, Armagnac, brandy, metaxa
Distilled from residue of the wine press: grappa, marc
Distilled from cereals (grain, rye, corn, oats, barley): whisky, whiskey, bourbon, vodka
Distilled from fruit or plants: gin, kirsch, calvados, midori, cachaça, tequila, mezcal, rum
Bitters: Fernet Branca, Campari, orange bitters, Unicum, Jägermeister
Champagne, sparkling, and prosecco wines: brut, extra-brut
Vermouth: white, red, dry, sweet
Sweet and fortified wines: port, sherry, madeira, Marsala
Liqueurs: amaretto, cherry brandy, Bailey's, Bénédectine, Cointreau, curaçao, Drambuie, crème de menthe, Galliano, Grand Marnier, mandarinetto, Maraschino, triple sec, Southern Comfort, anisette, Sambuca
Syrups: mint, amarene, raspberry
Sugar syrup
Juices: pineapple, orange, grapefruit, tomato
Grenadine (syrup made from pomegranates)
Soda water, Tonic water, White soda, Cola
Angostura: strong bitters made in Trinidad
Sweet-and-sour mix: syrup made from lemon juice and sugar
Worcestershire sauce
Fruit: lemons, limes, orange, grapefruit, olives, etc.

GARNISHES

A Martini without a green olive is not a Martini, just as the slice of orange must be included in a Negroni, and a cherry in a Manhattan—these are fundamental ingredients in each recipe. In other cocktails, the addition of a bunch of red currants, a wedge of lime or pineapple, a piece of lemon peel, a slice of peach, or a strawberry, raspberry, or grape on the rim of the glass are optional garnishes that do as much to please the eye as they do the palate. Some "purists" see garnishes as something to be strictly avoided. We suggest you follow your own tastes.

Long drinks can be made particularly attractive with the addition of a garnish or two. Colorful and often fruit-based, they can be finished with whole pieces of fresh fruit, such as a strawberry or cherry, or slices, wedges, or cubes of fruit cut to fit the glass, and by mint leaves and other herbs. Together with colored straws and cocktail umbrellas, these extras can make a simple cocktail seem right for a Hollywood pool party or a private beach in the Caribbean. A word of advice: less is usually better when it comes to garnishing a cocktail; choose just a very few elements of the highest quality. Fruit should not be overripe and should always be thoroughly rinsed, especially if it is not peeled.

Bent straws are perfect for long drinks with a lot of ice as they help to drink the drink. If liked, add little paper umbrellas, flags, and dolls, but—be warned—not everyone likes their drink laden with non-essentials.

Use sharp little knifes for cutting fruit into decorative star, moon, or fan shapes. A simple potato peeler is also useful for preparing strips of carrot, zucchini (courgettes), and celery, while a citrus peeler can be used to make perfect orange, lemon, or lime spirals. A small grater is useful for spices, such as nutmeg (which are so much tastier when grated fresh).

SNACKS

What nibbles should you offer with a cocktail? Olives—green and black, with or without the pit (stone), and stuffed, are absolute classics. Almonds, hazelnuts, peanuts, and pistachios, each in their own little bowl go beautifully with all kinds of cocktail. Salty or vinegary snacks are also good with drinks, so try pickles, such as gherkins and onions. Vegetables also make good—and healthy—cocktail snacks. Try carrot sticks, celery stalks, radishes, and slices of bell peppers (capsicums) or fennel. Always prepare vegetables shortly before serving and keep them in very cold water until just before serving. Potato chips, French fries, mini-pizzas, savory muffins, crackers, and cookies are other popular choices.

If you have time, prepare tiny toasted sandwiches, crostini, puff pastry savories, cheese straws, fried onion rings, savory pies, and a range of other delicious finger and party food. A really rich buffet offering can often take the place of dinner. If you are serving dinner to your guests straight afterward, just prepare small quantities of something really delicious so as not to spoil their appetites. Remember too, that the cocktails should always be the stars of the show, and they shouldn't be upstaged by food.

COCKTAIL PARTIES

Cocktail parties are an ideal way to entertain a lot of guests with a minimum of fuss, even in small, big city apartments. They normally start around 7 o'clock and last for about an hour or so. Guests mill happily around, drinks in hand, chatting to friends and networking, while snacking on tasty nibbles generally laid out on a buffet table or proffered by waiters with

trays. Despite the name, you often won't find a cocktail served at one of these parties and this is a mistake: be sure to serve at least one type of champagne cocktail or Bellini (an Italian apéritif based on sparkling prosecco wine and peach juice invented at Harry's Bar in Venice), along with dry white wine, fruit juices, and lots of iced mineral water. If you don't have a professional bar and a squadron of barmen it is difficult to serve a good cocktail at a cocktail party. Long drinks are usually the best choice since they can take more ice and last longer. If some guests ask for a Martini or a gin tonic the best thing is to leave the ingredients and equipment out so that they can prepare it for themselves.

For a touch of class, hire a barman and a waiter or two to do these jobs for you. This will leave you free to mingle with your guests without the worry of preparing and pouring drinks.

What food should you serve? Any of the snacks and finger food listed on the previous page are ideal for cocktail parties. You may also want to offer more substantial fare, including seafood cocktails and salads, sliced cold meats, and grilled or baked fish and vegetables. The important thing is to serve them in mini-portions in such a way that no knife is required and they can safely be eaten while standing up with a drink in hand. Most of the buffet will be made up of cold food; add a dish or two of hot offerings for variety. There should also be a part of the buffet devoted to cakes, cookies, and desserts which should be accompanied by dessert wines or bubblies, such as Asti Spumante or Moscato dolce.

How much wine and spirits should you allow for each guest? This is always difficult, but remember that it is always better to have something left over than to run out of supplies during the party.

TOASTS

Cheers, prosit, cin cin, skhol, à la santé... every country has its own special way of wishing themselves and each other good fortune, happiness, or efficient digestion as the case may be, when they raise their glasses in a toast. It is a very ancient gesture that highlights the happy occasion when people gather to celebrate a special person or event. A toast is often accompanied by a brief speech by the party-giver or a guest, although not always. Wine, champagne, and spirits are all suitable for a toast, although the sparkling bubbles of a good champagne are perhaps the best choice. On more intimate occasions, cocktails can also symbolize friendship, love, or the pleasure of being together. Alcohol is an excellent social glue, encouraging people to loosen up and become more outgoing. As David E. Embury, author of The Fine Art of Mixing Drinks (one of the best cocktail books ever written) put it: «This nectar overcomes reserve and shyness, relaxes the nerves, loosens tongues, and allows friendships to reveal their stronger sides».

51

HANGOVERS

One cocktail tends to encourage the next. Fresh and fragrant, colorful and full of spirit... it can be difficult to stop before the euphoria turns to headache and nausea, upset stomach, and all the other unpleasant symptoms of a hangover. Everyone has their own level of resistance to alcohol. For every drinker who can go ahead for hours with no apparent ill effect, there are others who after just one or two drinks begin to feel physically and mentally unstable. According to some barmen, the Negroni is the wickedest drink, sneaking up unawares on even the most experienced of drinkers. While a cocktail or two won't hurt anybody, you can

generally tell when its time to stop. Even so, sometimes things do get out of hand and we wake up next morning with a terrible hangover. Kingsley Amis gives us one of the best descriptions of a hangover in *Lucky Jim:* «Consciousness was upon him before he could get out of the way.... The light did him harm, but not as much as looking at things did; he resolved, having done it once, never to move his eyeballs again. A dusty thudding in his head made the scene before him beat like a pulse. His mouth had been used as a latrine by some small creature of the night, and then as its mausoleum. During the night, too, he'd somehow been on a cross-country run and then had been expertly beaten up by the secret police. He felt bad.»

What can you do about a hangover? Not a lot really, except wait it out. Drink plenty of fluids, get as much rest as possible, as well as a little light exercise (if you can move!), and wait for it to pass.

But then how many movies have we seen where the hero, forced by circumstances beyond his control, needs to be back on his feet after a night on the town? He usually gets thrown under a cold shower and then and then forced to ingest some weird mixture that is supposed to be the antidote to over indulgence. The experts—those among us who regularly face similar situations—suggest a drastic cure: a strong alcoholic drink, also known as "hair of the dog." If you can face it, try it!

These medicinal drinks are sometimes called "pick me ups" or "picker uppers" since this is what they are supposed to do. Even the ancient Greeks and Romans knew about them as the Latin author Petronius showed in his famous description of Trimalcione's dinner in the *Satyricon*.

53

The Bloody Mary is a cocktail that is especially recommended on these occasions: place a generous amount of vodka in a collins glass and top up with cold tomato juice, a teaspoon of lemon juice, salt, pepper, Tabasco, and Worcestershire sauce. Take a deep breath and then quaff it down. If it stays down, it will help! Morning Glory Fizz is another, ironically-named, cure: place a generous amount of Scotch whisky in a collins glass. Add a few drops of absinthe (optional), a teaspoon of lemon juice and another of sugar, a dash of Angostura, and an egg white. Add ice cubes and top up with soda water. Stir and drink.

Ernest Hemingway also had a favorite hangover cure. When the writer, Carlos Baker, went to stay with him at Key West in Florida, they ate and drank a little too much. The next morning Baker was unwell. To get him back on his geet, Hemingway filled a large glass with crushed ice, added a dash of Angostura bitters, some lime juice, and then topped it up with Dutch gin. This gin has a strong aromatic flavor and is not usually recommended for cocktails, but in this case it was perfect. It worked.

THE MAIN INGREDIENTS

Spirits, liqueurs, wines, vermouths, and so on, each have their own diverse origins, history, and character, just as the cocktails they make also take on their own distinct personalities. These spirits and liqueurs are an essential part of every home bar, and should be chosen on the basis of quality, even if—according to the experts—mixed drinks can sometimes be made using products that are not right at the top of their range; champagne for example, and also whisky and gin. Choose medium to fine quality brands.

Whisky, whiskey & co.

There are many different types of whisky. Scotland, Canada, the United States, and Ireland are the main whisky producers, although other countries also make some fine whiskies. Whisky is distilled from barley, rye, oats, wheat, and corn. Although traditionally associated with Scotland, the earliest known whiskies appear to have been made in Ireland where they are recorded from the 15th century onward. Nowadays there are two main types of whisky: single malt and blended.

Single malt Scotch whisky is made by steeping malted barley grains in spring water and then allowing the grains to germinate. When the grains have sprouted they are dried in a kiln, then ground and infused in hot water. Yeast is added to the infused liquid which is then distilled at least twice before being left to mature in oak barrels for a minimum of three years. Some single malt whiskies are also produced in Ireland.

Blended whiskies are made from various combinations of different grains which are carefully selected by the whisky-maker to produce flavorful, balanced, smooth, and harmonious drinks that can be easily duplicated for large-scale production. Bourbon

is a blended whisky originally produced in Bourbon County, Kentucky. Made with at least 51 percent corn, it is aged in oak barrels for a minimum of two years. Rye whisky, another popular American whisky, is made from rye mash. Canadian whiskies are usually made from a blend of rye and other whiskies.

Gin

Clear and innocent-looking, gin is a spirit that was originally made in Holland, although it became especially popular in England where it was produced in huge quantities in the 18th and 19th centuries. Gin is made from a neutral grain spirit that is then flavored, traditionally with juniper berries, but nowadays with a range of herbs, spices, and fruits. The earliest Dutch gins were full and aromatic, but the later London gins were dry, strong, and blander in flavor. This makes them ideal ingredients in a range of classic cocktails and long drinks, including Gin Fizz (see page 294), Gin and Tonic (see page 290) and Collins. The Martini is the classic gin cocktail and theories abound as to the correct mix of gin and vermouth. Churchill was famous for his love of very dry Martinis, so much so that he was said to just "show" the shaker a vermouth bottle rather than actually adding any to the drink. In reality, he probably did what many barmen do, which is to briefly shake the ice with vermouth and then tip it out before adding the gin to the vermouth-flavored ice cubes. Hemingway is said to have preferred a 15 to 1 formula, instead of the classic 8 parts gin to 2 parts of vermouth.

Rum and cachaça

Made from a base of cane sugar and melasses, a by-product of the sugar-making process, rum is now the biggest-selling spirit in the world. Caribbean pirates were famous for drinking it in large quantities, along with the Dutch of the West India Company who then

took it to Southeast Asia, producing large quantities in Java. Originally from Jamaica, rum is now made in many Caribbean countries, including Cuba, Haiti, Puerto Rico, and Barbados. Refined, delicate Cuban rum is one of the best. Jamaican rum is strong and pungent and is aged for at least five years. Rum made in Haiti is full and velvety and is aged for many years. There are three types of rum: white rum, which is dry and well suited to mixed drinks; gold rum, which is smooth and potent; and dark rum, which is heavier and spiced. Rum can be served neat or added to hot drinks such as grog. It is also the basis of many classic cocktails, such as the Daiquiri (see page 300), and some of the more exotic long drinks, such as Piña Colada (with coconut and pineapple) and the famous Cuba Libre (see page 304).

Cachaça is very similar to rum and is made in Brazil from a mix of cane juice and corn distillate. It is the basic ingredient in the very popular Caipiriña (see page 288), along with fresh lime and crushed ice.

Vodka

Vodka takes its name from the Russian word for "little water" and it probably originated in Russia, although the Poles also claim to have invented it. Today vodka is produced in many countries, especially in northern and eastern Europe, but is also made in the United States and Canada where it has become increasingly popular in recent years. Vodka is distilled from cereals, such as barley, wheat, and rye, and also from sugar beets. Usually crystal clear, the best vodkas have a distinctive flavor and are not more than 40° proof. Vodka is never aged and is famous for not leaving any odor on the breath, even when imbibed in large quantities. There are many different types of vodka, many of which are flavored with fruits, herbs, berries. Traditionally drunk ice cold and neat in special small glasses—often with

ABSOLU
VODK

ABSOLU
CITRO

wódka

0% vol.

IMPORTE

caviar as a nibble—it has come into its own in the world of mixed drinks. It is a vital ingredient in many cocktails, such as the Vodka Martini (see page 332), where it substitutes the gin, and in the Caipiroska, which is a Caipiriña with the Brazilian cachaça replaced by vodka.

Cognac and brandy

Cognac is a type of brandy and, like all brandies, it is distilled from wine. Cognac is made only in France, in the southwestern Charente region, which surrounds the city of Cognac. It is aged for at least three years and is generally classified as VS (Very Special), VSOP (Very Special Old Pale), and XO (Extra Old). Armagnac is another fine French brandy, made in the Gascony region. Calvados is an apple brandy made in Normandy, in northern France. Many other brandies are produced both in France and around the world. Spain, Italy, Germany, Cyprus, Mexico, and Chile are all major producers of good brandies. Brandy can be served neat in the traditional balloon-shaped snifter, and is also an excellent base for a range of cocktails. Sidecar (see page 302), French Connection (see page 494), and Brandy Alexander (see page 278), are three classic brandy-based cocktails.

Grappa, Marc, and Bagaceira

These are all pomace brandies. Pomace is the mixture of seeds, stalks, and skins that is left behind when winemakers press grapes. Grappa is made in Italy, Marc in France, and Bagaceira in Portugal. There are many different types and a wide range of flavors. These brandies are usually colorless and can be drunk neat or added to mixed drinks.

Tequila

This Mexican spirit is distilled from the heart of the blue algave fruit. It is related to an undistilled drink called

pulque, which is thought to date from the time of the Aztecs. Mexicans drink tequila neat and at room temperature, with just the addition of a slice of lemon and a little salt. The elegant and popular Margarita (see page 144) cocktail is based on tequila, with the addition of Cointreau and lime. The salt used to frost the rim of the glass recalls the traditional way to drink tequila.

Champagne and sparkling wines

Champagne is probably the most famous wine in the world. It is made from Chardonnay, Pinot Meunier, and Pinot Noir grapes, only in the region of the same name in northern France. It is made according to the classic *méthode champenoise*, which requires an extended fermentation time and the mechanical or manual turning of the bottles. Champagnes with no sugar added are labeled *Ultra Brut*, *Extra Brut*, *Brut Zero*, or *Brut Sauvage* and are very dry. *Brut* and *Extra-Sec* are slightly less dry, while *Sec* is medium-dry, *Demi-Sec*, sweet, and *Doux*, very sweet. Other sparkling wines are made in many different parts of the world, most notably in France, Italy, Spain, California, Australia, South Africa, and New Zealand. Some famous bubblies include the Asti and Prosecco wines of Italy, the various crémants made in France and elsewhere, Cava from Spain, and Cap Classique of South Africa, to name a few. There are many cocktails based on champagne and other fizzies. Light and refreshing, these cocktails make excellent apéritifs.

Vermouth

Vermouths are wine-based bitters mainly from Italy and France that have become classic apéritifs the world over. The first vermouth is said to have been made in 1786 in Italy, at the Carpano winery near Turin. There are white and red vermouths, although they are all made from high-quality white grapes. White vermouth is usually dry and strong, while the reds are normally sweeter and smoother. Punt e Mes, which originates from Milan, has a fairly bitter finish. Vermouths can be served neat, usually fairly well chilled, but they come into their own as a cocktail ingredient. They are a classic ingredient in Martinis, but are also present in other famous cocktails, such as the Manhattan and the Negroni, the latter invented in Florence in 1925.

Sweet and fortified wines

This group of still wines includes Sauternes from France, sherry from Spain, Port and Madeira from Portugal, and Marsala and Moscato from Italy. Often served as apéritifs or dessert wines, they can also be added to mixed drinks, and are especially popular in punches. Once very fashionable, they then fell from favor, only to enjoy a small renaissance in recent years when enterprising wine-makers have revived classic wines, perfecting and modernizing their flavors and appearance.

Liqueurs

There is a huge variety of more or less sweet liqueurs, made in every part of the world, and flavored with every imaginable ingredient, from herbs and fruit to coffee and chocolate. Many are frequently added to cocktails. Here, in alphabetical order, are some of the most popular liqueurs: Amaretto, almond-flavored; anisette, anise flavored; apricot brandy; Bénédictine, flavored with a mix of herbs; Chartreuse, flavored with herbs; cherry brandy; Cointreau, based on bitter and sweet oranges macerated in eau de vie; crème de cassis, flavored with blackcurrants, a basic ingredient in the Kir (see page 286); curaçao, made from orange peel and variously colored; Grand Marnier, based on Cognac and bitter oranges from the Antilles; kirsch, cherry flavored; Midori, a melon-flavored liqueur; mandarinetto, made from mandarins; Maraschino, based on cherries; Sambuca, made from anise and various aromas.

Bitters

Invented in Italy in the second half of the 19th century, Campari is one of the best and most popular bitters. Its secret formula contains a mix of herbs that give it a rich and harmonious taste. Bright red in color, it can be served neat, or lengthened with soda water and served as a classic apéritif. Campari Soda (see page 76) is the perfect combination of Campari and soda water. Campari is also present in the Negroni (see page 282), and the Americano (see page 280), a cocktail invented in Milan in the 1930s, which could perhaps have been named more appropriately The Italiano: it is made entirely of Italian products—vermouth and bitters—even the soda water was also invented in Milan in the 1920s. Angostura bitter, another fundamental ingredient in many cocktails, comes originally from Venezuela but is now made in Trinidad. It is very strong, and just a few drops are required to flavor a drink.

Cordials and soft drinks

Syrups based on sugar, coffee, mint, anise, coconut, and a range of other flavors are added to many cocktails, while tonic water, soda water, white soda, cola, and ginger ale are used to top up a host of long drinks. You will also need a range of fruit juices in your bar, from pineapple and tomato juice to grapefruit and other, more exotic flavors. For citrus juices, such as lemon, lime, and orange, be sure to always use freshly squeezed juices prepared just before serving.

HINTS & TIPS

Mixing glasses and shakers should always be chilled with ice before use. If they are warm they will make the cocktail or drink too watery. Never fill either more than three-quarters full.

Don't shake or mix for more than 6–8 seconds otherwise the drink will become watery.

Take care not to wash a mixing glass with hot water when it is still very cold; it could break.

If serving a cocktail without any added ice, be sure to chill the glass first. You can chill a glass either by filling it with ice cubes and leaving it for a few minutes or placing it in the freezer for 10 minutes.

Champagne should be kept cold in an ice bucket. Use a special stopper to keep in the bubbles when storing. In drinks containing fruit, the champagne should be poured in first followed by the fruit juices to avoid overflow. For obvious reasons, it should never be included among ingredients that require shaking.

Drinks containing citrus juices should always be prepared and served immediately, while other fruit juices can be prepared ahead of time and kept in the refrigerator. Add a few drops of freshly squeezed lemon juices to keep them fresh and to maintain the colors.

Finally, when pouring a number of drinks from a shaker or pitcher (jug), set out the glasses and fill them all half full. Then you can top them all up, keeping them all about the same size.

GLOSSARY OF LIQUEURS

Advocaat: a thick liqueur made from eggs and grain spirit or brandy

Amarula Cream: a South African liqueur made from the fruit of the marula tree

Butterscotch Schnapps: a liqueur based on butter and brown sugar

Buttershot Schnapps: a liqueur based on Jamaican rum and vanilla

Chambord: a French liqueur made from raspberries, cognac, and spices

Drambuie: a Scottish liqueur made from whisky, herbs, honey, and spices

Dubonnet: a red, French vermouth

Frangelico: an Italian liqueur flavored with hazelnuts, herbs, and vanilla

Galliano: an Italian liqueur with a complex mix of herb, flower, and vanilla flavors

Ginger beer: a sweet bubbly soft drink flavored with ginger

Ginger wine: a wine made from wine and ginger

Jägermeister: a herb bitter, usually served as a digestive

Kahlua: a coffee liqueur tinged with molasses and fruit

Kümmel: a caraway-seed liqueur

Kurant vodka: vodka made from blackcurrants

Lillet: liqueur made from wine, herbs, and fruit

Licor 43: an aromatic Spanish liqueur

Ouzo: a Greek and Cypriot aniseed and licorice flavored liqueur

Pernod: a French anise and herb-flavored liqueur

Pimm's: a liqueur based on gin (or vodka) flavored with fruit and spices

Sambuca: an Italian anise and elderberry-flavored liqueur

Sweet-and-sour mix: a syrup made with lemon juice and sugar

Strega: a herb-based spirit

Tia Maria: a sweet, coffee and vanilla flavored liqueur

Yukon Jack: a Canadian whisky with honey

APÉRITIFS

APPLE MARTINI

Fill a shaker two-thirds full with ice. Add the vodka, apple liqueur, and apple juice. Shake well and strain into a chilled martini glass. Garnish with the apple and, if liked, serve with the cheese.

- 1¹/₂ oz (45 ml) vodka
- 1 oz (30 ml) apple liqueur
- 1 oz (30 ml) apple juice
- Wedge of green apple, to garnish
- Wedge of cheddar or blue cheese, to serve (optional)

APPLE MARTINI • 1

1 oz (30 ml) green apple vodka
1 oz (30 ml) Midori melon liqueur
1 oz (30 ml) freshly squeezed lemon juice
Dash of sugar syrup

Fill a shaker two-thirds full with ice. Add the vodka, Midori, lemon juice, and sugar syrup and shake. Strain into a chilled martini glass.

APPLE MARTINI • 2

1¹/₂ oz (45 ml) apple vodka
¹/₂ oz (15 ml) Calvados
¹/₂ oz (15 ml) Cointreau

Fill a shaker two-thirds full with ice. Add the vodka, Calvados, and apple juice. Shake well and strain into a chilled martini glass.

APPLE PIE MARTINI

1¹/₂ oz (45 ml) vanilla vodka
¹/₂ oz (15 ml) apple brandy
¹/₂ oz (15 ml) dry vermouth
Thin wedge of green apple, to garnish

Fill a shaker two-thirds full with ice. Add the vodka, brandy, and vermouth. Shake well and strain into a chilled martini glass. Garnish with a wedge of apple.

CHERRY BLOSSOM

Moisten the rim of a chilled
martini glass with cherry brandy.
Dip into sugar to frost the rim.
Fill a shaker two-thirds full with
ice. Add the brandy, cherry
brandy, Cointreau, grenadine,
and lemon juice. Shake well
and strain into the glass.

- 1 oz (30 ml) brandy
- $2/3$ oz (20 ml) cherry brandy
- $1/2$ oz (15 ml) Cointreau
- $1/2$ oz (15 ml) grenadine
- $1/2$ oz (15 ml) freshly squeezed lemon juice
- Sugar

CHERRY BLOSSOM • 1

$1^1/_2$ oz (45 ml) anise liqueur
$2/3$ oz (20 ml) grenadine
Milk, to fill
Fresh cherries, to garnish

Fill a shaker two-thirds full
with ice. Add the anise
liqueur and grenadine.
Shake well and strain into
a chilled martini glass.
Top up with milk. Garnish
with the cherries.

FRUITY APPLE MARTINI

1 oz (30 ml) green apple
vodka
$1/2$ oz (15 ml) sour apple
liqueur
$1/2$ oz (15 ml) raspberry
liqueur
$1/2$ oz (15 ml) banana liqueur
2 oz (60 ml) apple juice

Fill a shaker two-thirds full
with ice. Add the green
apple vodka, apple liqueur,
raspberry liqueur, banana
liqueur, and apple juice.
Shake well and strain into
a chilled martini glass.

CANDY APPLE

$1^1/_2$ oz (45 ml) apple vodka
$1/2$ oz (15 ml) sour apple
liqueur
$1/2$ oz (15 ml) caramel
schnapps
2 oz (60 ml) apple juice
Wedge of green apple,
to garnish (optional)

Fill a shaker two-thirds full
with ice. Add the apple
vodka, apple liqueur,
schnapps, and apple juice.
Shake well and strain into
a chilled martini glass.
Garnish with the slice
of apple, if liked.

CAMPARI AND SODA

Place 3–4 ice cubes in an old-fashioned glass. Add the campari, soda water, and orange. Stir well.

- **2 oz (60 ml) Campari**
- **2 oz (60 ml) soda water**
- **Wedge of orange, zest and flesh**

CAMPARI ORANGE

1½ oz (45 ml) Campari
2 oz (60 ml) freshly squeezed orange juice

Fill a hurricane or highball glass with ice cubes. Pour in the Campari and orange juice. Stir well.

GOODNIGHT KISS

1 oz (30 ml) Campari
1 cube sugar
2–3 drops Angostura bitters
Chilled dry champagne or other good quality dry sparkling wine, to fill

Put the Angostura bitters on the sugar cube. Drop the cube into a champagne flute. Pour in the Campari and top up with the sparkling wine.

MAÈEK

1 oz (30 ml) bourbon
2/3 oz (20 ml) Campari
½ oz (15 ml) freshly squeezed orange juice
Orange zest, to garnish

Fill an old-fashioned glass with ice cubes. Pour in the bourbon, Campari, and orange juice. Mix well. Garnish with the orange zest.

CASANOVA COBBLER

Place the strawberries, lime, and sugar in an old-fashioned glass and muddle until the sugar has dissolved. Add 3–4 ice cubes and vermouth. Stir well.

- **3–4 medium strawberries, chopped**
- **1/4 lime, with zest, chopped**
- **2 teaspoons sugar**
- **2 oz (60 ml) dry vermouth**

ORANGE AFFINITY

1 oz (30 ml) Scotch whisky
1 oz (15 ml) sweet vermouth
1 oz (15 ml) dry vermouth
2 dashes orange bitters

Half fill a mixing glass with ice cubes. Add the whisky, sweet vermouth, dry vermouth, and bitters and stir well. Strain into a martini glass.

ALGONQUIN

1¹/₂ oz (45 ml) rye whisky
1 oz (30 ml) dry vermouth
1 oz (30 ml) pineapple juice

Fill a shaker two-thirds full with ice. Add the whisky, vermouth, and pineapple juice. Shake well and strain into a martini glass.

WHISKY FLIP

1¹/₂ oz (45 ml) blended whisky
2 teaspoons heavy (double) cream
1 teaspoon sugar
1 egg
Freshly grated nutmeg

Fill a shaker two-thirds full with ice. Add the whisky, cream, sugar, and egg. Shake well and strain into an old-fashioned glass. Dust with nutmeg.

FRENCH 75

Half fill a shaker with ice. Add the cognac, lemon juice, and syrup and shake. Strain into two champagne flutes and top up with the champagne.

- **1¹/₂ oz (45 ml) cognac**
- **2 teaspoons freshly squeezed lemon juice**
- **1 teaspoon sugar syrup**
- **Dry champagne, well chilled, to fill**

80

■ ■ ■ *This cocktail was named after an artillery gun used by allied troops in France during World War I, presumably because drinking more than one or two was a bit like being zapped by it!*

FRENCH 76

²/₃ oz (20 ml) vodka
²/₃ oz (20 ml) Cointreau
1 teaspoon freshly squeezed lemon juice
¹/₂ teaspoon sugar syrup
1 drop orange flower water
Dry champagne, well chilled, to fill

Fill a shaker two-thirds full with ice. Add the vodka, Cointreau, lemon juice, syrup, and orange flower water. Shake well and strain into a chilled martini glass. Top up with champagne.

FRENCH 75 • 1

1¹/₂ oz (45 ml) gin
2 teaspoons sugar
1¹/₂ oz (45 ml) freshly squeezed lemon juice
5 oz (150 ml) dry champagne, well chilled
Maraschino cherry, to garnish

Fill a shaker two-thirds full with ice. Add the gin, sugar, and lemon juice. Shake well and strain into a Collins glass. Top up with the champagne and garnish with the cherry.

FRENCH 68

1 oz (30 ml) Calvados
¹/₃ oz (10 ml) brandy
¹/₃ oz (10 ml) freshly squeezed lemon juice
Dash grenadine
Dry champagne, well chilled, to fill

Fill a shaker two-thirds full with ice. Add the Calvados, brandy, lemon juice, and grenadine. Shake well and strain into a champagne flute. Top up with champagne.

CAPE COD

Half fill an old-fashioned glass with ice. Pour in the vodka and cranberry juice. Stir well and garnish with the lime.

- 1$^{1}/_{2}$ oz (450 ml) vodka
- 3 oz (90 ml) cranberry juice
- Wedge of lime, to garnish

CAPE COD CRUSH

2 oz (60 ml) Southern Comfort
3 oz (90 ml) cranberry juice
$^{1}/_{2}$ cup crushed ice

Place the Southern Comfort, cranberry juice, and ice in a blender, Blend on slow speed until smooth. Pour into a hurricane glass.

CAPE COD COOLER

1$^{1}/_{2}$ oz (45 ml) sloe gin
1$^{1}/_{2}$ oz (45 ml) gin
5 oz (150 ml) cranberry juice
$^{1}/_{2}$ oz (15 ml) freshly squeezed lime juice
$^{1}/_{2}$ oz (15 ml) almond syrup
Wedge of lime, to garnish

Fill a shaker two-thirds full with ice. Add the sloe gin, gin, cranberry juice, lime juice, and almond syrup. Shake well and strain into a Collins glass half filled with ice cubes. Garnish with the lime.

CAPE CODDER

1 oz (30 ml) vodka
3 oz (90 ml) cranberry juice
1 oz (30 ml) white soda, such as 7–Up or Sprite
$^{1}/_{2}$ oz (15 ml) coconut rum
$^{1}/_{2}$ oz (15 ml) pineapple juice

Half fill an old-fashioned glass with ice cubes. Pour in the vodka, cranberry juice, and white soda. Add the coconut rum and pineapple juice. Do not stir the drink.

GENOA SLING

Fill a shaker two-thirds full with ice. Add the vodka, campari, and orange juice and shake. Strain into two chilled old-fashioned glasses over 2–3 cubes of ice.

- 1¹/₂ oz (45 ml) vodka
- 1 oz (30 ml) Campari
- 3 oz (90 ml) freshly squeezed orange juice

BLUE EDISON

1¹/₂ oz (45 ml) Campari
1¹/₂ oz (45 ml) Brandy
1 oz (30 ml) freshly squeezed lemon juice

Fill a shaker two-thirds full with ice. Add the Campari, brandy, and lemon juice. Shake well and strain into a chilled martini glass.

CAMPARI WITH LEMON

1¹/₂ oz (45 ml) Campari
1 teaspoon freshly squeezed lemon juice
Twist of lime zest

Fill a shaker two-thirds full with ice. Add the Campari and lemon juice. Shake well and strain into a chilled martini glass. Garnish with the twist of lime.

NICKY FINN

1 oz (30 ml) brandy
1 oz (30 ml) Cointreau
1 oz (30 ml) freshly squeezed lemon juice
Dash of anise liqueur, such as Pastis, Sambuca, Pernod
Maraschino cherry, to garnish

Fill a shaker two-thirds full with ice. Add the brandy, Cointreau, lemon juice, and anise liqueur. Shake well and strain into a chilled martini glass. Garnish with the cherry.

VESPER MARTINI

Fill a shaker two-thirds full with ice. Add the gin, vodka, and Lillet Blonde. Shake well and strain into a chilled martini glass or champagne goblet. Garnish with the lemon zest.

- **3 oz (90 ml) gin**
- **1 oz (30 ml) vodka**
- **1/2 oz (15 ml) Lillet Blonde (French vermouth)**
- **Lemon zest, to garnish**

■ ■ ■ *This famous variation on the martini was invented by James Bond in Ian Fleming's 1953 novel* Casino Royale. *Bond named it for female double agent Vesper Lynd. A martini man, Bond ordered Vesper "in a deep champagne goblet.... Three measures of Gordon's, one of vodka, half a measure of Kina Lillet. Shake it very well until it's ice-cold, then add a large thin slice of lemon peel."*

KEY LIME MARTINI

Fill a shaker two-thirds full with ice. Add the vodka, lime juice, and cream and shake. Strain into a chilled martini glass. Garnish with the lime.

- 2 oz (60 ml) vanilla vodka
- $2/3$ oz (20 ml) freshly squeezed lime juice
- 1 oz (30 ml) heavy (double) cream
- Twist of lime zest

KIR MARTINI

2 oz (60 ml) gin
$2/3$ oz (20 ml) dry vermouth
$1/3$ oz (10 ml) crème de cassis
Twist of lemon, to garnish

Fill a shaker two-thirds full with ice. Add the gin, vermouth, and crème de cassis. Shake well and strain into a chilled martini glass. Garnish with the lemon.

MILKY WAY MARTINI

2 oz (60 ml) vanilla vodka
$1^1/2$ oz (45 ml) chocolate liqueur
1 oz (30 ml) Irish cream

Fill a shaker two-thirds full with ice. Add the vodka, chocolate liqueur, and Irish cream. Shake well and strain into a martini glass.

COFFEE MARTINI

2 oz (60 ml) vodka
1 oz (30 ml) dark crème de cacao
$2/3$ oz (20 ml) coffee liqueur

Fill a shaker two-thirds full with ice. Add the vodka, crème de cacao, and coffee liqueur. Shake well and strain into a chilled martini glass.

COSMOPOLITAN

Fill a shaker two-thirds full with ice. Add the vodka, Cointreau, cranberry juice, and lime juice. Shake well and strain into a chilled martini glass. Garnish with the lemon zest.

- 1¹/₂ oz (45 ml) vodka
- 1 oz (30 ml) Cointreau
- 1 oz (30 ml) cranberry juice
- ¹/₂ oz (15 ml) freshly squeezed lime juice
- **Twist of lemon zest, to garnish**

COSMOPOLITAN • 1

1 oz (30 ml) vodka
¹/₂ oz (15 ml) Cointreau
¹/₂ oz (15 ml) cranberry juice
1 teaspoon freshly squeezed lime juice
¹/₂ oz (15 ml) Chambord raspberry liqueur
Twist of lemon zest, to garnish

Fill a shaker two-thirds full with ice. Add the vodka, Cointreau, cranberry juice, and lime juice. Shake well and strain into a chilled martini glass. Float the Chambord on top and garnish with the lemon zest.

WHITE COSMOPOLITAN

1¹/₂ oz (45 ml) lemon vodka
¹/₂ oz (15 ml) Cointreau
¹/₂ oz (15 ml) freshly squeezed lime juice
³/₄ oz (25 ml) white cranberry juice
Twist of lemon zest, to garnish

Fill a shaker two-thirds full with ice. Add the vodka, Cointreau, lime juice, and white cranberry juice. Shake well and strain into a chilled martini glass. Garnish with the lemon zest.

COSMOPOLITAN • 2

1¹/₂ oz (45 ml) raspberry vodka
²/₃ oz (20 ml) Cointreau
¹/₃ oz (10 ml) Chambord raspberry liqueur
1 oz (30 ml) sweet-and-sour mix
1 oz (30 ml) cranberry juice

Fill a shaker two-thirds full with ice. Add the vodka, Cointreau, Chambord, sweet-and-sour mix, and cranberry juice. Shake well and strain into a chilled martini glass.

CAJUN MARTINI

Place the vodka, garlic, chile, and onions in a small bowl. Cover and refrigerate for two hours. Fill a shaker two-thirds full with ice. Add the vodka mixture and shake. Strain into a martini glass. Garnish with a couple of slices of fresh red or green jalapeno.

- 2 oz (60 ml) vodka
- Dash of dry vermouth
- 1 clove garlic, peeled and cut in half
- 3–4 slices fresh jalapeno chile + extra slices to garnish
- 2–3 cocktail onions, rinsed to remove vinegar flavor

SPICY MARTINI

$1^{1}/_{2}$ oz (45 ml) gin
1 oz (30 ml) dry vermouth
Few drops Tabasco

Fill a shaker two-thirds full with ice. Add the gin and vermouth. Shake well and strain into a chilled martini glass. Add Tabasco to taste and stir gently.

PINK MARTINI

$1^{1}/_{2}$ oz (45 ml) gin
1 oz (30 ml) red vermouth
Twist of orange zest, to garnish

Fill a shaker two-thirds full with ice. Add the gin and vermouth. Shake well and strain into a chilled martini glass. Garnish with the orange zest.

CAJUN COMFORTER

$1^{1}/_{2}$ oz (45 ml) Southern Comfort
$1/_{2}$ oz (15 ml) bourbon
Few drops Tabasco

Fill an old-fashioned glass with ice cubes. Pour in the Southern Comfort and bourbon. Add Tabasco to taste and stir gently.

ANDALUSIA

Fill a shaker two-thirds full with ice. Add the sherry, brandy, and rum. Shake well and strain into a chilled martini glass. Squeeze the orange zest over the glass so that the fruit's fragrant oils gently flavor the drink.

- 1½ oz (45 ml) dry sherry
- ½ oz (15 ml) brandy
- ½ oz (15 ml) white rum
- **Piece of orange zest**

STONE COCKTAIL

1 oz (30 ml) dry sherry
½ oz (15 ml) sweet white vermouth
½ oz (15 ml) light rum

Fill a shaker two-thirds full with ice. Add the sherry, vermouth, and rum. Shake well and strain into a martini glass.

BLARNEY STONE COCKTAIL

2 oz (60 ml) Irish whisky
½ teaspoon anise liqueur
½ teaspoon Cointreau
¼ teaspoon Maraschino cherry liqueur
Twist of orange zest

Fill a shaker two-thirds full with ice. Add the whisky, anise liqueur, Cointreau, and Maraschino. Shake well and strain into a martini glass. Garnish with the orange zest.

SCOTCH BISHOP

1 oz (30 ml) Scotch whisky
½ oz (15 ml) dry vermouth
½ teaspoon Cointreau
½ oz (15 ml) freshly squeezed orange juice
¼ teaspoon sugar
Piece of orange zest

Fill a shaker two-thirds full with ice. Add the whisky, vermouth, Cointreau, orange juice, and sugar. Shake well and strain into a martini glass. Squeeze the orange zest over the glass so that the fruit's fragrant oil gently flavor the drink.

BOMBAY

Fill a shaker two-thirds full with ice. Add the brandy, dry vermouth, sweet vermouth, blue curaçao, and Pernod. Shake well and strain into an old-fashioned glass half-filled with ice.

- 1 oz (30 ml) brandy
- 1/2 oz (15 ml) dry vermouth
- 1/2 oz (15 ml) sweet white vermouth
- Dash of blue curaçao
- Drop of Pernod

BOMBAY COCKTAIL

1 oz (30 ml) brandy
2/3 oz (20 ml) dry vermouth
1/2 oz (15 ml) sweet white vermouth
1/2 teaspoon Cointreau
1/4 teaspoon anise liqueur

Fill a shaker two-thirds full with ice. Add the brandy, dry vermouth, sweet vermouth, Cointreau, and anise liqueur. Shake well and strain into a martini glass.

DUCHESS

1 oz (30 ml) sweet red vermouth
1 oz (30 ml) dry vermouth
1 oz (30 ml) anise liqueur
Slice of orange, to garnish

Fill a shaker two-thirds full with ice. Add the sweet vermouth, dry vermouth, and anise liqueur. Shake well and strain into a martini glass. Garnish with the orange.

WHIP COCKTAIL

11/2 oz (45 ml) Cognac
1/2 oz (15 ml) dry vermouth
1/2 oz (15 ml) sweet red vermouth
1 teaspoon Cointreau
1/4 teaspoon anise liqueur

Fill a shaker two-thirds full with ice. Add the Cognac, dry vermouth, sweet vermouth, Cointreau, and anise liqueur. Shake well and strain into a martini glass.

BOBBY BURNS

Place 2–3 ice cubes in a chilled Martini glass. Pour in the Scotch, vermouth, and Benedictine. Mix gently with a bar spoon. Squeeze the lemon zest over the glass so that the fruit's fragrant oils gently flavor the drink.

- 1 oz (30 ml) Scotch whisky
- 1/2 oz (15 ml) sweet red vermouth
- 3 drops Benedictine
- Piece of lemon zest

BOBBY BURNS • 1

1¹/₂ oz (45 ml) Scotch whisky
2/3 oz (20 ml) sweet red vermouth
2 dashes Drambuie
Dash of Angostura bitters

Half fill a mixing glass with ice cubes. Add the whisky, vermouth, Drambuie, and Angostura bitters. Mix gently with a bar spoon. Strain into a martini glass.

HOOTS MON

1¹/₂ oz (45 ml) Scotch whisky
1/2 oz (15 ml) Lillet Blonde (French vermouth)
1/2 oz (15 ml) sweet vermouth

Half fill a mixing glass with ice cubes. Add the whisky, Lillet, and vermouth. Mix gently with a bar spoon. Strain into a martini glass.

TARTANTULA

1¹/₂ oz (45 ml) bourbon
1 oz (30 ml) sweet white vermouth
1/2 oz (15 ml) Chartreuse
Twist of lemon zest

Half fill a mixing glass with ice cubes. Add the bourbon, vermouth, and Chartreuse. Mix gently with a bar spoon. Strain into a martini glass. Garnish with the lemon zest.

ARNAUD

Fill a shaker two-thirds full with ice. Add the gin, crème de cassis, and vermouth. Shake well and strain into a chilled martini glass. Garnish with the white currants, if liked.

- 1 oz (30 ml) gin
- 1 oz (30 ml) crème de cassis
- 1 oz (30 ml) dry vermouth
- Tiny bunch white currants (optional)

DOWNTOWN COCKTAIL

1 oz (30 ml) gin
1/2 oz (15 ml) sweet white vermouth
1/2 oz (15 ml) dry vermouth
1 sprig fresh mint

Half fill a mixing glass with ice cubes. Add the gin, sweet vermouth, and dry vermouth. Mix gently with a bar spoon. Strain into a martini glass. Garnish with the mint.

DOWNTOWN COCKTAIL • 1

1 oz (30 ml) gin
2/3 oz (20 ml) dry vermouth
2/3 oz (20 ml) Dubonnet vermouth

Fill a shaker two-thirds full with ice. Add the gin, dry vermouth, and Dubonnet. Shake well and strain into a martini glass.

FRUITY COCKTAIL

1 oz (30 ml) dry vermouth
1/3 oz (10 ml) gin
1/3 oz (10 ml) Midori melon liqueur
1/3 oz (10 ml) pineapple juice

Fill a shaker two-thirds full with ice. Add the vermouth, gin, Midori, and pineapple juice. Shake well and strain into a martini glass.

BLACK CURRANT MARTINI

Fill a shaker two-thirds full with ice. Add the vodka, crème de cassis, grenadine, and lime juice. Shake well and strain into a chilled martini glass.

- 2 oz (60 ml) vodka
- 1/2 oz (15 ml) crème de cassis
- 2 dashes grenadine
- 1/3 oz (10 ml) freshly squeezed lime juice

BLACK AND BLUE

2 oz (60 ml) Chambord raspberry liqueur
1 oz (30 ml) blue curaçao
1/2 oz (15 ml) vodka

Fill a shaker two-thirds full with ice. Add the Chambord, blue curaçao, and vodka. Shake well and strain into a martini glass.

TEQUILA BLACK

1 oz (30 ml) tequila
1 oz (30 ml) blackberry brandy
1 oz (30 ml) soda water, well chilled, to fill

Place 2–3 ice cubes in an old-fashioned glass. Pour in the tequila and blackberry brandy. Top up with the soda water.

BLACK CHERRY

1 1/2 oz (45 ml) oz raspberry vodka
3/4 oz (25 ml) Irish cream
3/4 oz (25 ml) coffee liqueur
3/4 oz (25 ml) heavy (double) cream
Maraschino cherry, to garnish

Fill an old-fashioned glass with ice cubes. Add the vodka, Irish cream, coffee liqueur, and cream. ingredients. Mix gently with a bar spoon. Garnish with the cherry.

CAMPARI AND GIN

Place 4–5 ice cubes in an old-fashioned glass. Pour in the gin and campari and stir gently.

- 1 oz (30 ml) gin
- 1 oz (30 ml) Campari

GIN AND CAMPARI

1¹/₂ oz (45 ml) gin
¹/₂ oz (15 ml) Campari
Tonic water

Place 4–5 ice cubes in an old-fashioned glass. Add the gin and campari. Stir gently and add tonic water to taste.

NORTHERN CAMPARI

1 oz (30 ml) gin (or vodka)
1 oz (30 ml) Grand Marnier
1 oz (30 ml) Campari
Slice of orange, to garnish

Place 4–5 ice cubes in an old-fashioned glass. Add the gin (or vodka), Grand Marnier, and Campari. Stir gently. Garnish with the orange.

BITTER GIN TWIST

1¹/₂ oz (45 ml) gin
¹/₂ oz (15 ml) sweet vermouth
¹/₂ oz (15 ml) Campari
Twist of lemon zest

Half fill a mixing glass with ice cubes. Add the gin, vermouth, and Campari. Mix gently with a bar spoon. Garnish with the lemon zest.

FLYING DUTCHMAN

Fill a shaker two-thirds full with ice. Add the gin, vermouth, and blue curaçao. Shake well and strain into a chilled martini glass. Garnish with the lemon.

- **2 oz (60 ml) gin**
- **1/2 oz (15 ml) dry vermouth**
- **Dash of blue curaçao**
- **Twist of lemon zest**

AMSTERDAM

1¹/₂ oz (45 ml) Bols gin
¹/₂ oz (15 ml) Cointreau
³/₄ oz (25 ml) freshly squeezed orange juice

Fill a shaker two-thirds full with ice. Add the gin, Cointreau, and orange juice. Shake well and strain into an old-fashioned glass with 2–3 cubes of ice.

APPLE AND GIN

3 oz (90 ml) sweet apple cider
1 oz (30 ml) gin
¹/₃ oz (10 ml) triple sec

Place 4–5 cubes of ice in an old-fashioned glass. Pour in the cider, gin, and triple sec. Mix gently with a bar spoon.

PEACHY

1 oz (30 ml) gin
1 oz (30 ml) peach vodka
1 oz (30 ml) triple sec

Fill a shaker two-thirds full with ice. Add the gin, peach vodka, and triple sec. Shake well and strain into a martini glass.

BELLINI MARTINI

Fill a shaker two thirds full with ice. Add the vodka and peach schnapps. Shake well and strain into a chilled martini glass. Garnish with the peach.

- 1¹/₂ oz (45 ml) vodka
- 1 oz (30 ml) peach schnapps
- **Wedge of fresh peach, peeled, to garnish**

BELLINI MARTINI • 1

1 fresh peach, peeled
3 oz (90 ml) vodka
1¹/₂ oz (45 ml) peach brandy

Chop the peach in a blender. Fill a shaker two-thirds full with ice. Add the vodka, peach brandy, and 1 tablespoon of the puréed peach. Shake well and strain into a martini glass.

GOLF MARTINI

2 oz (60 ml) gin
²/₃ oz (20 ml) dry vermouth
2–3 dashes Angostura bitters
1 cocktail olive

Fill a shaker two-thirds full with ice. Add the gin, dry vermouth, and Angostura. Shake well and strain into a chilled martini glass. Garnish with the olive.

FRUITY MARTINI

2 oz (60 ml) grape vodka
Splash Grand Marnier
¹/₂ oz (15 ml) grapefruit juice
¹/₂ oz (15 ml) pineapple juice

Fill a shaker two-thirds full with ice. Add the vodka, Grand Marnier, grapefruit juice, and pineapple juice. Shake well and strain into a chilled martini glass.

BRANDY SOUR

Fill a shaker two-thirds full with ice. Add the brandy, lemon juice, orange juice, and sugar syrup. Shake well and strain into a chilled old-fashioned glass over 2–3 ice cubes. Garnish with the cherry.

- 1¹/₂ oz (45 ml) brandy
- 1 oz (30 ml) freshly squeezed lemon juice
- ¹/₂ oz (15 ml) freshly squeezed orange juice
- 1 teaspoon sugar syrup
- Maraschino cherry, to garnish

APPLE MANHATTAN

Fill a shaker two-thirds full with ice. Add the Calvados, dry vermouth, and sweet vermouth. Shake well and strain into a chilled martini glass. Drop the slice of apple into the drink.

- 1½ oz (45 ml) Calvados
- ½ oz (15 ml) dry vermouth
- ½ oz (15 ml) sweet vermouth
- Wedge of red apple

APPLE MANHATTAN • 1

1½ oz (45 ml) bourbon
1 oz (30 ml) sweet apple schnapps
Wedge of red apple, to garnish

Half fill a mixing glass with ice cubes. Add the bourbon and schnapps. Mix well and strain into a chilled martini glass. Garnish with the apple.

TEQUILA AND CIDER

1 oz (30 ml) tequila
4 oz (120 ml) apple cider

Place 2–3 ice cubes in an old-fashioned glass. Pour in the tequila and cider.

APPLE JACK

1½ oz (45 ml) apple brandy
1 oz (30 ml) bourbon
1 oz (30 ml) freshly squeezed lemon juice
1 teaspoon sugar syrup
Soda water, to fill

Fill a shaker two-thirds full with ice. Add the brandy, bourbon, lemon juice, and sugar syrup. Shake well and strain into an old-fashioned glass with 2–3 cubes of ice. Top up with soda water.

APRICOT SOUR

Fill a shaker two-thirds full with ice. Add the apricot brandy, lemon juice, orange juice, and and sugar syrup. Shake well and strain into a chilled martini glass. Garnish with the lemon.

- 2 oz (60 ml) apricot brandy
- 1/2 oz (15 ml) freshly squeezed lemon juice
- 1/2 oz (15 ml) freshly squeezed orange juice
- 1/2 teaspoon sugar syrup
- Wedge of lemon, to garnish

APPLEJACK SOUR

2 oz (60 ml) Applejack brandy
1 oz (30 ml) freshly squeezed lemon juice
1 teaspoon sugar syrup
Soda water
Wedge of lemon, to garnish

Fill a shaker two-thirds full with ice. Add the brandy, lemon juice, and sugar syrup. Shake well and strain into an old-fashioned glass. Top up with soda water to taste. Garnish with the lemon.

AMARETTO SOUR

1 1/2 oz (45 ml) vodka
1 1/2 oz (45 ml) amaretto
1 oz (30 ml) freshly squeezed lemon juice
1 teaspoon sugar syrup

Fill a shaker two-thirds full with ice. Add the vodka, amaretto, lemon juice, and sugar syrup. Shake well and strain into a chilled martini glass.

RYE WHISKY SOUR

1 1/2 oz (45 ml) rye whisky
1 oz (30 ml) freshly squeezed lemon juice
1/2 oz (15 ml) sugar syrup

Fill a shaker two-thirds full with ice. Add the whisky, lemon juice, and sugar syrup. Shake well and strain into an old-fashioned glass over 2–3 ice cubes.

FLYING GRASSHOPPER

Fill a shaker two-thirds full with ice. Add the vodka, green crème de menthe, and white crème de menthe. Shake well and strain into a chilled old-fashioned glass.

- ³/₄ oz (25 ml) vodka
- ³/₄ oz (25 ml) green crème de menthe
- ³/₄ oz (25 ml) white crème de menthe

116

■ ■ ■ *All four cocktails on this page can also be served after dinner.*

CREAMY GRASSHOPPER

²/₃ oz (20 ml) vodka
²/₃ oz (20 ml) green crème de menthe
²/₃ oz (20 ml) white crème de cacao

Fill a shaker two-thirds full with ice. Add the vodka, crème de menthe, and crème de cacao. Shake well and strain into a martini glass.

GRASSHOPPER CAFÉ

1 oz (30 ml) green crème de menthe
1 oz (30 ml) coffee liqueur
1 oz (30 ml) heavy (double) cream

Fill a shaker two-thirds full with ice. Add the crème de menthe, coffee liqueur, and cream. Shake well and strain into a chilled old-fashioned glass, over 2–3 ice cubes.

TEQUILA GRASSHOPPER

1 oz (30 ml) tequila
1 oz (30 ml) crème de menthe

Fill a shaker two-thirds full with ice. Add the tequila and crème de menthe. Shake well and strain into an old-fashioned glass over 2–3 ice cubes.

CHABLIS COOLER

Place 3–4 ice cubes in a large wine goblet. Add the vodka, grenadine, lemon juice, vanilla, and wine and stir gently.
Top up with soda water.

- 1 oz (30 ml) vodka
- $1/2$ teaspoon grenadine
- $1/2$ oz (15 ml) freshly squeezed lemon juice
- Dash of vanilla extract (essence)
- 4 oz (120 ml) chablis
- Soda water, to fill

CAPTAIN'S COCKTAIL

2 oz (60 ml) dry white wine
$1^1/2$ oz (45 ml) spiced rum
Cola, such as Pepsi or Coca-Cola, to fill
Wedge of lime

Half fill an old-fashioned glass with ice cubes. Pour in the white wine and then the rum. Top up with cola. Garnish with the lime.

SPICED COLADA

$1^1/2$ oz (45 ml) spiced rum
2 oz (60 ml) pineapple juice
1 oz (30 ml) cream of coconut

Fill a shaker two-thirds full with ice. Add the spiced rum, pineapple juice, and cream of coconut. Shake well and strain into a wine goblet.

WHITE WINE MARTINI

2 oz (60 ml) gin
$1/2$ oz (15 ml) chablis
Green cocktail olive

Fill a shaker two-thirds full with ice. Add the gin and wine. Shake well and strain into a chilled martini glass. Add the olive.

BLUE FROSTBITE

Fill a shaker two-thirds full with ice. Add the tequila, crème de menthe, blue curaçao, and cream. Shake well and strain into a wine goblet filled with ice. Garnish with the mint leaves.

- 2 oz (60 ml) white tequila
- 1 oz (30 ml) white crème de menthe
- 1/2 oz (15 ml) blue curaçao
- 2 oz (60 ml) heavy (double) cream
- Fresh mint leaves, to float on top

120

FROSTBITE •1

1 1/2 oz (45 ml) white tequila
1 1/2 oz (45 ml) crème fraîche
1 1/2 oz (45 ml) crème de cacao

Fill a shaker two-thirds full with ice. Add the tequila, crème fraîche, and crème de cacao. Shake well and strain into a chilled martini glass.

TEQUILA ORANGE

2 oz (60 ml) gold tequila
1/2 oz (15 ml) Cointreau
Twist of orange peel

Fill a shaker two-thirds full with ice. Add the tequila and Cointreau, Shake well and strain into a chilled martini glass. Garnish with the orange.

TEQUILA CREAM

1 oz (30 ml) white tequila
1 oz (30 ml) Kahlua
1/2 oz (15 ml) Chambord raspberry liqueur
1 1/2 oz (45 ml) heavy (double) cream

Fill a shaker two-thirds full with ice. Add the tequila, Kahlua, Chambord, and cream. Shake well and strain into a chilled martini glass.

CORTINA COCKTAIL

Fill a shaker two-thirds full with ice. Add the port, vodka, Campari, and grenadine. Shake well and strain into a chilled martini glass. Garnish with the orange, if liked.

- 1½ oz (45 ml) white port
- 1 oz (30 ml) vodka
- ½ oz (15 ml) Campari
- **Dash of grenadine**
- **Wedge of orange, to garnish (optional)**

CORTINA COCKTAIL • 1

1 oz (30 ml) brandy
1½ oz (45 ml) port
½ oz (15 ml) Cointreau
⅓ oz (10 ml) freshly squeezed lemon juice
1 teaspoon sugar
Lemon wedge, to garnish

Fill a shaker two-thirds full with ice. Add the brandy, port, Cointreau, lemon juice, and sugar. Shake well and strain into a chilled martini glass. Garnish with the lemon.

JAMAICA LULLABY

1 oz (30 ml) dark rum
½ oz (15 ml) port
½ oz (15 ml) orange curaçao
⅔ oz (20 ml) freshly squeezed lemon juice

Moisten the rim of a martini glass with rum. Dip into sugar to coat. Half fill a mixing glass with ice cubes. Add the rum, port, orange curaçao, and lemon juice. Stir well. Strain into the martini glass.

GIN VERMOUTH

2 oz (60 ml) gin
½ oz (15 ml) sweet vermouth
½ oz (15 ml) dry vermouth
½ oz (15 ml) freshly squeezed orange juice

Fill a shaker two-thirds full with ice. Add the gin, sweet vermouth, dry vermouth, and orange juice. Shake well and strain into a chilled martini glass.

DEATH IN THE AFTERNOON

Pour the Pernod into a champagne flute and top up with the champagne.

- 1¹/₂ oz (45 ml) Pernod
- **4 oz (120 ml) very dry champagne, well chilled**

■ ■ ■ *This drink is said to have been one of Hemingway's favorites during his time in Paris in the 1920s.*

VODKA CHAMPAGNE

3 oz (90 ml) vodka
1 oz (30 ml) cherry juice
1 oz (30 ml) freshly squeezed lemon juice
Dry champagne, well chilled, to fill

Fill a shaker two-thirds full with ice. Add the vodka, cherry juice, and lemon juice. Shake well and strain into two champagne flutes. Top up with champagne.

MONK'S BLESSINGS

1 oz (30 ml) brandy
1 oz (30 ml) Cointreau
1 oz (30 ml) Benedictine
Dry champagne, well chilled, to fill

Pour the brandy, Cointreau, and Benedictine into a wine goblet over 2–3 ice cubes. Top up with champagne.

CARIBBEAN CURE

1¹/₂ oz (45 ml) white rum
1 oz (30 ml) brandy
2 oz (60 ml) freshly squeezed lime juice
2 oz (60 ml) freshly squeezed lime juice
1 teaspoon sugar syrup
1 teaspoon grenadine
Dry champagne, well chilled, to fill

Fill a shaker two-thirds full with ice. Add the rum, brandy, lime juice, lemon juice, sugar syrup, and grenadine. Shake well and strain into a wine goblet. Top up with champagne.

MALIBU MONSOON

Fill a shaker two-thirds full with ice. Add the the rum, Grand Marnier, pineapple juice, and cranberry juice. Shake well and strain into a chilled wine goblet. Garnish with the cherry.

- 1½ oz (45 ml) Malibu rum
- 1 oz (30 ml) Grand Marnier
- 1 oz (30 ml) pineapple juice
- ½ oz (15 ml) cranberry juice
- Maraschino cherry, to garnish

ANISE FRAPPÉ

Fill a shaker two-thirds full with ice. Add the Pernod, Sambuca, and Angostura. Shake well and strain into a chilled martini glass.

- 1¹/₂ oz (45 ml) **Pernod**
- ¹/₂ oz (15 ml) **Sambuca**
- 3–4 dashes **Angostura bitters**

128

CITRUS PERNOD FLIP

1¹/₂ oz (45 ml) **Pernod**
¹/₂ oz (15 ml) **Cointreau**
¹/₂ oz (15 ml) **freshly squeezed lemon juice**
1 teaspoon **sugar syrup**

Fill a shaker two-thirds full with ice. Add the Pernod, Cointreau, lemon juice, and sugar syrup. Shake well and strain into a chilled martini glass.

SEAHORSE MARTINI

2 oz (60 ml) **gin**
1 oz (30 ml) **dry vermouth**
1 teaspoon **Pernod**
2 dashes **orange bitters**

Fill a shaker two-thirds full with ice. Add the gin, vermouth, Pernod, and bitters. Shake well and strain into a chilled martini glass.

SCOTCH QUAKE

1¹/₂ oz (30 ml) **Scotch whisky**
1 oz (30 ml) **gin**
1 oz (30 ml) **Pernod**

Fill a shaker two-thirds full with ice. Add the whisky, gin, and Pernod. Shake well and strain into a chilled martini glass.

LA JOLLARITA

Fill a shaker two-thirds full with ice. Add the tequila, Cointreau, and Chambord. Shake well and strain into a chilled martini glass.

- 2 oz (60 ml) white tequila
- 1 oz (30 ml) Cointreau
- 1 oz (30 ml) Chambord raspberry liqueur

130

TEQUILA DEVIL

Wedge of lime
1$^1/_2$ oz (45 ml) white tequila
$^1/_2$ oz (15 ml) crème de cassis
Chilled ginger ale, to fill

Place 3–4 ice cubes in an old-fashioned glass. squeeze in the lime juice then drop the peel into the drink. Pour in the tequila and crème de cassis. Top up with ginger ale.

TEQUILA SLING

2 oz (60 ml) white tequila
$^1/_2$ oz (15 ml) freshly squeezed lime juice
1 teaspoon sugar syrup
Soda water, to fill
Wedge of lime, to garnish

Place 5–6 ice cubes in an old-fashioned glass. Pour in the tequila, lime juice, and sugar syrup. Stir gently and top up with soda water.

ABSOLUTE HB

1$^1/_2$ oz (45 ml) gold tequila
1$^1/_2$ oz (45 ml) vodka
$^2/_3$ oz (20 ml) Southern Comfort
$^2/_3$ oz (20 ml) dry vermouth
1 oz (30 ml) white soda, such as 7-Up or Sprite

Half fill an old-fashioned glass with ice cubes. Pour in the tequila, vodka, Southern Comfort, vermouth, and white soda. Stir gently.

132

TEQUILA SANGRITA

Place the tequila, tomato juice, orange juice, lime juice, chilies, and salt in a pitcher (jug) and stir gently until well mixed. Taste and adapt the amount of chile and salt to suit your taste. Pour into four glasses or mugs.

- **6 oz (180 ml) white tequila**
- **8 oz (250 ml) tomato juice**
- **4 oz (120 ml) freshly squeezed orange juice**
- **2 oz (60 ml) freshly squeezed lime juice**
- **Minced fresh green serrano or jalapeno chilies, to taste**
- **Salt**

Sangrita is a fiery combo of tomato juice, orange and/or lime juice, chilies, and salt. In Mexico it is served in its own glass alongside a glass of good quality tequila. You take a sip of tequila and then a chaser of sangrita.

EL TORO SANGRIENTO

Place 4–6 ice cubes in an old-fashioned glass and pour in the tequila, tomato juice, beef bouillon, lemon juice, and Worcestershire sauce. Stir gently. Taste and season with salt and white pepper as liked.

- **2 oz (60 ml) white tequila**
- **3 oz (90 ml) tomato juice**
- **3 oz (90 ml) beef bouillon**
- **1 teaspoon freshly squeezed lemon juice**
- **3–4 dashes Worcestershire sauce**
- **Salt**
- **Freshly ground white pepper**

BLOODY MARIA

1 oz (30 ml) tequila
2 oz (60 ml) tomato juice
Dash of lemon juice
Dash of Tabasco
2 pinches celery salt
Slice of lemon, to garnish

Fill a shaker two-thirds full with ice. Add the tequila, tomato juice, lemon juice, Tabasco, and celery salt. Shake well and strain into an old-fashioned glass over 2–3 ice cubes. Garnish with the lemon

VT SUNRISE

1¹/₂ oz (45 ml) vodka
1 oz (30 ml) gold tequila
3 oz (90 ml) orange juice
3 oz (90 ml) tomato juice

Place the vodka, tequila, orange juice, and tomato juice in a mixing glass. Mix well. Place 3–4 ice cubes in an old-fashioned glass. Pour the drink into the glass.

RISE AND SHINE

2 oz (60 ml) vodka
¹/₂ oz (15 ml) gin
¹/₂ oz (15 ml) gold tequila
¹/₂ oz (15 ml) dry vermouth
2 oz (60 ml) tomato juice
Salt

Fill a shaker two-thirds full with ice. Add the vodka, gin, tequila, vermouth, tomato juice, and a pinch of salt. Shake well and strain into an old-fashioned glass half-filled with ice.

MATADOR

Fill a shaker two-thirds full with ice. Add the tequila, pineapple juice, lime juice, and honey. Shake well and strain into two chilled martini glasses.

- 3 oz (90 ml) white tequila
- 3 oz (90 ml) pineapple juice
- 1 oz (30 ml) freshly squeezed lime juice
- 1/2 teaspoon honey

TEQUILA SPIKE

1 1/2 oz (45 ml) white tequila
3 oz (90 ml) freshly squeezed grapefruit juice
Dash of orange bitters
Wedge of orange, to garnish

Fill a shaker two-thirds full with ice. Add the tequila, grapefruit juice, and orange bitters. Shake well and strain into a chilled old-fashioned glass. Garnish with the orange.

TEQUILA COCKTAIL

2 oz (60 ml) gold tequila
1 1/2 oz (45 ml) freshly squeezed lime juice
1 teaspoon honey
3 dashes orange bitters
1 egg white
Soda water, to fill

Fill a shaker two-thirds full with ice. Add the tequila, lime juice, honey, orange bitters, and egg white. Shake well and strain into an old-fashioned glass half filled with ice cubes. Top up with soda water.

LOLITA

1 oz (30 ml) white tequila
1/2 oz (15 ml) freshly squeezed lime juice
1 teaspoon honey
2 dashes Angostura bitters

Fill a shaker two-thirds full with ice. Add the tequila, lime juice, honey, and Angostura. Shake well and strain into a chilled martini glass.

FROSTBITE

Fill a shaker two-thirds full with ice. Add the tequila, crème de cacao, blue curaçao, and cream. Shake well and strain into a chilled martini glass.

- 1¹/₂ oz (45 ml) white tequila
- 1 oz (30 ml) white crème de cacao
- ²/₃ oz (20 ml) blue curaçao
- 2 oz (60 ml) heavy (double) cream

138

ACAPULCO CREAM

1 oz (30 ml) gold tequila
¹/₂ oz (15 ml) cream of coconut
2 oz (60 ml) freshly squeezed orange juice
¹/₄ teaspoon cinnamon, to dust

Fill a shaker two-thirds full with ice. Add the tequila, cream of coconut, and orange juice. Shake well and strain into a chilled martini glass. Dust with the cinnamon.

ACAPULCO VERTIGO

2 oz (60 ml) gold tequila
1 oz (45 ml) sweet-and-sour mix
1 oz (30 ml) cranberry juice
1 oz (30 ml) freshly squeezed lime juice

Place 4–6 ice cubes in an old-fashioned glass. Pour in the tequila, sweet-and-sour mix, cranberry juice, and lime juice. Stir well.

ACAPULCO NIGHTS

1 oz (30 ml) gold tequila
1 oz (30 ml) vodka
1 oz (30 ml) Kahlua
3 oz (90 ml) milk
3 oz (90 ml) chilled cola, such as Pepsi or Coca-Cola

Half fill two old-fashioned glasses with ice. Pour in the tequila, vodka and Kahlua. Half fill each glass with cola and top up with milk. Stir gently.

YALE COCKTAIL

Fill a shaker two-thirds full with ice. Add the gin, vermouth, blue curaçao, and bitters. Shake well and strain into a chilled martini glass.

- 2 oz (60 ml) gin
- 1/2 oz (15 ml) dry vermouth
- 2 dashes blue curaçao
- Dash of orange bitters

GINNY'S FAVORITE

1 1/2 oz (45 ml) gin
1/2 oz (15 ml) dry vermouth
1/2 oz (15 ml) sweet vermouth
2 dashes orange bitters

Fill a shaker two-thirds full with ice. Add the gin, dry vermouth, sweet vermouth, and orange bitters. Shake well and strain into a chilled martini glass.

GIN COCKTAIL

1 oz (30 ml) gin
3/4 oz (25 ml) dry vermouth
1 oz (30 ml) freshly squeezed orange juice
2 dashes orange bitters

Fill a shaker two-thirds full with ice. Add the gin, dry vermouth, orange juice, and bitters. Shake well and strain into a chilled martini glass.

BITTER AND BLUE

1 1/2 oz (45 ml) gin
1 oz (30 ml) Cointreau
3 dashes aromatic bitters
1/3 oz (10 ml) blue curaçao

Fill an old-fashioned glass three-quarters full with ice. Pour in the gin, Cointreau, and bitters. Stir gently. Pour the blue curaçao into the center.

WEDDING BELLE

Fill a shaker two-thirds full with ice. Add the gin, Dubonnet, cherry brandy, and orange juice. Shake well and strain into a chilled martini glass. Garnish with the fresh fruit.

- 1½ oz (45 ml) gin
- 1 oz (30 ml) Dubonnet
- ½ oz (15 ml) cherry brandy
- 1½ oz (45 ml) freshly squeezed orange juice
- Fresh fruit, to garnish

HONEYMOON SPECIAL

1 oz (30 ml) vodka
1 oz (30 ml) Galliano
½ oz (15 ml) Campari
2 oz (60 ml) freshly squeezed range juice
Wedge of fresh pineapple, to garnish

Fill a shaker two-thirds full with ice. Add the vodka, Galliano, Campari, and orange juice. Shake well and strain into a chilled martini glass. Garnish with the pineapple.

BELLE DE JOUR

1½ oz (45 ml) gin
1 oz (30 ml) Cointreau
1 oz (30 ml) apricot brandy
½ oz (15 ml) freshly squeezed lemon juice

Fill a shaker two-thirds full with ice. Add the gin, Cointreau, apricot brandy, and lemon juice. Shake well and strain into a chilled martini glass.

FLYING TIGER

1 oz (30 ml) vodka
1 oz (30 ml) Galliano
1 oz (30 ml) white crème de cacao
3 oz (90 ml) freshly squeezed range juice

Half fill an old-fashioned glass with ice cubes. Pour in the vodka, and Galliano, crème de cacao. Top up with the orange juice and stir gently.

VODKA MARGARITA

Moisten the rim of a chilled margarita glass and dip in salt to coat. Fill a shaker two-thirds full with ice. Add the vodka, Cointreau, and lime juice. Shake well and strain into the margarita glass. Garnish with the lime.

- 1¹/₂ oz (45 ml) vodka
- ¹/₂ oz (15 ml) Cointreau
- 1 oz (30 ml) freshly squeezed lime juice
- Salt
- Slice of lime, to garnish

144

CURAÇAO MARGARITA

1¹/₂ oz (45 ml) white tequila
1 oz (30 ml) blue curaçao
1 oz (30 ml) freshly squeezed lime juice
Salt

Moisten the rim of a martini glass with lime juice. Dip into salt to coat. Fill a shaker two-thirds full with ice. Add the tequila, blue curaçao, and lime juice. Shake well and strain into the martini glass.

ORANGE MARGARITA

2 oz (60 ml) gold tequila
²/₃ oz (20 ml) oz Grand Marnier
1¹/₂ oz (45 ml) freshly squeezed orange juice
Wedge of orange, to garnish
Salt

Moisten the rim of a martini glass with orange juice. Dip into salt to coat. Fill a shaker two-thirds full with ice. Add the tequila, Grand Marnier, and orange juice. Shake well and strain into the martini glass. Garnish with the orange.

LIME MARGARITA

2 oz (60 ml) gold tequila
1 oz (30 ml) Grand Marnier
1 oz (30 ml) freshly squeezed lime juice
Salt

Moisten the rim of a martini glass with lime juice. Dip into salt to coat. Fill a shaker two-thirds full with ice. Add the tequila, Grand Marnier, and lime juice. Shake well and strain into the martini glass.

TROJAN HORSE

Fill a shaker two-thirds full with ice. Add the brandy, Dubonnet, Maraschino, and lime juice. Shake well and strain into a chilled martini glass. Garnish with the cherry.

- 1 oz (30 ml) brandy
- 1/2 oz (15 ml) Dubonnet
- 1/3 oz (10 ml) Maraschino liqueur
- 1/2 oz (15 ml) freshly squeezed lime juice
- Maraschino cherry, to garnish

ALESSIA'S SPECIAL

1 1/2 oz (45 ml) brandy
1/2 oz (15 ml) Maraschino liqueur
1/2 oz (15 ml) Cointreau
1 oz (30 ml) pineapple juice
2 dashes orange bitters

Fill a shaker two-thirds full with ice. Add the brandy, Maraschino, Cointreau, pineapple juice, and bitters. Shake well and strain into a chilled martini glass.

FANTASY

1 oz (30 ml) brandy
2/3 oz (20 ml) dry vermouth
1/3 oz (10 ml) white crème de menthe
1/3 oz (10 ml) Maraschino liqueur

Half fill a mixing glass with ice cubes. Add the brandy, vermouth, crème de menthe, and Maraschino. Strain into a chilled martini glass.

DUBONNET SQUEEZE

1 oz (30 ml) brandy
1 oz (30 ml) Dubonnet rouge
Dash of Maraschino liqueur
1 oz (30 ml) freshly squeezed lime juice

Fill a shaker two-thirds full with ice. Add the brandy, Dubonnet, Maraschino, and lime juice. Shake well and strain into a chilled martini glass.

TIPPERARY

Fill a shaker two-thirds full with ice. Add the whiskey, Chartreuse, and vermouth. Shake well and strain into a chilled martini glass.

- 1¹/₂ oz (45 ml) Irish whiskey
- 1 oz (30 ml) green Chartreuse
- 1 oz (30 ml) dry vermouth

PEARL'S COCKTAIL

1¹/₂ oz (45 ml) Scotch whisky
¹/₂ oz (15 ml) dry vermouth
¹/₂ oz (15 ml) sweet vermouth

Half ill a mixing glass with ice cubes. Pour in the whisky, dry vermouth, and sweet vermouth and stir well. Strain into a chilled martini glass.

ORTENSIA

1¹/₂ oz (45 ml) Scotch whisky
²/₃ oz (20 ml) dry vermouth
²/₃ oz (20 ml) Aperol

Fill a shaker two-thirds full with ice. Add the whisky, vermouth, and Aperol. Shake well and strain into a chilled martini glass.

ODIN'S SPECIAL

1¹/₂ oz (45 ml) Scotch whisky
1 oz (30 ml) Irish whiskey
¹/₂ oz (15 ml) freshly squeezed lemon juice
Dash of orange bitters

Fill a shaker two-thirds full with ice. Add the Scotch whisky, Irish whiskey, lemon juice, and bitters. Shake well and strain into a chilled martini glass.

ANTI FREEZE MARTINI

Fill a shaker two-thirds full with ice. Add the vodka, blue curaçao, melon liqueur, and passion fruit juice. Shake well and strain into a chilled martini glass.

- 1½ oz (45 ml) vodka
- ½ oz (15 ml) blue curaçao
- ½ oz (15 ml) Midori melon liqueur
- ½ oz (15 ml) passion fruit juice

ABSINTHE SANDWICH

1 oz (30 ml) absinthe
1 oz (30 ml) gin
½ oz (15 ml) Grand Marnier
½ oz (15 ml) dry vermouth

Half fill a mixing glass with ice cubes. Pour in the absinthe and gin and stir well. Pour the vermouth into a chilled martini glass. Strain the contents of the mixing glass into the martini glass. Float the Grand Marnier on top.

POLSKA MARTINI

2 oz (60 ml) vodka
3–4 dashes kirsch
Dash of Pernod
Blackberry, to garnish

Fill a shaker two-thirds full with ice. Add the vodka, kirsch, and Pernod. Shake well and strain into a chilled martini glass. Garnish with the blackberry.

CLOUDBERRY MARTINI

1 oz (30 ml) vodka
½ oz (15 ml) blue curaçao
½ oz (15 ml) dry vermouth
1½ oz (45 ml) cloudberry juice

Fill a shaker two-thirds full with ice. Add the vodka, blue curaçao, vermouth, and cloudberry juice. Shake well and strain into a chilled martini glass.

MANDARINETTO DRINK

Place 3–4 ice cubes in an old-fashioned glass and pour in the mandarinetto, gin, and dry vermouth. Add the orange peel and stir well.

- 1 oz (30 ml) Mandarinetto
- 1 oz (30 ml) gin
- 1 oz (30 ml) dry vermouth
- Sliver of orange peel

■■■ *Mandarinetto is an Italian liqueur strongly flavored with Mediterranean tangerines. Often imbued with just a hint of cinnamon, it is an excellent ingredient for cocktails. Try this one on the rocks.*

GREAT GATSBY

Fill a shaker two-thirds full with ice. Add the vodka, gin, vermouth, and lime juice. Shake well and strain into a chilled martini glass.

- 2 oz (60 ml) vodka
- 2 oz (60 ml) gin
- 1/2 oz (15 ml) sweet vermouth
- 1/2 oz (15 ml) freshly squeezed lime juice

RED SPOT COCKTAIL

1 oz (30 ml) peach schnapps
1 oz (30 ml) vodka
1 oz (30 ml) coconut rum
Pineapple juice, to fill
Splash of cranberry juice

Pour the peach schnapps, vodka, and rum into a chilled martini glass. Top up with the pineapple juice and a splash of cranberry juice.

FRUITY BOURBON

2 oz (60 ml) bourbon
1 oz (30 ml) peach schnapps
1 oz (30 ml) banana liqueur
1/2 oz (15 ml) freshly squeezed lemon juice
2 oz (60 ml) cola, such as Pepsi or Coca-Cola

Half fill a highball glass with ice cubes. Pour in the bourbon, schnapps, banana liqueur, and lemon juice. Top up with cola, stirring well.

NORDIC STAR

1 oz (30 ml) aquavit
1/2 oz (15 ml) cherry brandy
1/2 oz (15 ml) orange bitters
Dash of cranberry juice

Fill a shaker two-thirds full with ice. Add the aquavit, cherry brandy, bitters, and cranberry juice. Shake well and strain into a chilled martini glass.

GOLDEN DAWN

Fill a shaker two-thirds full with ice. Add the gin, apricot brandy, orange juice, and grenadine. Shake well and strain into a chilled martini glass.

- 2 oz (60 ml) gin
- 1/2 oz (15 ml) apricot brandy
- 1/2 oz (15 ml) freshly squeezed orange juice
- Dash of grenadine

BRONX EGG

2 oz (60 ml) gin
1/3 oz (10 ml) dry vermouth
1/3 oz (10 ml) sweet vermouth
1/2 oz (15 ml) freshly squeezed orange juice
1 egg yolk

Fill a shaker two-thirds full with ice. Add the gin, dry vermouth, sweet vermouth, orange juice, and egg. Shake well and strain into an old-fashioned or highball glass.

GOLDEN BRONX

1 1/2 oz (45 ml) gin
1/3 oz (10 ml) dry vermouth
1/2 oz (15 ml) freshly squeezed orange juice

Fill a shaker two-thirds full with ice. Add the gin, dry vermouth, and orange juice. Shake well and strain into a chilled martini glass.

WILL ROGERS

1 1/2 oz (45 ml) gin
1/2 oz (15 ml) dry vermouth
Dash of Cointreau
1/2 oz (15 ml) freshly squeezed orange juice

Fill a shaker two-thirds full with ice. Add the gin, vermouth, Cointreau, and orange juice. Shake well and strain into a chilled martini glass.

GIBSON

Place the pearl onions in a chilled martini glass. Fill a shaker two-thirds full with ice. Add the gin and vermouth. Shake well and strain into the martini glass.

- **2 oz (60 ml) gin**
- **$1/2$ oz (15 ml) dry vermouth**
- **1–2 pearl onions**

■ ■ ■ *A Gibson is a martini garnished with 1–2 pearl onions instead of an olive.*

AMSTERDAMER

Fill a shaker two-thirds full with ice. Add the cherry brandy and advocaat. Shake well and strain into a chilled martini glass. Garnish with the cherry.

- 1¹/₂ oz (45 ml) cherry brandy
- 1¹/₂ oz (45 ml) advocaat
- Maraschino cherry, to garnish

FAITH'S BEST

1¹/₂ oz (45 ml) gin
¹/₂ oz (15 ml) Cointreau
¹/₂ oz (15 ml) freshly squeezed lime juice
2 dashes Angostura

Fill a shaker two-thirds full with ice. Add the gin, Cointreau, lime juice, and Angostura. Shake well and strain into a chilled martini glass.

YELLOW FLIP

2 oz (60 ml) advocaat
2 oz (60 ml) dry sherry
¹/₂ oz (15 ml) freshly squeezed lime juice

Fill a shaker two-thirds full with ice. Add the advocaat, sherry, and lemon juice. Shake well and strain into a chilled martini glass.

GOLDEN DREAM

1 oz (30 ml) apricot brandy
1 oz (30 ml) amaretto
1¹/₂ oz (45 ml) freshly squeezed orange juice

Fill a shaker two-thirds full with ice. Add the brandy, amaretto, and orange juice. Shake well and strain into a chilled martini glass.

BLOODY MARY

Fill a shaker two-thirds full with ice. Add the tequila, tomato juice, lime juice, Tabasco, and Worcestershire sauce. Shake well and strain into a large chilled collins glass over ice.

- 1½ oz (45 ml) tequila
- 4 oz (120 ml) tomato juice
- Freshly squeezed juice from ½ lime
- 4 dashes Tabasco
- 2 dashes Worcestershire sauce
- Salt
- Freshly ground black pepper

CITRUS MERINGUE

Fill a shaker two-thirds full with ice. Add the orange vodka, lemon liqueur, and crème de cacao. Shake well and strain into a chilled martini glass. Drop the slices of lime in so that they float in the drink.

- 1¹/₂ oz (45 ml) orange vodka
- ³/₄ oz (25 ml) lemon liqueur
- ¹/₂ oz (15 ml) white crème de cacao
- 2 very thin slices of lime, to garnish

CITRUS THRILL

1¹/₂ oz (45 ml) rum
1¹/₂ oz (45 ml) Cointreau
1 oz (30 ml) sweet-and-sour mix
Freshly squeezed grapefruit juice, to fill
Wedge of lemon, to garnish

Half fill a highball glass with ice cubes. Pour in the rum, Cointreau, and sweet-and-sour mix. Top up with grapefruit juice. Stir gently. Garnish with the lemon.

ORANGE PSYCHO

1 oz (30 ml) vodka
1 oz (30 ml) tequila
¹/₂ oz (15 ml) Grand Marnier
¹/₂ oz (15 ml) peppermint schnapps
Swirl of freshly squeezed lime juice
Freshly squeezed orange juice, to fill

Half fill an old-fashioned glass with ice cubes. Pour in the vodka, tequila, Grand Marnier, schnaaps, and lime juice. Top up with orange juice. Stir gently.

ORANGE VODKA

1 oz (30 ml) vodka
¹/₂ oz (15 ml) white curaçao
Freshly squeezed orange juice, to fill

Half fill a highball glass with ice cubes. Pour in the vodka and curaçao. Top up with orange juice. Stir gently.

STRAWBERRY MIMOSA

Place the strawberries in a small bowl and mash well with a fork (or chop in a blender). Pour in the orange juice. Strain into two champagne flutes. Top up with champagne. Garnish with the whole strawberries.

- **6 large tasty strawberries**
- **2–3 oz freshly squeezed orange juice**
- **Very dry champagne, well chilled, to fill**
- **Whole strawberries, to garnish**

■ ■ ■ *Light and cooling, this recipe makes a healthy apéritif for two.*

RASPBERRY BELLINI

Place the raspberries and sugar in a small bowl and mash well with a fork. Spoon the mixture into six champagne flutes and carefully top up with prosecco.

- **16–20 fresh raspberries**
- **2 tablespoons sugar**
- **1 (750 ml) bottle prosecco (Italian dry sparkling wine) or dry champagne, well chilled, to fill**

FRUITY BELLINI

2 slices fresh peach, peeled
8 raspberries
3 oz (90 ml) freshly squeezed orange juice
2–3 drops grenadine
1 teaspoon freshly squeezed lime juice
1 oz (30 ml) vanilla syrup
1 oz (30 ml) citrus vodka
Champagne or prosecco, well chilled, to fill

Chop the peach, raspberries, orange juice, grenadine, lime, and vanilla in a blender until smooth. Pour the vodka into 2 champagne flutes. Fill with blended mixture and champagne.

MANGO BELLINI

2 slices fresh mango
2 oz (60 ml) mango juice
Champagne or prosecco, well chilled, to fill

Mash the mango with a fork in a small bowl. Place in two champagne flutes. Pour in the mango juice and top up with champagne.

FALL BELLINI

1 oz (30 ml) lemon vodka
1/2 oz (15 ml) Cointreau
1/2 oz (15 ml) cranberry juice
1/2 oz (15 ml) white peach purée
1 teaspoon freshly squeezed lime juice
Champagne or prosecco, well chilled, to fill

Fill a shaker two-thirds full with ice. Add the vodka, Cointreau, cranberry juice, peach purée, and lime juice. Shake well and strain into a champagne flute. Top up with champagne.

PASSION FRUIT MARGARITA

Moisten the edges of a chilled margarita glass with some of the lemon juice. Dip in the sugar and salt mix to coat the rim. Fill a shaker two-thirds full with ice. Add the tequila, Chambord, Cointreau, passion fruit juice, and remaining lemon juice. Shake well and strain into the margarita glass.

- 1 oz (30 ml) white tequila
- 1/2 oz (15 ml) Chambord raspberry liqueur
- 1/2 oz (15 ml) Cointreau
- 1 oz (30 ml) passion fruit juice
- 1 oz (30 ml) freshly squeezed lemon juice
- 1 tablespoon mixed sugar and salt

FRESH FRUIT CAIPIROVSKA

Place the blueberries and raspberries in an old-fashioned glass. Add the sugar and muddle with the fruit. Add 4–6 ice cubes and pour in the vodka, raspberry liqueur, and lime juice. Add the lime wedge and stir gently.

- 4 fresh blueberries
- 4 fresh raspberries
- 2 teaspoons sugar
- 2 oz (60 ml) vodka
- $1/2$ oz (15 ml) Chambord raspberry liqueur
- 2 tablespoons freshly squeezed lime juice
- Wedge of lime

STRAWBERRY DREAM

2 oz (60 ml) vodka
1 oz (30 ml) kirsch
$1/3$ oz (10 ml) strawberry liqueur
5 fresh strawberries
Tonic water, to fill

Mash the strawberries with a fork in a small bowl. Fill a shaker two-thirds full with ice. Add the vodka, kirsch, strawberry liqueur, and strawberries. Shake well and strain into a highball glass with 4–5 cubes of ice. Top up with tonic water.

MIDSUMMER MARTINI

3 oz (90 g) very ripe, peeled watermelon flesh
3 oz (90 ml) vodka
$1^1/2$ oz (45 ml) freshly squeezed lime juice
1 oz (30 ml) sugar syrup

Mash the watermelon with a fork in a small bowl. Remove any seeds. Fill a shaker two-thirds full with ice. Add the watermelon, vodka, lime juice, and sugar syrup. Shake well and strain into 2 martini glasses.

KIWI VODKA ORANGE

2 oz (60 ml) vodka, chilled
1 oz (30 ml) orange soda, such as Fanta
$1/2$ oz (15 ml) kiwi juice, concentrate

Pour the vodka in a chilled martini glass. Add the orange soda and kiwi juice and stir gently.

WATERMELON MARGARITA

Peel the watermelon, remove the seeds, and cut the flesh into small cubes. Freeze well spaced on a tray so they don't stick together. Depending on the size of the watermelon, you will have quite a lot of cubes. Place 2 cups of them in a blender (store the rest in a plastic bag for more margaritas) along with the mescal, Grand Marnier, lime juice, and mint leaves. Blend until smooth. Salt the rims of four chilled margarita glasses. Carefully pour in the watermelon mixture. Garnish each glass with a sprig of mint.

- 1 fresh, ripe watermelon
- 5 oz (150 ml) mescal (or tequila)
- 1 oz (30 ml) Grand Marnier
- 2 oz (60 ml) freshly squeezed lime juice
- 4 fresh mint leaves
- Fresh mint sprigs, to garnish

JAMAICAN DUST

Fill a shaker two-thirds full with ice. Add the rum, Tia Maria, and pineapple juice. Shake well and strain into a chilled martini glass. Garnish with the lime.

- 1 oz (30 ml) 151 rum
- 1 oz (30 ml) Tia Maria
- 2 oz (60 ml) pineapple juice
- Wedge of lime, to garnish

FRUIT RUM COCKTAIL

2 oz (60 ml) dark rum
2 dashes Angostura bitters
2 oz (60 ml) freshly squeezed lemon juice
1 oz (30 ml) pineapple juice
1 oz (30 ml) freshly squeezed orange juice
1/3 oz (10 ml) grenadine

Half fill a mixing glass with crushed ice. Pour in the rum, Angostura, lemon juice, pineapple juice, orange juice, and grenadine. Stir well. Strain into a highball glass with 3–4 cubes of ice.

JAMAICAN COCKTAIL

2 oz (60 ml) dark rum
1 oz (30 ml) white rum
Dash of Campari
Splash grenadine
3 oz (90 ml) pineapple juice
1 oz (30 ml) cream of coconut

Half fill a mixing glass with crushed ice. Pour in the dark rum, white rum, Campari, grenadine, and cream of coconut. Stir well. Strain into a highball glass with 3–4 cubes of ice.

JAMAICAN BREEZE

1 oz (30 ml) dark rum
1/2 oz (15 ml) coconut rum
Pineapple juice, to fill
Small wedge fresh pineapple, to garnish

Place 4–5 ice cubes in an old-fashioned glass. Pour in the dark rum and coconut rum. Top up with pineapple juice. Garnish with the pineapple.

WHY NOT? INDEED!

Fill a shaker two-thirds full with ice. Add the apricot brandy, gin, dry vermouth, and lime juice. Shake well and strain into a chilled martini glass.

- 1 oz (30 ml) apricot brandy
- 1 oz (30 ml) gin
- $3/4$ oz (25 ml) dry vermouth
- 1 teaspoon freshly squeezed lime juice

180

BLACKEYE MARTINI

$2^1/_2$ oz (75 ml) gin
$1/_2$ oz (15 ml) dry vermouth
1 black olive

Fill a shaker two-thirds full with ice. Add the gin and vermouth. Shake well and strain into a chilled martini glass. Add the olive.

APRICOT COCKTAIL

1 oz (30 ml) apricot brandy
$1/_2$ oz (15 ml) gin
$1/_2$ oz (15 ml) dry vermouth
$1/_3$ oz (10 ml) freshly squeezed lime juice

Fill a shaker two-thirds full with ice. Add the apricot brandy, gin, vermouth, and lime juice. Shake well and strain into a chilled martini glass.

APRICOT COCKTAIL • 1

1 oz (30 ml) gin
$2/_3$ oz (20 ml) apricot brandy
$2/_3$ oz (20 ml) dry vermouth
$1/_3$ oz (10 ml) freshly squeezed lemon juice
Wedge of lemon, to garnish

Fill a shaker two-thirds full with ice. Add the gin, apricot brandy, vermouth, and lemon juice. Shake well and strain into a chilled martini glass. Garnish with the lemon.

SLEDGEHAMMER

Fill a shaker two-thirds full with ice. Add the rum, brandy, apple brandy, and Pernod. Shake well and strain into a chilled martini glass. Garnish with the apple and serve with the cheese, if liked.

- 3/4 oz (25 ml) dark rum
- 3/4 oz (25 ml) brandy
- 1/2 oz (15 ml) apple brandy
- **Dash of Pernod**
- **Wedge green apple, to garnish (optional)**
- **Tiny wedge of cheese, to serve (optional)**

RUM AND SAMBUCA

2 oz (60 ml) white rum
2 dashes Sambuca
1–2 dashes Angostura bitters
1 cube sugar
Chilled mineral water, to fill

Place the sugar cube in an old-fashioned glass. Soak with the Angostura and crush the sugar. Add 3–4 ice cubes, then pour in the rum and Sambuca. Top up with the water.

HUMMINGBIRD

1 oz (30 ml) white rum
2/3 oz (20 ml) dark rum
1–2 dashes Angostura bitters
2 1/2 oz (75 ml) freshly squeezed orange juice

Fill a shaker two-thirds full with ice. Add the white rum, dark rum, Angostura, and orange juice. Shake well and strain into an old-fashioned glass over 3–4 ice cubes.

SAINT PAUL

1 oz (30 ml) gin
1 oz (30 ml) white rum
1–2 dashes Angostura bitters
Bitter lemon, to fill

Half fill an old-fashioned glass with ice cubes. Pour in the gin, rum, and Angostura. Top up with bitter lemon. Stir gently.

ORANGE BLOSSOM

Fill a shaker two-thirds full with ice. Add the gin, vermouth, and orange juice. Shake well and strain into a chilled martini glass. Garnish with the orange.

- 1 oz (30 ml) gin
- 1 oz (30 ml) dry vermouth
- 1 oz (30 ml) freshly squeezed orange juice
- **Slice of orange, to garnish**

ORANGE BLOSSOM

2 oz (60 ml) peach schnapps

2 oz (60 ml) lemon soda

3 oz (90 g) orange sherbet

1¹/₂ oz (45 ml) vanilla ice cream

2 oz (60 ml) double (heavy) cream

Slice of orange, to garnish

Place the peach schnapps, soda, sherbet, ice cream, and cream in a blender with 4-5 ice cubes. Blend until smooth. Pour into a wine goblet. Garnish with the orange.

HAWAIIAN ORANGE B.

1¹/₂ oz (45 ml) gin

1 oz (30 ml) white curaçao

2 oz (60 ml) freshly squeezed orange juice

1 oz (30 ml) pineapple juice

1 slice orange

Fill a shaker two-thirds full with ice. Add the gin, curaçao, orange juice, and pineapple juice. Shake well and strain into a chilled martini glass. Garnish with the orange.

ROYAL BLOSSOM

1¹/₂ oz (45 ml) gin

1 oz (30 ml) pineapple juice

¹/₂ oz (15 ml) freshly squeezed lemon juice

¹/₃ oz (10 ml) sugar syrup

Fill a shaker two-thirds full with ice. Add the gin, pineapple juice, lemon juice, and sugar syrup. Shake well and strain into a chilled martini glass.

SHERRY COBBLER

Fill a wine goblet with cracked ice. Pour in the sherry, Cointreau, and sugar syrup. Stir gently. Twist the lemon peel over the drink to release the fragrant oils then drop it into the drink. Garnish with chunks of pineapple or other fresh fruit.

- **3 oz (100 ml) sherry**
- **1/2 oz (15 ml) Cointreau**
- **1 teaspoon sugar syrup**
- **Lemon peel**
- **Pineapple (or other fresh fruit), to garnish**

BOURBON COBBLER

2^1/$_2$ oz (75 ml) bourbon
1^1/$_2$ oz (45 ml) soda water
1 teaspoon sugar
Maraschino cherry
1 slice orange
1 slice lemon

Place the sugar in an old-fashioned glass. Add the soda water and stir until dissolved. Fill the glass three-quarters full with cracked ice. Pour in the bourbon and stir well. Garnish with the cherry, orange. and lemon.

BRANDY COBBLER

2^1/$_2$ oz (75 ml) brandy
1^1/$_2$ oz (45 ml) soda water
1 teaspoon sugar
Maraschino cherry
1 slice lime
1 slice orange

Place the sugar in an old-fashioned glass. Add the soda water and stir until dissolved. Fill the glass three-quarters full with cracked ice. Pour in the brandy and stir well. Garnish with the cherry, orange, and lime.

GIN COBBLER

2 oz (60 ml) gin
1^1/$_2$ oz (45 ml) soda water
1 teaspoon sugar
Wedge of lemon

Place the sugar in an old-fashioned glass. Add the soda water and stir until dissolved. Fill the glass three-quarters full with cracked ice. Pour in the gin and stir well. Garnish with the lemon.

ACAPULCO

Fill a shaker two-thirds full with ice. Add the tequila, Cointreau, rum, and lime juice. Shake well and strain into a chilled martini glass. Garnish with the wedge of lemon.

- 1¹/₂ oz (45 ml) tequila
- ¹/₂ oz (15 ml) Cointreau
- ¹/₂ oz (15 ml) white rum
- ¹/₂ oz (15 ml) freshly squeezed lime juice
- Wedge of lemon, to garnish

BUSTED IN ACAPULCO

1 oz (30 ml) vodka
1 oz (30 ml) white tequila
1 oz (30 ml) white rum
Dash of white crème de menthe
2 oz (60 ml) freshly squeezed orange juice
2 oz (60 ml) freshly squeezed grapefruit juice

Place 3–4 ice cubes in a highball glass. Pour in the vodka, tequila, rum, and crème de menthe. Top up with the orange and grapefruit juices.

WHITE RUM SPECIAL

2 oz (60 ml) white rum
¹/₃ oz (10 ml) Maraschino liqueur
1 oz (30 ml) freshly squeezed lime juice
1 oz (30 ml) freshly squeezed grapefruit juice

Fill a shaker two-thirds full with ice. Add the rum, Maraschino, lime juice, and lemon juice. Shake well and strain into a chilled martini glass.

RUM AND LIME

1¹/₂ oz (45 ml) white rum
¹/₂ oz (15 ml) freshly squeezed lime juice
1 teaspoon sugar

Fill a shaker two-thirds full with ice. Add the rum, lime juice, and sugar. Shake well and strain into a chilled martini glass.

TWIN PEAKS

Half fill a mixing glass with ice cubes. Pour in the whisky, vermouth, and Cointreau and stir gently. Strain into a chilled martini glass. Twist the lemon peel over the drink to release its fragrant oils then drop it into the drink.

- **2 oz (60 ml) blended whisky**
- **$1/2$ oz (15 ml) sweet white vermouth**
- **$1/2$ oz (15 ml) Cointreau**
- **Lemon peel**

BILL'S HILLS

$1^1/_2$ oz (45 ml) blended whisky
$1/_2$ oz (15 ml) Benedictine
$1/_2$ oz (15 ml) freshly squeezed lemon juice
$1/_2$ oz (15 ml) freshly squeezed lime juice
1 teaspoon sugar
1 slice lemon

Fill a shaker two-thirds full with ice. Add the whisky, Benedictine, lemon juice, lime juice, and sugar. Shake well and strain into a chilled martini glass.

BILL ON LEAVE

2 oz (60 ml) blended whisky
$1/_2$ oz (15 ml) sweet vermouth
1 teaspoon grenadine
Maraschino cherry

Fill a shaker two-thirds full with ice. Add the whisky, vermouth, and grenadine. Shake well and strain into a chilled martini glass. Garnish with the cherry.

SIMPLE BILL

3 oz (90 ml) blended whisky
Freshly squeezed juice of $1/_2$ lemon
Cola, such as Pepsi or Coca-Cola, to fill

Half fill an old-fashioned glass with ice cubes. Pour in the whisky. Squeeze in the lemon juice and top up with cola.

GREEN DRAGON

Fill a shaker two-thirds full with ice. Add the gin, kümmel, crème de menthe, and lemon juice. Shake well and strain into a chilled martini glass. Garnish with the lemon peel tied into a knot.

- **2 oz (60 ml) gin**
- **1/2 oz (15 ml) kümmel caraway liqueur**
- **1/2 oz (15 ml) green crème de menthe**
- **1/2 oz (15 ml) freshly squeezed lemon juice**
- **Lemon peel, cut in a long thin piece, to garnish**

GREEN DRAGON • 1

11/2 oz (45 ml) cognac
11/2 oz (45 ml) green Chartreuse

Fill a shaker two-thirds full with ice. Add the cognac and Chartreuse. Shake well and strain into a chilled martini glass.

CARAWAY DRAGON

11/2 oz (45 ml) gin
1/2 oz (15 ml) kümmel caraway liqueur
1/2 oz (15 ml) apricot brandy
1/2 oz (15 ml) freshly squeezed lemon juice
Twist of lemon peel

Fill a shaker two-thirds full with ice. Add the gin, kümmel, apricot brandy, and lemon juice. Shake well and strain into a chilled martini glass. Garnish with the lemon peel.

GINNY'S DRAGON

1 oz (30 ml) gin
1 oz (30 ml) dry vermouth
1/2 oz (15 ml) kümmel caraway liqueur

Fill a shaker two-thirds full with ice. Add the gin, vermouth, and kümmel. Shake well and strain into a chilled martini glass.

CHAMPAGNE CHARLIE

Pour the apricot brandy into a chilled champagne flute and top up with the champagne.

- **2 oz (60 ml) apricot brandy**
- **Dry champagne, well chilled, to fill**

RASPBERRY CHAMPAGNE

4 oz (120 ml) dry champagne, well chilled

1/2 oz (15 ml) Chambord raspberry liqueur

Pour the champagne into a chilled champagne flute. Splash in the Chambord.

LEMON CHAMPAGNE

3 oz (90 ml) dry champagne, well chilled

2/3 oz (20 ml) gin

1/2 oz (15 ml) freshly squeezed lemon juice

1/2 oz (15 ml) sugar syrup

Pour the champagne into a chilled champagne flute. Add the gin, lemon juice, and sugar syrup. Stir gently.

BLACKBERRY CHAMPAGNE

4 oz (120 ml) dry champagne, well chilled

1/2 oz (15 ml) blackberry brandy

1/2 oz (15 ml) honey liqueur

Pour the champagne into a chilled champagne flute. Splash in the brandy and honey liqueur.

JADE

Fill a shaker two-thirds full with ice. Add the Midori, blue curaçao, lime juice, and Angostura. Shake well and strain into a chilled champagne flute. Top up with champagne.

- 1 oz (30 ml) Midori melon liqueur
- 1 oz (30 ml) blue curaçao
- 1 oz (30 ml) freshly squeezed lime juice
- Dash of Angostura bitters
- Dry champagne, well chilled, to fill

JADE • 1

1¹/₂ oz (45 ml) vanilla vodka
¹/₂ oz (15 ml) Midori melon liqueur
2 oz (60 ml) pineapple juice
1 oz (30 ml) freshly squeezed lime juice
¹/₂ oz (15 ml) freshly squeezed lime juice
¹/₂ oz (15 ml) sugar syrup

Fill a shaker two-thirds full with ice. Add the vodka, Midori, pineapple juice, lime juice, lemon juice, and sugar syrup. Shake well and strain into a chilled martini glass.

JADE • 2

2 oz (60 ml) Midori melon liqueur
1 oz (30 ml) blue curaçao
1 oz (30 ml) vodka
3 oz (90 ml) sweet-and-sour mix
White soda, such as 7-Up or Sprite, to fill
Maraschino cherry, to garnish

Fill a shaker two-thirds full with ice. Add the Midori, curaçao, vodka, and sweet-and-sour mix. Shake well and strain into a hurricane glass over 3–4 ice cubes. Top up with soda. Garnish with the cherry.

JADED

1¹/₂ oz (45 ml) white rum
¹/₂ oz (15 ml) green crème de menthe
¹/₂ oz (15 ml) Cointreau
¹/₂ oz (15 ml) freshly squeezed lime juice
1 teaspoon sugar
Wedge of lime, to garnish

Fill a shaker two-thirds full with ice. Add the rum, crème de menthe, Cointreau, lime juice, and sugar. Shake well and strain into a chilled martini glass. Garnish with the lime.

TEQUILA MOCKINGBIRD

Fill a shaker two-thirds full with ice. Add the apple cider, tequila, crème de cassis, and lemon juice. Shake well. Place 4–6 ice cubes in an old-fashioned glass and strain the drink in over the top.

- 3 oz (90 ml) apple cider
- 1 oz (30 ml) white tequila
- 1 oz (30 ml) crème de cassis
- 2 teaspoons freshly squeezed lemon juice

T. MOCKINGBIRD •1

1¹/₂ oz (45 ml) white tequila
²/₃ oz (20 ml) green peppermint liqueur
1¹/₂ oz (45 ml) freshly squeezed lime juice

Fill a shaker two-thirds full with ice. Add the tequila, peppermint liqueur, and lime juice. Shake well and strain into a chilled martini glass.

BLUE TEQUILA

1¹/₂ oz (45 ml) white tequila
²/₃ oz (20 ml) blue curaçao
1 oz (30 ml) freshly squeezed lime juice

Fill a shaker two-thirds full with ice. Add the tequila, blue curaçao, and lime juice. Shake well and strain into a chilled martini glass.

TEQUILA HIGHBALL

1¹/₂ oz (45 ml) white tequila
¹/₂ oz (15 ml) crème de cassis
¹/₃ oz (10 ml) freshly squeezed lime juice
4 oz (120 ml) ginger ale

Fill a shaker two-thirds full with ice. Add the tequila, crème de cassis, and lime juice. Shake well and strain into a highball glass half filled with ice cubes. Top up with ginger ale.

LONG
DRINKS

ROMAN COOLER

Fill a shaker two-thirds full with ice. Add the gin, Punt e Mes, lemon juice, syrup, and vermouth. Shake well and strain into a chilled collins glass. Top up with soda water. Garnish with the orange.

- 2 oz (60 ml) gin
- 1/2 oz (15 ml) Punt e Mes
- 1/2 oz (15 ml) freshly squeezed lemon juice
- 1 tablespoon sugar syrup
- Dash of sweet vermouth
- Soda water
- Wedge of orange, to garnish

206

MELON COOLER

1 1/2 oz (45 ml) vodka
1 oz (30 ml) Midori melon liqueur
2/3 oz (20 ml) Cointreau
2 oz (60 ml) sweet-and-sour mix
White soda, such as 7-Up or Sprite, to fill

Half fill a collins glass with ice cubes. Pour in the vodka, Midori, Cointreau, and sweet-and-sour mix. Stir gently. Top up with white soda.

VERMOUTH COOLER

2 oz (60 ml) dry vermouth
1/3 oz (10 ml) grenadine
Soda water, to fill
Wedge of lemon or lime
Twist of orange zest

Half fill a collins glass with ice cubes. Pour in the vermouth and grenadine. Top up with soda water and stir gently. Add the wedge of lemon or lime to the glass and garnish with the orange zest.

GIN COOLER

2 oz (60 ml) gin
1/2 oz (15 ml) dry vermouth
1/2 teaspoon sugar
Soda water, to fill
Slice of orange, to garnish

Half fill a collins glass with ice cubes. Pour in the gin and vermouth. Add the sugar and top up with soda water. Stir gently. Add the the orange.

MOJITO

Fill a shaker two-thirds full with ice. Add the gin, Punt e Mes, lemon juice, sugar syrup, and vermouth. Shake well and strain into a chilled highball or collins glass. Top up with soda water. Garnish with the orange.

- **2 oz (60 ml) gin**
- **1/2 oz (15 ml) Punt e Mes**
- **1/2 oz (15 ml) freshly squeezed lemon juice**
- **1/2 oz (15 ml) sugar syrup**
- **Dash of sweet vermouth**
- **Soda water, to fill**
- **Wedge of orange, to garnish**

■ ■ ■ *Reputedly Hemingway's favorite drink, the cool and refreshing Mojito comes from Havana, Cuba.*

SORRENTO SLING

Fill a shaker two-thirds full with ice. Add the Limoncello, gin, and lemon juice. Shake well and strain into a chilled collins glass. Top up with soda water or champagne. Garnish with the lemon or lime.

- **2 oz (60 ml) Limoncello**
- **1 oz (30 ml) gin**
- **1 oz (30 ml) freshly squeezed lemon juice**
- **Soda water or very dry champagne, well chilled, to fill**
- **Wedge of lemon or lime, to garnish**

■ ■ ■ *Limoncello is a sweet but feisty lemon liqueur traditionally made in Naples and the Bay of Sorrento, where lemon groves stretch down to the sea. It needs to be kept in the freezer. Generally served neat after dinner, this is a delicious way to enjoy it as a lazy, hot summer's day long drink*

KIWI COLADA

Cut the kiwi in half. Cut off a slice to garnish and set aside. Peel the rest and place in a blender with the crushed ice, rum, Midori, cream of coconut, and pineapple. Blend for a few seconds until just slushy. Strain into a hurricane glass or wine goblet. Garnish with the slice of kiwi.

214

- 1 kiwi
- $1/2$ cup (125 ml) crushed ice
- 1 oz (30 ml) white rum
- 1 oz (30 ml) Midori melon liqueur
- $1/2$ oz (15 ml) cream of coconut
- 4 tablespoons crushed pineapple, with juice

CANADA KIWI

$1^1/_2$ oz (45 ml) Canadian whisky
1 oz (30 ml) kiwi liqueur
$1/_3$ oz (10 ml) freshly squeezed lemon juice
Lemonade, well chilled, to fill

Half fill an old-fashioned glass with ice cubes. Pour in the whisky, kiwi liqueur, and lemon juice. Stir gently then top up with lemonade.

KIWI AND RUM

2 oz (60 ml) white rum
2 oz (60 ml) kiwi juice
White soda, such as 7-Up or Sprite, to fill
Slice of kiwi, to garnish

Half fill a hurricane glass with ice cubes. Pour in the rum and kiwi juice. Stir gently then top up with white soda. Garnish with the kiwi.

KIWI SPARKLE

3 oz (90 ml) dry champagne, well chilled
$1/_2$ oz (15 ml) kiwi liqueur
1 oz (30 ml) kiwi juice

Pour the kiwi liqueur and juice into a chilled champagne flute. Top up with champagne.

CITRUS CRUSH

Fill a shaker two-thirds full with ice. Add one kafir lime leaf, the lemon, lime, gin, and triple sec and shake. Fill a chilled collins glass with ice. Strain the drink into the glass and drop the remaining kafir lime leaf in on top.

- 1¹/₂ oz (45 ml) gin
- ¹/₂ oz (15 ml) triple sec
- 2 kafir lime leaves
- ¹/₂ lemon, cut in small wedges
- ¹/₂ lime, cut in small wedges

FLUFFY DUCK

218

Fill a shaker two-thirds full with ice. Add the gin, Cointreau, advocaat, and orange juice. Shake well. Half fill a collins glass with ice and strain the drink into it. Top up with soda water or lemonade. Garnish with the cherry.

- 1 oz (30 ml) gin
- 1/2 oz (15 ml) Cointreau
- 1 oz (30 ml) advocaat
- 3 oz (90 ml) freshly squeezed orange juice
- Soda water or lemonade, to fill
- Maraschino cherry, to garnish

BLONDIE

2 oz (60 ml) advocaat
1/2 oz (15 ml) rum
1/2 oz (15 ml) banana liqueur
Freshly squeezed orange juice, to fill

Fill a shaker two-thirds full with ice. Add the advocaat, rum, and banana liqueur. Shake well and strain into a hurricane glass over 3–4 ice cubes. Top up with orange juice and stir gently.

SNOWBOARDER

2 oz (60 ml) advocaat
1/2 oz (15 ml) lime cordial
Lemonade, well chilled, to fill

Half fill a collins glass with ice cubes. Pour in the advocaat and lime cordial. Stir gently and top up with lemonade.

SNOWBALL

1 1/2 oz (45 ml) vodka
1/2 oz (15 ml) Galliano
1/2 oz (15 ml) Southern Comfort
1/2 oz (15 ml) advocaat
Freshly squeezed orange juice, to fill

Fill a shaker two-thirds full with ice. Add the vodka, Galliano, Southern Comfort, and advocaat. Shake well and strain into a collins glass over 3–4 ice cubes. Top up with orange juice.

FUZZY NAVEL

Half fill a collins glass with ice cubes. Pour in the peach schnapps. Top up with orange juice.

- **2 oz (60 ml) peach schnapps**
- **Freshly squeezed orange juice, to fill**

FIZZY FUZZY NAVEL

1¹/₂ oz (45 ml) peach schnapps
2 oz (60 ml) freshly squeezed orange juice
Dry champagne, well chilled, to fill

Half fill a collins glass with ice cubes. Pour in the peach schnapps and orange juice. Stir gently and top up with champagne.

BERRY FUZZY NAVEL

1 oz (30 ml) peach schnapps
¹/₂ oz (15 ml) vodka
4 oz (120 ml) freshly squeezed orange juice
Splash blackberry brandy

Half fill a collins glass with ice cubes. Pour in the peach schnapps, vodka, and orange juice. Stir gently then add a splash of blackberry brandy.

VERY FUZZY NAVEL

2¹/₂ oz (75 ml) peach schnapps
1¹/₂ oz (45 ml) Cointreau
Freshly squeezed orange juice, to fill

Half fill a collins glass with ice cubes. Pour in the peach schnapps and Cointreau. Stir gently and top up with orange juice.

HORSE'S NECK

Peel the lemon with a potato peeler in one long strip. Place in a chilled collins glass. Half fill with ice cubes and pour the brandy in over the top. Squeeze about 1/2 tablespoon of lemon juice into the glass. Fill up with ginger ale, stirring gently.

- 2 1/2 oz (75 ml) brandy
- 1 lemon
- Ginger ale, to fill

HORSE'S NECK • 1

2 oz (60 ml) blended whisky
Dash of Angostura bitters
Ginger ale, to fill

Half fill an old-fashioned glass with ice. Pour in the whisky and bitters and top up with ginger ale.

HORSE AND JOCKEY

1 1/2 oz (45 ml) dark rum
1 oz (30 ml) Southern Comfort
1/2 oz (15 ml) sweet vermouth
2 dashes orange bitters
Soda water, to fill

Half fill a collins glass with ice. Pour in the rum, Southern Comfort, vermouth, and bitters. Stir well and top up with soda water.

FLORIDA

2 oz (60 ml) brandy
3 oz (90 ml) freshly squeezed grapefruit juice
1 oz (30 ml) freshly squeezed lime juice
1 teaspoon sugar syrup
Soda water, to fill

Half fill a collins glass with ice. Pour in the brandy, grapefruit juice, lime juice, and sugar syrup. Stir gently then top up with soda water.

ADONIS
SHORT AND LONG

Fill a shaker two-thirds full with ice. Add the sherry, vermouth, and bitters. Shake well and strain into a chilled martini glass. Squeeze the orange peel over the glass so that the fruit's fragrant oils gently flavor the drink. Drop the orange peel into the drink.

For a long drink, strain the cocktail into a chilled collins glass half-filled with ice. Top up with ginger ale. Garnish with the orange peel as for the short drink.

- 1$^1/_2$ oz (45 ml) dry sherry
- $^3/_4$ oz (25 ml) sweet vermouth
- Dash of orange bitters
- Piece of orange peel

- Ginger ale, to fill

SCARLET PIMPERNEL

Half fill a collins glass with ice. Pour in the Cointreau, Pimm's, cranberry juice, apple juice, and lime juice. Stir gently. Garnish with the lime.

- **1 oz (30 ml) Cointreau**
- **1 oz (30 ml) Pimm's**
- **3 oz (90 ml) cranberry juice**
- **3 oz (90 ml) apple juice**
- **Dash of freshly squeezed lime juice**
- **Slice of lime, to garnish**

226

SCARLET LETTER

1¹/₂ oz (45 ml) vodka
1 oz (30 ml) white rum
¹/₂ oz (15 ml) gin
3 oz (90 ml) cranberry juice
Slice of lime, to garnish

Half fill a mixing glass with ice cubes. Add the vodka, rum, gin, and cranberry juice and stir well. Place 3–4 ice cubes in a collins glass and pour the drink in over the top. Garnish with the lime.

SCARLET LONG DRINK

1¹/₂ oz (45 ml) Southern Comfort
2 oz (60 ml) cranberry juice
1 oz (30 ml) freshly squeezed lemon juice
Soda water, to fill
Slice of lemon, to garnish

Half fill a mixing glass with ice cubes. Add the Southern Comfort, cranberry juice, and lemon juice. Stir well and pour into a collins glass over 4–5 ice cubes. Top up with soda water. Garnish with the lemon.

SOUTHERN LONG DRINK

2 oz (60 ml) coconut rum
1 oz (30 ml) white rum
1 oz (30 ml) Midori melon liqueur
¹/₂ oz (15 ml) spiced rum
¹/₂ oz (15 ml) freshly squeezed lime juice
Pineapple juice, to fill

Half fill a collins glass with ice cubes. Pour in the three types of rum, the Midori, and lime juice. Stir well and top up with pineapple juice.

PIMM'S CUP

Half fill a collins glass with ice cubes. Add the Pimm's, orange, lemon, and cucumber. Top up with lemon soda. Stir gently.

- **1^1/$_2$ oz (45 ml) Pimm's**
- **Lemon soda, to fill**
- **Slice of orange (with peel)**
- **Slice of lemon (with peel)**
- **Stick of cucumber (don't peel it)**

228

PIMM'S CUP • 1

1^1/$_2$ oz (45 ml) Pimm's
5 oz (150 ml) white soda, such as 7-Up or Sprite
Twist of lemon peel
Stick of cucumber

Place 4–5 ice cubes in a highball or collins glass. Add the lemon peel and cucumber stick. Pour in the Pimm's and white soda.

PIMM'S CUP • 2

1^1/$_2$ oz (45 ml) Pimm's
Twist of lemon peel
Twist of orange peel
Stick of cucumber
Ginger ale, to fill

Half fill a collins glass with ice cubes. Add the lemon, orange, and cucumber. Pour in the Pimm's and top up with ginger ale.

PIMM'S CUP • 3

1^1/$_2$ oz (45 ml) Pimm's
Dry champagne, well chilled, to fill
Slice of orange
Strawberry
Mint leaves

Half fill a collins glass with ice cubes. Add the orange and strawberry. Pour in the Pimm's and top up with champagne. Garnish with the mint.

FLYING KANGAROO

Fill a shaker two-thirds full with ice. Add the vodka, rum, Galliano, pineapple juice, orange juice, cream of coconut, and cream. Shake well and strain into a highball glass filled with ice.

- 1 oz (30 ml) vodka
- 1 oz (30 ml) white rum
- $1/3$ oz (10 ml) Galliano
- $1^1/_2$ oz (45 ml) pineapple juice
- 1 oz (30 ml) freshly squeezed orange juice
- $3/_4$ oz (25 ml) cream of coconut
- $1/_2$ oz (15 ml) heavy (double) cream

GINGER DRAGON

Place 5–6 ice cubes in a collins glass. Pour in the vodka and ginger wine. Stir gently and top up with soda water

- **3 oz (90 ml) vodka**
- **2 oz (60 ml) ginger wine**
- **Soda water, to fill**

■ ■ ■ *Serve this unusual drink with a piece of candied ginger to nibble on.*

GINGER IN THE BREEZE

Fill a shaker two-thirds full with ice. Add the rum, cherry brandy, and orange juice. Shake well and strain into a highball glass filled with ice. Top up with ginger ale. Garnish with the lime.

- 2 oz (60 ml) white rum
- $1/2$ oz (15 ml) cherry brandy
- 4 oz (120 ml) freshly squeezed orange juice
- Ginger ale, to fill
- Wedge of lime, to garnish

GINGER SPICE

2 oz (60 ml) spiced rum
Ginger ale, to fill

Half fill a collins glass with ice. Pour in the spiced rum and top up with ginger ale.

GINGER BREEZE

$1^1/2$ oz (45 ml) white curaçao
Ginger ale, to fill

Half fill a collins glass with ice. Pour in the curaçao and top up with ginger ale.

GINGER FIRE

2 oz (60 ml) dark rum
$1^1/2$ oz (45 ml) white rum
1 oz (30 ml) pineapple juice
1 oz (30 ml) freshly squeezed grapefruit juice
Ginger ale, to fill

Fill a shaker two-thirds full with ice. Add the two types of rum and the pineapple and grapefruit juice. Strain into a collins glass over 5–6 ice cubes. Top up with ginger ale.

PEARL HARBOR LONG ONE

Fill a shaker two-thirds full with ice. Add the Midori, vodka, and pineapple juice and shake well. Place 4–6 ice cubes in a highball glass and add the melon. Strain the cocktail in over the top.

- **2 oz (60 ml) Midori melon liqueur**
- **2 oz (60 ml) vodka**
- **4 oz (120 ml) pineapple juice**
- **Slice of cantaloupe (rock) melon, chopped**

PEARL HARBOR • 1

2 oz (60 ml) Scotch whisky
4 oz (120 ml) cola, such as Pepsi or Coca-Cola
$1/2$ teaspoon vanilla extract (essence)

Half fill a collins glass with ice. Pour in the whisky and top up with cola. Add the vanilla and stir gently.

PEARL DIVER

$1^1/_2$ oz (15 ml) white rum
$1/2$ oz (15 ml) Cointreau
$1/2$ oz (15 ml) Midori melon liqueur
$1/2$ oz (15 ml) freshly squeezed lime juice
$1/2$ teaspoon sugar syrup
Soda water, to fill

Fill a shaker two-thirds full with ice. Add the rum, Cointreau, Midori, lime juice, and sugar syrup. Shake well and strain into a highball glass over 4–5 ice cubes. Top up with soda water.

CRANBERRY SPLASH

1 oz (30 ml) vodka
1 oz (30 ml) Midori melon liqueur
Pineapple juice, to fill
4–5 splashes of cranberry juice

Half fill a collins glass with ice. Pour in the vodka and Midori and top up with pineapple juice. Splash in the cranberry juice.

DUBONNET FIZZ

Place 4–5 ice cubes in a chilled collins glass. Pour in the Dubonnet, cherry brandy, orange juice, and lime juice. Stir gently and top up with champagne.

- 4 oz (120 ml) Dubonnet rouge
- 1/2 oz (15 ml) cherry brandy
- 3 oz (90 ml) freshly squeezed orange juice
- 1 oz (30 ml) freshly squeezed lime juice
- Dry champagne, well chilled, to fill

APPLE DUBONNET

1 1/2 oz (45 ml) apple brandy
1 oz (30 ml) Dubonnet rouge
2 oz (60 ml) apple juice
Soda water, to fill
Twist of lemon peel

Fill a shaker two-thirds full with ice. Add the apple brandy, Dubonnet, and apple juice. Shake well and strain into a collins glass over 4–5 ice cubes. Top up with soda water. Garnish with the lemon.

ALMOND FIZZ

5 oz (150 ml) dry champagne, well chilled
2 dashes white curaçao
2 dashes amaretto
1/2 oz (15 ml) freshly squeezed lemon juice
Twist of lemon peel

Half fill a collins glass with ice cubes. Pour in the champagne followed by the curaçao, amaretto, and lemon juice. Stir gently and garnish with the lemon.

CHAMPER BLUES

5 oz (150 ml) dry champagne, well chilled
1/2 oz (15 ml) blue curaçao
2 strawberries

Half fill a collins glass with ice cubes. Pour in the champagne and blue curaçao. Garnish with the strawberries.

LADY KILLER

Fill a shaker two-thirds full with ice. Add the vodka, Galliano, passion fruit juice, orange juice, and pineapple juice and shake. Strain into two chilled hurricane glasses. Top up with soda water. Garnish with the orange.

- 3 oz (90 ml) vodka
- 2 oz (60 ml) Galliano
- 2 oz (60 ml) passion fruit juice
- 2 oz (60 ml) freshly squeezed orange juice
- 2 oz (60 ml) pineapple juice
- Soda water, to fill
- Slices of orange, to garnish

GOLDEN OLDIE

Half fill a highball glass with ice cubes. Pour in the rum and banana liqueur. Top up with pineapple juice.

- 1¹/₂ oz (45 ml) dark rum
- ¹/₂ oz (15 ml) banana liqueur
- Pineapple juice, well chilled

GOLDEN DAZE

1¹/₂ oz (45 ml) gin
¹/₂ oz (15 ml) peach brandy
2 oz (60 ml) freshly squeezed orange juice
White soda, such as 7-Up or Sprite, to fill

Fill a shaker two-thirds full with ice. Add the gin, brandy, and orange juice. Shake well and strain into a collins glass half filled with ice. Top up with white soda.

GOLDEN MILE

1 oz (30 ml) amaretto
1 oz (30 ml) Grand Marnier
1 oz (30 ml) white crème de cacao
2 oz (60 ml) freshly squeezed orange juice

Half fill an old-fashioned glass with ice cubes. Pour in the amaretto, Grand Marnier, crème de cacao, and orange juice. Stir well.

WEEKENDER

2 oz (60 ml) coconut rum
1 oz (30 ml) dark rum
1 oz (30 ml) banana liqueur
Splash of grenadine
3 oz (90 ml) freshly squeezed orange juice
Ginger ale, well chilled, to fill

Place 3–4 ice cubes in a collins glass. Pour in both types of rum, the banana liqueur, grenadine, and orange juice. Top up with ginger ale.

WHITE CARNATION

Place 4–6 ice cubes in a collins glass and pour in the vodka, lemon juice, and pineapple juice. Stir gently then top up with soda water.

- 2 oz (60 ml) vodka
- 1$^1/_2$ oz (45 ml) freshly squeezed lemon juice
- 1 oz (30 ml) pineapple juice
- Soda water, to fill

WHITE CARNATION • 1

1$^1/_2$ oz (45 ml) vodka
$^1/_2$ oz (15 ml) peach schnapps
2$^1/_2$ oz (75 ml) freshly squeezed orange juice
2 oz (60 ml) soda water
Splash of heavy (double) cream

Place 4–6 ice cubes in a collins glass. Pour in the vodka, peach schnapps, orange juice, and soda water. Stir gently then splash in the cream.

RED CARNATION

1 oz (30 ml) vodka
1 oz (30 ml) peach schnapps
3 oz (90 ml) freshly squeezed orange juice
3 oz (90 ml) cranberry juice

Place 4–6 ice cubes in a collins glass. Pour in the vodka, peach schnapps, orange juice, and cranberry juice. Shake the glass gently; do not stir.

CARNATION

1 oz (30 ml) vodka
1 oz (30 ml) amaretto
1 oz (30 ml) peach schnapps
1 oz (30 ml) freshly squeezed orange juice
1 oz (30 ml) cranberry juice
Soda water, to fill

Fill a shaker two-thirds full with ice. Add the vodka, amaretto, peach schnapps, orange juice, and cranberry juice. Shake well and strain into a highball glass over 5–6 ice cubes. Top up with soda water.

ANESTHETIC

Fill a shaker two-thirds full with ice. Add the gin, cognac, sweet vermouth, dry vermouth, lime juice, and sugar syrup. Shake well and strain into a chilled hurricane glass. Garnish with the orange.

- 3 oz (90 ml) gin
- 1 oz (30 ml) cognac
- 1 oz (30 ml) sweet vermouth
- 1 oz (30 ml) dry vermouth
- 1/2 oz (15 ml) freshly squeezed lime juice
- 1 teaspoon sugar syrup
- Slice of orange, to garnish

ORANGE VERMOUTH

1 1/2 oz (45 ml) dry vermouth
1/2 oz (15 ml) gin
1/2 oz (15 ml) freshly squeezed orange juice
Dash of orange bitters
Ginger ale, to fill

Fill a shaker two-thirds full with ice. Add the vermouth, gin, orange juice, and bitters. Shake well and strain into a collins glass over 4–5 ice cubes. Top up with ginger ale.

SWEET AND LONG

1 oz (30 ml) gin
1 oz (30 ml) sweet vermouth
1 oz (30 ml) dry vermouth
2 oz (60 ml) freshly squeezed orange juice
Dash of Angostura bitters
White soda, such as 7-Up or Sprite, to fill
Slice of orange, to garnish

Fill a shaker two-thirds full with ice. Add the gin, both types of vermouth, the orange juice, and bitters. Shake well and strain into a collins glass over 4–5 ice cubes. Top up with white soda and garnish with the orange.

BANGKOK SPECIAL

1 oz (30 ml) Midori melon liqueur
1/2 oz (15 ml) vodka
1/2 oz (15 ml) rum
1/2 oz (15 ml) gin
1/2 oz (15 ml) tequila
1/2 oz (15 ml) Cointreau
Ginger ale, to fill
Slice of lime, to garnish

Fill a shaker two-thirds full with ice. Add the Midori, vodka, rum, gin, tequila, and Cointreau. Shake well and strain into a collins glass over 4–5 ice cubes. Top up with ginger ale. Garnish with the lime.

GENTLE BEN

Half fill a collins glass with ice cubes. Pour in the tequila, gin, and vodka. Top up with orange juice, stirring gently. Garnish with the cherry.

- $1/2$ oz (15 ml) white tequila
- $1/2$ oz (15 ml) gin
- $1/2$ oz (15 ml) vodka
- **Freshly squeezed orange juice, chilled**
- **Maraschino cherry, to garnish**

LESS GENTLE BEN

$1^1/2$ oz (45 ml) gin
1 oz (30 ml) brandy
1 oz (30 ml) sweet vermouth
Freshly squeezed orange juice, to fill

Place 4–6 ice cubes in an old-fashioned glass. Pour in the gin, brandy, vermouth, and orange juice. Stir gently.

VICTOR'S BEN

$1^1/2$ oz (45 ml) gin
$1/2$ oz (15 ml) brandy
$1/2$ oz (15 ml) sweet vermouth
1 oz (30 ml) freshly squeezed orange juice
Soda water, to fill

Fill a shaker two-thirds full with ice. Add the gin, brandy, vermouth, and orange juice. Shake well and strain into a collins glass over 4–6 ice cubes. Top up with soda water.

VICTOR'S BEN • 1

1 oz (30 ml) gin
$1/2$ oz (15 ml) brandy
$1/2$ oz (15 ml) dry vermouth
$1/2$ oz (15 ml) sweet vermouth
1 oz (30 ml) freshly squeezed lemon juice
1 teaspoon sugar syrup
Soda water, to fill

Fill a shaker two-thirds full with ice. Add the gin, brandy, both types of vermouth, lemon juice, and sugar syrup. Shake well and strain into a collins glass over 4–6 ice cubes. Top up with soda water.

252

ASSASSIN

Place 4–6 ice cubes in a collins or highball glass. Pour in the whisky, vermouth, and pineapple juice. Top up with soda water and stir gently. Finish with a dash or two of Sambuca.

- **2 oz (60 ml) Scotch whisky**
- **1 oz (30 ml) dry vermouth**
- **1 oz (30 ml) pineapple juice**
- **Soda water**
- **1–2 dashes Sambuca**

■ ■ ■ *Sambuca is an anise- and elderberry-flavored liqueur made in Italy.*

ASSASSIN • 1

1¹/₂ oz (45 ml) Scotch whisky
1 oz (30 ml) dry vermouth
1¹/₂ oz (45 ml) freshly squeezed lemon juice
Soda water, to fill

Half fill a collins or highball glass with ice cubes. Pour in the whisky, vermouth, and lemon juice. Top up with soda water and stir gently.

ASSASSIN • 2

1¹/₂ oz (45 ml) Scotch whisky
1 oz (30 ml) bourbon
2 oz (60 ml) pineapple juice
White soda, such as 7–up or Sprite, to fill

Half fill a collins or highball glass with ice cubes. Pour in the whisky, bourbon, and pineapple juice. Top up with white soda.

ASSASSIN • 3

1 oz (30 ml) blended whisky
1/2 oz (15 ml) gold tequila
1/3 oz (10 ml) peppermint schnapps
Cola, such as Pepsi or Coca-Cola, to fill

Fill a shaker two-thirds full with ice. Add the whisky, tequila, and peppermint schnapps. Shake well and strain into a highball glass over 3–4 ice cubes. Top up with cola.

WILD IRISH ROSE

Half fill a collins glass with cracked ice. Pour in the Irish whiskey, grenadine, and lime juice. Top up with ginger ale.

- **2 oz (60 ml) Irish whiskey**
- **1 oz (30 ml) grenadine**
- **1 oz (30 ml) freshly squeezed lime juice**
- **Ginger ale, to fill**

IRISH HIGHBALL

2 oz (60 ml) Irish whiskey
5 oz (150 ml) ginger ale
Slice of lemon, to garnish

Place 2–3 ice cubes in a highball glass. Pour in the whiskey. Top up with ginger ale. Drop the slice of lemon into the drink.

IRISH WHISKEY COCKTAIL

1¹/₂ oz (45 ml) Irish whiskey
¹/₂ oz (15 ml) peach brandy
2 oz (60 ml) freshly squeezed orange juice
1 oz (30 ml) freshly squeezed lemon juice
1 teaspoon sugar syrup
Soda water, to fill

Place 3–4 ice cubes in a highball glass. Pour in the whiskey, peach brandy, orange juice, lemon juice, and sugar syrup. Mix well. Top up with soda water.

LEPRECHAUN

2 oz (60 ml) Irish whiskey
¹/₂ oz (15 ml) Drambuie
¹/₂ oz (15 ml) freshly squeezed lemon juice
Ginger ale, to fill

Fill a shaker two-thirds full with ice. Add the whiskey, Drambuie, and lemon juice. Shake well and strain into a highball glass over 3–4 ice cubes. Top up with ginger ale.

YELLOW BIRD

Fill a shaker two-thirds full with ice. Add the rum, Galliano, Cointreau, and lemon juice. Shake well and strain into a collins glass half filled with ice. Top up with pineapple juice. Garnish with the lime.

- 2¹/₂ oz (75 ml) white rum
- 1 oz (30 ml) Galliano
- 1 oz (30 ml) Cointreau
- 1 oz (30 ml) freshly squeezed lemon juice
- Pineapple juice, to fill
- Wedge of lime, to garnish

YELLOW BIRD • 1

1 oz (30 ml) dark rum
1 oz (30 ml) white rum
¹/₃ oz (1 ml) Galliano
1 oz (30 ml) freshly squeezed orange juice
¹/₂ oz (15 ml) freshly squeezed lime juice
Sprig of fresh mint, to garnish

Fill a shaker two-thirds full with ice. Add both types of rum, the Galliano, orange juice, and lemon juice. Shake well and strain into a collins glass half-filled with ice cubes. Garnish with the mint.

YELLOW BIRD • 2

1¹/₂ oz (45 ml) vodka
1 oz (30 ml) banana liqueur
White soda, such as 7-Up or Sprite, to fill

Place 4–5 ice cubes in a collins glass. Pour in the vodka and banana liqueur. Top up with white soda, stirring gently.

FRUITY YELLOW BIRD

1 oz (30 ml) peach schnapps
¹/₂ oz (15 ml) banana liqueur
¹/₂ oz (15 ml) Cointreau
4 oz (120 ml) pineapple juice

Place 4–5 ice cubes in a highball glass. Pour in the peach schnapps, banana liqueur, Cointreau, and pineapple juice. Stir gently.

JACK COLLINS

Fill a shaker two-thirds full with ice. Add the brandy, lemon juice, bitters, and sugar. Shake well and strain into a chilled collins glass. Top up with soda water. Garnish with the orange.

258

- 2¹/₂ oz (75 ml) applejack brandy
- 1 oz (30 ml) freshly squeezed lemon juice
- 2 dashes orange bitters
- 1 teaspoon sugar
- Soda water, to fill
- Slice of orange, to garnish

TOM COLLINS

2 oz (60 ml) gin
1 oz (30 ml) freshly squeezed lemon juice
1 teaspoon sugar
3 oz (90 ml) soda water
Slice of orange, to garnish

Fill a shaker two-thirds full with ice. Add the gin, lemon juice, and sugar. Shake well and strain into a collins glass almost filled with ice cubes. Top up with soda water and garnish with the orange.

BRANDY COLLINS

2 oz (60 ml) brandy
1 oz (30 ml) freshly squeezed lemon juice
1 teaspoon sugar syrup
3 oz (90 ml) soda water
Slice of orange, to garnish

Fill a shaker two-thirds full with ice. Add the brandy, lemon juice, and sugar syrup. Shake well and strain into a collins glass almost filled with ice cubes. Top up with soda water and garnish with the orange.

APPLEJACK CHAMPERS

2 oz (60 ml) applejack brandy
1/3 oz (10 ml) Cointreau
1 oz (30 ml) freshly squeezed lemon juice
Dry champagne, well chilled, to fill

Place 4–6 ice cubes in an old-fashioned glass. Pour in the brandy, Cointreau, and lemon juice. Stir gently and top up with champagne.

MOULIN ROUGE

Place 4–6 ice cubes in a highball glass and pour in the brandy and pineapple juice. Add the chunks of pineapple and top up with the champagne or wine. Garnish with the orange.

- **2 oz (60 ml) brandy**
- **4 oz (120 ml) pineapple juice**
- **Chunks of fresh pineapple**
- **Dry champagne or sparkling white wine, well chilled, to fill**
- **Slice of orange, to garnish**

MOULIN ROUGE • 1

1¹/₂ oz (45 ml) sloe gin
²/₃ oz (20 ml) sweet vermouth
2 dashes Angostura bitters
Dry champagne, well chilled, to fill

Fill a shaker two-thirds full with ice. Add the gin, vermouth, and bitters. Shake well and strain into an old-fashioned glass over 3–4 ice cubes. Top up with champagne.

PEACH COOLER

1¹/₂ oz (45 ml) peach brandy
2 oz (60 ml) freshly squeezed orange juice
Dry champagne, well chilled, to fill
Slice of fresh peach, to garnish

Fill a shaker two-thirds full with ice. Add the peach brandy and orange juice. Shake well and strain into an old-fashioned glass over 3–4 ice cubes. Top up with champagne. Garnish with the peach.

RUSSIAN BRUNCH

1¹/₂ oz (45 ml) vodka
1 oz (30 ml) freshly squeezed orange juice
Dry champagne, well chilled, to fill

Fill a shaker two-thirds full with ice. Add the vodka and orange juice. Shake well and strain into an old-fashioned glass over 3–4 ice cubes. Top up with champagne.

HUATUSCO WHAMMER

Fill a shaker two-thirds full with ice. Add the tequila, rum, vodka, gin, triple sec, lemon juice, and sugar syrup and shake well. Half fill a highball glass with ice cubes and strain the drink over the top. Top up with cola.

- **2 oz (60 ml) white tequila**
- **2 oz (60 ml) white rum**
- **1 oz (30 ml) vodka**
- **1 oz (30 ml) gin**
- **1 oz (30 ml) triple sec**
- **2 oz (60 ml) freshly squeezed lemon juice**
- **1 teaspoon sugar syrup**
- **Cola, such as Pepsi or Coca-Cola, well chilled, to fill**

SALTY DOG

Moisten the rim of an old-fashioned glass with grapefruit juice and dip in the salt to coat. Fill with ice. Pour in the gin and top up with grapefruit juice. Stir gently.

- 1½ oz (45 ml) gin
- **Freshly squeezed grapefruit juice**
- **Salt**

270

SALTY DOG • 1

1½ oz (45 ml) vodka
Freshly squeezed grapefruit juice to fill
Salt

Moisten the rim of a highball glass with grapefruit juice and dip in the salt to coat. Fill the glass with ice cubes. Pour in the vodka and top up with grapefruit juice.

SALTY DOG • 2

1½ oz (45 ml) vodka
½ oz (15 ml) Midori melon liqueur
Freshly squeezed orange juice to fill
Salt

Moisten the rim of a highball glass with orange juice and dip in the salt to coat. Fill the glass with ice cubes. Pour in the vodka and Midori and top up with orange juice. Stir gently.

SALTY CHIHUAHUA

1½ oz (45 ml) white tequila
Lemon soda, well chilled, to fill
Wedge of lime
Salt

Moisten the rim of a highball glass with lime juice and dip in the salt to coat. Fill the glass with ice cubes. Pour in the tequila and top up with lemon soda.

SCARLET O'HARA

Half fill an old-fashioned glass with ice. Pour in the Southern Comfort and top up with cranberry juice. Squeeze the lime peel over the glass so that the fruit's fragrant oils gently flavor the drink. Drop the lime peel into the drink.

- 1¹/₂ oz (45 ml) Southern Comfort
- Cranberry juice
- Piece of lime peel

SOUTHERN COOLER

1¹/₂ oz (45 ml) Southern Comfort
1 oz (30 ml) amaretto
5 oz (150 ml) cranberry juice
Wedge of lime, to garnish

Half fill an old-fashioned glass with ice cubes. Pour in the Southern Comfort and amaretto. Top up with cranberry juice. Garnish with the lime.

SPIKED BOURBON

1 oz (30 ml) bourbon
1 oz (30 ml) Jägermeister
2 oz (60 ml) freshly squeezed orange juice
Cola, such as Pepsi or Coca-Cola, to fill

Half fill an old-fashioned glass with ice cubes. Pour in the bourbon, Jägermeister, and orange juice. Top up with cola.

BOURBON COMFORT

1¹/₂ oz (45 ml) Southern Comfort
1¹/₂ oz (45 ml) bourbon
Cranberry juice, to fill

Half fill a collins glass with ice cubes. Pour in the Southern Comfort and bourbon. Stir well and top up with cranberry juice.

CLASSICS

GRASSHOPPER

Fill a shaker two-thirds full with ice. Add the crème de menthe, crème de cacao, and cream. Shake well and strain into a chilled martini glass. Garnish with the chocolate.

- **1 oz (30 ml) green crème de menthe**
- **1 oz (30 ml) white crème de cacao**
- **1 oz (30 ml) heavy (double) cream**
- **Grated bittersweet (dark) chocolate, to garnish**

■ ■ ■ *Serve this one after dinner. Use light (single) cream, if preferred.*

FROZEN GRASSHOPPER

1 oz (30 ml) green crème de menthe
1 oz (30 ml) white crème de cacao
2 scoops vanilla ice cream

Place the ice cream in a blender with the crème de menthe and the crème de cacao and blend until smooth. Pour into a hurricane glass and serve with a long-handled dessert spoon.

COFFEE GRASSHOPPER

1 oz (30 ml) white crème de menthe
1 oz (30 ml) coffee liqueur
Milk, well chilled, to fill
Grated milk chocolate, to garnish (optional)

Place 3–4 ice cubes in a highball glass. Pour in the crème de menthe and coffee liqueur. Top up with milk and stir gently. Garnish with the chocolate, if liked.

VODKA CREAM

1 oz (30 ml) vodka
1 oz (30 ml) white crème de cacao
1/2 oz (15 ml) green crème de menthe

Fill a shaker two-thirds full with ice. Add the vodka, crème de cacao, and crème de menthe. Shake well and strain into a chilled martini glass.

BRANDY ALEXANDER

Fill a shaker two-thirds full with ice. Add the brandy, crème de cacao, and cream. Shake well and strain into a chilled martini glass. Dust with the nutmeg.

- **1¹/₂ oz (45 ml) brandy**
- **1 oz (30 ml) white crème de cacao**
- **1 oz (30 ml) heavy (double) cream**
- **Grated nutmeg, to dust**

■ ■ ■ *This classic cocktail can be made using either white or dark crème de cacao.*

GIN ALEXANDER	GIN ALEXANDER • 1	ALEXANDER THE GREAT
1 oz (30 ml) gin	2 oz (60 ml) gin	1¹/₂ oz (45 ml) vodka
²/₃ oz (20 ml) white crème de cacao	1 oz (30 ml) dark crème de cacao	¹/₂ oz (15 ml) white crème de cacao
1 oz (30 ml) light (single) cream	1 oz (30 ml) heavy (double) cream	¹/₂ oz (15 ml) coffee liqueur
	Grated nutmeg, to dust	¹/₂ oz (15 ml) heavy (double) cream
Fill a shaker two-thirds full with ice. Add the gin, crème de cacao, and cream. Shake well and strain into a chilled martini glass.	Fill a shaker two-thirds full with ice. Add the gin, crème de cacao, and cream. Shake well and strain into into a chilled martini glass. Dust with the nutmeg.	Fill a shaker two-thirds full with ice. Add the vodka, crème de cacao, coffee liqueur, and cream. Shake well and strain into a chilled martini glass.

AMERICANO

Half fill a highball glass with ice cubes. Pour in the Campari and vermouth. Stir well and top up with soda water. Garnish with the lemon or orange.

- **1 oz (30 ml) Campari**
- **1 oz (30 ml) sweet vermouth**
- **Soda water, to fill**
- **Slice of lemon or orange, to garnish**

■ ■ ■ *This cocktail was invented in Italy just after the World War One.*

AMERICANO HIGHBALL

1 oz (30 ml) Campari
2 oz (60 ml) dry vermouth
Soda water, to fill
Twist of lemon peel, to garnish

Half fill a highball glass with ice cubes. Pour in the Campari and vermouth and top up with soda water. Garnish with the lemon.

BLACKTHORN

1$^{1}/_{2}$ oz (45 ml) sloe gin
1 oz (30 ml) sweet vermouth
4 dashes orange bitters
Twist of orange peel, to garnish

Fill a shaker two-thirds full with ice. Add the sloe gin, vermouth, and orange bitters. Shake well and strain into a chilled martini glass. Garnish with the orange.

CHUM COCKTAIL

1$^{1}/_{2}$ oz (45 ml) sloe gin
1 oz (30 ml) sweet vermouth
Wedge of orange

Fill a shaker two-thirds full with ice. Add the sloe gin and vermouth. Shake well and strain into a chilled martini glass. Squeeze the juice from the orange wedge into the drink and drop the peel in on top.

281

NEGRONI

Fill a shaker two-thirds full with ice. Add the gin, vermouth, and Campari. Shake well and strain into a chilled martini glass. Garnish with the orange.

- 1 oz (30 ml) gin
- 1 oz (30 ml) sweet vermouth
- 1 oz (30 ml) Campari
- Slice of orange, to garnish

282

■ ■ ■ *This cocktail was born when the noble Florentine, count Camillo Negroni, asked his favorite barman at the Giacosa caffè in Florence, to replace the soda water in his Americano with a little gin.*

NEGRONI DUBONNET

1¹/₂ oz (45 ml) gin
1¹/₂ oz (45 ml) Campari
1¹/₂ oz (45 ml) Dubonnet Blanc
Slice of orange, to garnish

Fill a shaker two-thirds full with ice. Add the gin, Campari, and Dubonnet. Shake well and strain into a chilled martini glass. Garnish with the orange.

ORANGE NEGRONI

1 oz (30 ml) gin
¹/₂ oz (15 ml) Campari
¹/₂ oz sweet vermouth
2 oz (60 ml) freshly squeezed orange juice
Sugar

Rub the rim of an old-fashioned glass with orange juice and dip into sugar to coat. Add 3–4 ice cubes to the glass. Fill a shaker two-thirds full with ice. Add the gin, Campari, vermouth, and orange juice. Shake well and strain into the glass.

DRY NEGRONI

1 oz (30 ml) gin
1 oz (30 ml) Campari
1 oz (30 ml) dry vermouth
Orange zest, to garnish

Half fill an old-fashioned glass with ice cubes. Pour in the gin, Campari, and vermouth. Stir well and garnish with the orange.

SINGAPORE SLING

Fill a shaker two-thirds full with ice. Add the gin, cherry brandy, Cointreau, pineapple juice, lime juice, and bitters. Shake well and strain into a chilled collins glass. Top up with soda water. Garnish with the pineapple and mint.

- **2 oz (60 ml) gin**
- **1/2 oz (15 ml) cherry brandy**
- **Dash of Cointreau**
- **2 oz (60 ml) pineapple juice**
- **1/2 oz (15 ml) freshly squeezed lime juice**
- **Dash of orange bitters**
- **Soda water, to fill**
- **Wedge of fresh pineapple, to garnish**
- **Fresh mint leaf, to garnish**

■ ■ ■ *Perfect for a hot day in the tropics, this classic was invented by Ngaim Tong Boon, barman at the famous Raffles Hotel in Singapore sometime around 1910. The exact date of its invention, and even the recipe itself, are now disputed. There are many versions; we prefer a longer drink, with fruity tones to help mellow out the strong alcoholic content. After all this was traditionally a ladies' drink!*

KIR

Pour the crème de cassis into a chilled wine glass. Top up with the wine. Garnish with the lemon, if liked.

- 1 oz (30 ml) crème de cassis
- Dry white wine, well chilled
- Slice of lemon, to garnish (optional)

■ ■ ■ *A classic French aperitif, made originally with white burgundy and crème de cassis (blackcurrant juice). It is named for the Abbot of Kir, who was also the mayor of Djion. For a Kir royale, replace the white wine with champagne.*

CAIPIRIÑA

Place the crushed ice in an old-fashioned glass. Place the lime and sugar in a mixing glass. Muddle until well blended and the sugar has dissolved. Pour in the cachaça and the ice from the old-fashioned glass. Stir well. Pour back into the old-fashioned glass. Garnish with the lime.

- 1/2 cup (125 ml) crushed ice
- 1/2 lime, cut into four wedges
- 2 teaspoons sugar
- 21/2 oz (75 ml) cachaça
- Slice of lime, to garnish

CAMPESINA COCKTAIL

2 oz (60 ml) white tequila
2 teaspoons sugar
1/2 lime
1/2 cup (125 ml) crushed ice

Cut the the lime into small wedges and place in an old-fashioned glass. Sprinkle with the sugar and muddle until the sugar has dissolved. Add the ice and pour in the tequila. Stir gently.

VIVA VILLA

11/2 oz (45 ml) white tequila
11/2 oz (45 ml) freshly squeezed lime juice
1 teaspoon sugar syrup
Salt

Moisten the rim of an old-fashioned glass with lime juice and dip in salt to coat. Place 2–3 ice cubes in the glass. Fill a shaker two-thirds full with ice. Add the tequila, lime juice, and sugar syrup. Shake well and strain into the glass.

MELZINHO COCKTAIL

3 oz (90 ml) cachaça
11/2 oz (45 ml) honey

Fill a shaker two-thirds full with ice. Add the cachaça and honey. Shake well and strain into a pousse café or shot glass over 1–2 cubes of ice.

GIN AND TONIC

Place the ice in an old-fashioned or collins glass. Pour in the gin and top up with tonic water. Garnish with the lime.

- **2 oz (60 ml) gin**
- **Tonic water, to fill**
- **Wedge of lime, to garnish**

■ ■ ■ *This classic cocktail is as simple to make as it is good to drink. According to legend, it was invented in India after it was discovered that the quinine in tonic water helped to ward off malaria. Loyal as the British were to their king and country, asking them to drink tonic water on its own was apparently too much to ask. The addition of a double shot of gin was just what was needed to make this a popular drink. For a pink gin tonic, add 3 dashes of bitters.*

RUSTY NAIL

Half fill an old-fashioned glass with ice cubes. Pour in the whisky. Hold a teaspoon just above the glass and pour the Drambuie over the top. This will help it spread out evenly in the whisky.

- 1½ oz (45 ml) Scotch whisky
- 1 oz (30 ml) Drambuie

LOCH LOMOND

2 oz (60 ml) Scotch whisky
½ oz (15 ml) Drambuie
½ oz (15 ml) dry vermouth
Twist of lemon peel

Half fill a mixing glass with ice cubes. Pour in the whisky, Drambuie, and vermouth and stir well. Strain into a chilled martini glass. Garnish with the lemon.

DRY ROB ROY

2 oz Scotch whisky
⅔ oz (20 ml) dry vermouth
Twist of lemon zest

Half fill a mixing glass with ice cubes. Pour in the whisky and vermouth and stir well. Strain into a chilled martini glass. Garnish with the lemon.

RUSTY SCREW

1½ oz (45 ml) Scotch whisky
½ oz (15 ml) Grand Marnier
Twist of lemon peel

Place 3–4 ice cubes in an old-fashioned glass. Pour in the whisky and Grand Marnier and stir well. Garnish with the lemon.

GIN FIZZ

Fill a shaker two-thirds full with ice. Add the gin, lemon juice, and sugar syrup. Shake well and strain into an old-fashioned glass with 2–3 ice cubes. Top up with soda water. Garnish with the lemon.

- **2 oz (60 ml) gin**
- **1¹/₂ oz (45 ml) freshly squeezed lemon juice**
- **2 teaspoons sugar syrup**
- **Soda water, to fill**
- **Slice of lemon, to garnish**

DIAMOND FIZZ

2 oz (60 ml) gin
1 oz (30 ml) freshly squeezed lemon juice
1 teaspoon sugar syrup
Dry champagne, well chilled, to fill

Fill a shaker two-thirds full with ice. Add the gin, lemon juice, and sugar syrup. Shake well and strain into an old-fashioned glass over 2–3 ice cubes. Top up with champagne.

GIN BUCK

1¹/₂ oz (45 ml) gin
1 oz (30 ml) freshly squeezed lemon juice
Ginger ale, to fill

Fill a shaker two-thirds full with ice. Add the gin and lemon juice. Shake well and strain into an old-fashioned glass over 2–3 ice cubes. Top up with ginger ale.

WHISKY FIZZ

1¹/₂ oz (45 ml) bourbon
1 oz (30 ml) freshly squeezed lemon juice
1 teaspoon sugar syrup
Lemon soda, to fill

Fill a shaker two-thirds full with ice. Add the whisky and lemon juice. Shake well and strain into an old-fashioned glass over 2–3 ice cubes. Top up with lemon soda.

BELLINI

Place the peach and raspberry in a blender and blend until smooth. Transfer to a large chilled champagne flute and top up with the champagne. Garnish with the peach, if liked.

- 1 medium ripe white peach, peeled and pitted
- $1/2$ teaspoon raspberry preserves (jam), strained to remove pips
- 5 oz (150 ml) dry champagne, well chilled
- Slice of peach, to garnish (optional)

■ ■ ■ *Popular the world over, this all-occasions cocktail was invented by Giuseppe Cipriani, proprietor of the famous Harry's Bar in Venice. Cipriani's original drink, invented to honor the painter Giovanni Bellini at his 1950 exhibition opening, was based on crushed white peach flesh and champagne, with a dash of raspberry purée for its classic pink tinge.*

MAI TAI

Fill a shaker two-thirds full with ice. Add the dark rum, light rum, curaçao, orange syrup, lime juice, and ginger. Shake well and strain into a chilled old-fashioned glass. Garnish with the pineapple and mint.

- $1^1/_2$ oz (45 ml) gold rum
- 1 oz (30 ml) white rum
- $1/_2$ oz (15 ml) white curaçao
- 1 oz (30 ml) orange syrup
- Juice from $1/_2$ freshly squeezed lime
- $1/_2$ teaspoon ground ginger
- Fresh pineapple wedge, to garnish
- Mint leaves, to garnish

■ ■ ■ *Invented by legendary restaurant owner Victor Bergron, better known as Trader Vic, and his barman at the Oakland Trader Vic's on an afternoon in 1944. Since then many different versions of the cocktail have been served. This is our favorite.*

DAIQUIRI

Fill a shaker two-thirds full with ice. Add the rum, lime juice, and sugar. Shake well and strain into a chilled martini glass.

- **2 oz (60 ml) dark rum**
- **Freshly squeezed juice of 1/2 lime**
- **2 teaspoons sugar**

PASSION DAIQUIRI

1¹/₂ oz (45 ml) white rum
1¹/₂ oz (45 ml) freshly squeezed lime juice
¹/₂ oz (15 ml) passion fruit juice
1 teaspoon sugar syrup

Fill a shaker two-thirds full with ice. Add the rum, lime juice, passion fruit juice, and sugar syrup. Shake well and strain into a chilled martini glass.

SANTIAGO COCKTAIL

1¹/₂ oz (45 ml) white rum
¹/₃ oz (10 ml) grenadine
1¹/₂ oz (45 ml) freshly squeezed lime juice
¹/₂ teaspoon sugar syrup

Fill a shaker two-thirds full with ice. Add the rum, grenadine, lime juice, and sugar syrup. Shake well and strain into a chilled martini glass.

HOP TOAD

1 oz (30 ml) white rum
1 oz (30 ml) apricot brandy
1 oz (30 ml) freshly squeezed lime juice

Fill a shaker two-thirds full with ice. Add the rum, apricot brandy, and lime juice. Shake well and strain into a chilled martini glass.

301

SIDECAR

If liked, moisten the rim of the glass with a little lemon juice and dip into the sugar to coat. Fill a shaker two-thirds full with ice. Add the brandy, Cointreau, and lemon juice. Shake well and strain into the martini glass.

- **$1^1/_2$ oz (45 ml) brandy**
- **$3/_4$ oz (25 ml) Cointreau**
- **$1/_2$ oz (15 ml) freshly squeezed lemon juice**
- **Sugar (optional)**

■ ■ ■ *Legend has it that this classic cocktail was invented at the Ritz in Paris during World War One. A certain captain was regularly driven to the hotel for dinner in the sidecar of a motorcycle and arrived frozen to the bone. He requested a pre-dinner drink that would warm him up. While brandy is a traditional "warmer" it is usually served after dinner; in this case the bartender added lemon juice and Cointreau to make the drink suitable as an apéritif.*

CUBA LIBRE

Fill a collins glass three-quarters full with ice. Pour in the rum and top up with cola. Add the wedge of lime and stir well.

- **2 oz (60 ml) white rum**
- **Cola, such as Pepsi or Coca-Cola, to fill**
- **Wedge of lime**

RUM GIMLET

2 oz (60 ml) white rum
1/2 oz (15 ml) lime cordial
Wedge of lime

Fill a shaker two-thirds full with ice. Add the rum and lime cordial. Shake well and strain into a chilled martini glass. Garnish with the lime.

DARK'N'DIRTY

1 1/2 oz (45 ml) dark rum
Cola, such as Pepsi or Coca-Cola, to fill

Place 3–4 ice cubes in an old-fashioned glass. Pour in the rum and top up with cola.

QUARTER DECK

1 1/2 oz (45 ml) white rum
1/2 oz (15 ml) cream sherry
1/2 oz (15 ml) freshly squeezed lime juice

Half fill a mixing glass with ice cubes. Pour in the rum, sherry, and lime juice. Stir well and strain into a chilled martini glass.

HARVEY WALLBANGER

Half fill a collins or highball glass with ice cubes. Pour in the vodka and orange juice. Hold a teaspoon upside down over the drink and pour the Galliano over it into the drink. Garnish with the orange, if liked.

- **2 oz (60 ml) vodka**
- **4 oz (120 ml) freshly squeezed orange juice**
- **1/2 oz (15 ml) Galliano**
- **Slice of orange, to garnish (optional)**

ALEXANDER NEVSKY

1 1/2 oz (45 ml) vodka
1 oz (30 ml) apricot liqueur
4 oz (120 ml) freshly squeezed orange juice
1/2 oz (15 ml) freshly squeezed lemon juice
Slice of orange, to garnish

Fill a shaker two-thirds full with ice. Add the vodka, apricot liqueur, orange juice, and lemon juice. Shake well and strain into a chilled wine goblet. Garnish with the orange.

BORODINO

1 oz (30 ml) vodka
1 oz (30 ml) gin
1 oz (30 ml) Cointreau

Fill a shaker two-thirds full with ice. Add the vodka, gin, and Cointreau. Shake well and strain into a chilled martini glass.

BAYWATCH

1 1/2 oz (45 ml) vodka
1 1/2 oz (45 ml) Galliano
2 oz (60 ml) freshly squeezed orange juice
1/2 oz (15 ml) light (single) cream

Fill a shaker two-thirds full with ice. Add the vodka, Galliano, and orange juice. Shake well and strain into a hurricane glass over 2–3 ice cubes. Pour the cream in on top.

SCREWDRIVER

Place 2–3 ice cubes in an old-fashioned glass. Pour in the vodka and orange juice. Garnish with the orange, if liked.

- 1½ oz (45 ml) vodka
- 4 oz (120 ml) freshly squeezed orange juice
- **Slice of orange, to garnish (optional)**

ADDISON SPECIAL

1 oz (30 ml) vodka
½ oz (15 ml) grenadine
3 oz (90 ml) freshly squeezed orange juice
Wedge of orange, to garnish

Fill a shaker two-thirds full with ice. Add the vodka, grenadine, and orange juice. Shake well and strain into an old-fashioned glass over 3–4 ice cubes. Garnish with the orange.

VODKA SUNRISE

1½ oz (45 ml) vodka
½ oz (15 ml) Grand Marnier
3 oz (90 ml) freshly squeezed orange juice
2 oz (60 ml) pineapple juice
Slice of orange, to garnish

Fill a shaker two-thirds full with ice. Add the vodka, Grand Marnier, orange juice, and pineapple juice. Shake well and strain into a highball glass over 4–5 ice cubes. Garnish with the orange.

BRASS MONKEY

1 oz (30 ml) vodka
1 oz (30 ml) white rum
4 oz (120 ml) freshly squeezed orange juice

Half fill a highball glass with ice cubes. Pour in the vodka and rum and top up with the orange juice. Stir well.

superb vodka
from grain grown
of Southern Sweden
at the famous
with more than
Swedish tradition

GIMLET

Fill a shaker two-thirds full with ice. Add the gin, lime juice, and sugar, if using. Shake well and strain into a chilled martini glass. Twist the lime peel over the drink and drop into the glass.

- **2 oz (60 ml) gin**
- **1 oz (30 ml) freshly squeezed lime juice**
- **1 teaspoon sugar (optional)**
- **Long spiral of lime peel**

GIMLET • 1

1¹/₂ oz (45 ml) gin
¹/₂ oz (15 ml) lime cordial

Half fill a mixing glass with ice cubes. Pour in the gin and lime cordial and mix well. Strain into a chill old-fashioned glass over 2–3 ice cubes.

FIZZY GIMLET

2 oz (60 ml) gin
¹/₂ oz (15 ml) freshly squeezed lime juice
3 oz (90 ml) white soda, such as 7-Up or Sprite
Wedge of lime, to garnish

Fill a shaker two-thirds full with ice. Add the gin and lime juice. Shake well and strain into a highball glass over 3–4 ice cubes. Top up with white soda. Garnish with the lime.

GIN CASSIS

1¹/₂ oz (45 ml) gin
¹/₂ oz (15 ml) crème de cassis
¹/₂ oz (15 ml) freshly squeezed lemon juice

Fill a shaker two-thirds full with ice. Add the gin, crème de cassis, and lemon juice. Shake well and strain into a chilled martini glass.

MANHATTAN

Place the bourbon, vermouth, and bitters in a mixing glass with 4–5 cubes of ice. Stir well, then strain into a chilled martini glass. Garnish with the cherry.

- **2 oz (60 ml) bourbon**
- **³/₄ oz (25 ml) sweet vermouth**
- **Dash of orange bitters**
- **Maraschino cherry, with stem**

■ ■ ■ *Reportedly invented at the Manhattan Club in Manhattan in 1894, when the socialite Jennie Jerome (Lady Randolph Churchill, Winston Churchill's mother), was hosting a party to celebrate the election of Samuel Tilden as governor and requested that a new drink be created for the occasion.*

MINT JULEP

Place the mint leaves, sugar, and a few drops of water in a collins glass and muddle well. Add half the bourbon, then fill the glass almost to the brim with crushed ice. Pour in the remaining bourbon. Garnish with the sprig of mint.

- **2 oz (60 ml) bourbon**
- **8–10 mint leaves**
- **1 teaspoon sugar**
- **Sprig of mint, to garnish**

■ ■ ■ *A grand old drink from the South. No one knows quite where it came from, although both Virginia and Kentucky lay claim to its invention. The Mint Julep is now the official drink at the Kentucky Derby. More 80,000 Mint Juleps are served over the two-day event.*

MINT JULEP • 1

2¹/₂ oz (75 ml) bourbon
4 sprigs fresh mint
1 teaspoon sugar
2 teaspoons water

Place the mint leaves, sugar, and water in a collins glass and muddle well. Fill the glass with crushed ice and pour in the bourbon. Stir well. Serve with a straw.

MINT JULEP • 2

2 oz (60 ml) bourbon
¹/₂ teaspoon Angostura bitters
6 sprigs fresh mint
¹/₂ oz (15 ml) sugar syrup

Place 5 sprigs of mint and the sugar syrup in a blender and blend until smooth. Strain into a highball glass full of crushed ice. Garnish with the remaining sprig of mint.

QUICK JULEP

2¹/₂ oz (75 ml) bourbon
1 teaspoon sugar syrup
3 sprigs fresh mint

Fill a collins glass with crushed ice. Pour in the bourbon and sugar syrup. Add the mint and stir well. Serve with a straw.

MIMOSA

Place 3–4 ice cubes in a collins glass. Pour the orange juice in over the top. Top up with the champagne. Add the Cointreau and stir gently.

- **Dry champagne, well chilled, to fill**
- **Dash of Cointreau**
- **3 oz (90 ml) freshly squeezed orange juice**

POINSETTIA

2 oz (60 ml) prosecco (or other dry, sparkling wine)

1 oz (30 ml) blackcurrant juice

Place 4–5 ice cubes in an old-fashioned glass. Pour in the blackcurrant juice and top up with the prosecco. Stir gently.

MOSCOW MIMOSA

1/2 oz (15 ml) vodka

2 oz (60 ml) prosecco (or other dry, sparkling wine)

2 oz (60 ml) freshly squeezed orange juice

Place 4–5 ice cubes in an old-fashioned glass. Pour in the vodka and orange juice and top up with the prosecco. Stir gently.

VALENCIA

1 1/2 oz (45 ml) apricot brandy

2–3 dashes orange bitters

1/2 oz (15 ml) freshly squeezed orange juice

Prosecco (or other dry, sparkling wine), to fill

Fill a shaker two-thirds full with ice. Add the apricot brandy, bitters, and orange juice. Shake well and strain into a chilled wine goblet. Top up with prosecco.

OLD-FASHIONED COCKTAIL

Muddle the sugar cube, water, bitters, and orange in a chilled old-fashioned glass. Add 4–5 ice cubes and pour in the bourbon.

- **2 oz (60 ml) bourbon (or blended, Canadian, or rye whisky)**
- **1 sugar cube**
- **1 teaspoon of water**
- **2 dashes orange bitters**
- **Slice of orange**

318

BOURBON SOUR

2 oz (60 ml) bourbon
1 oz (30 ml) freshly squeezed lemon juice
1/2 teaspoon sugar
Slice of orange, to garnish
Maraschino cherry, to garnish

Fill a shaker two-thirds full with ice. Add the bourbon, lemon juice, and sugar. Shake well and strain into an old-fashioned glass. Garnish with the orange and cherry.

ROB ROY

1½ oz (45 ml) Scotch whisky
3/4 oz (25 ml) sweet vermouth
Dash of Angostura bitters
Twist of lemon peel, to garnish

Half fill a mixing glass with ice cubes. Pour in the whisky, vermouth, and bitters and stir well. Strain into a chilled martini glass. Garnish with the lemon.

BLIMEY

2 oz (60 ml) Scotch whisky
1/2 oz (15 ml) freshly squeezed lime juice
1/2 teaspoon sugar

Fill a shaker two-thirds full with ice. Add the whisky, lime juice, and sugar. Shake well and strain into a chilled martini glass.

WHITE LADY

Fill a shaker two-thirds full with ice. Add the gin, Cointreau, and lemon juice. Shake well and strain into a chilled martini glass.

- 1¹/₂ oz (45 ml) gin
- ¹/₂ oz (15 ml) Cointreau
- 1 oz (30 ml) freshly squeezed lemon juice

320

■ ■ ■ *Reputedly created in 1919 at Ciro's Club in London by Harry MacElhone. The original recipe featured white crème de menthe, but when MacElhone substituted that ingredient for gin in 1929 the cocktail became a hit.*

LONG ISLAND ICED TEA

Fill a shaker two-thirds full with ice. Add the gin, vodka, tequila, rum, Cointreau, and lemon juice. Shake well and strain into a chilled collins or highball glass over 4–5 ice cubes. Top up with cola. Garnish with the lemon.

■ ■ ■ *True to its name, this powerful drink was invented on Long Island at the Oak Beach Inn in Hampton Bay by a barman known as Rosebud (Robert Butt) sometime in the 1970s.*

- $1/2$ oz (15 ml) gin
- $1/2$ oz (15 ml) vodka
- $1/2$ oz (15 ml) white tequila
- $1/2$ oz (15 ml) white rum
- $1/2$ oz (15 ml) Cointreau
- 1 oz (30 ml) freshly squeezed lemon juice
- Cola, such as Pepsi or Coca-Cola, to fill
- Lemon wedge, to garnish

LONG ISLAND ICED TEA • 1

$1/2$ oz (15 ml) vodka
$1/2$ oz (15 ml) white tequila
$1/2$ oz (15 ml) white rum
$1/2$ oz (15 ml) gin
3–4 dashes of Cola, such as Pepsi or Coca-Cola
Twist of lemon or lime zest

Fill a collins glass with crushed ice. Pour in the vodka, tequila, rum, and gin. Splash in the cola and garnish with the lemon or lime.

LONG ISLAND ICED TEA • 2

$1/2$ oz (15 ml) vodka
$1/2$ oz (15 ml) gold tequila
$1/2$ oz (15 ml) gold rum
$1/2$ oz (15 ml) gin
$1/2$ oz (15 ml) triple sec
1 oz (30 ml) sweet-and-sour mix
Cola, such as Pepsi or Coca-Cola, to fill

Fill a collins glass with crushed ice. Pour in the vodka, tequila, rum, gin, triple sec, and sweet-and-sour mix. Stir gently and top up with cola.

LONG ISLAND ICED TEA • 3

$1/3$ oz (10 ml) vodka
$1/3$ oz (10 ml) white tequila
$1/3$ oz (10 ml) gold rum
$1/3$ oz (10 ml) gin
$1/3$ oz (10 ml) Cointreau
3 oz (90 ml) freshly squeezed lemon or lime juice
Cola, such as Pepsi or Coca-Cola, to fill

Fill a collins glass with crushed ice. Pour in the vodka, tequila, rum, gin, Cointreau, and lemon or lime juice. Stir gently and top up with cola.

BLACK RUSSIAN

Fill a shaker two-thirds full with ice. Add the vodka and Kahlua. Shake well and strain into a chilled old-fashioned glass half filled with ice.

- 2 oz (60 ml) vodka
- 1 oz (30 ml) Kahlua

■ ■ ■ *This cocktail was invented in Brussels in the 1950s where barman Gustave Tops first made it at the Hotel Metropole for the American ambassador, Pearl Mesta.*

BLACK RUSSIAN • 1

1 oz (30 ml) vodka
1 oz (30 ml) Kahlua
5 oz (150 ml) cola, such as Pepsi or Coca-Cola

Place 4–5 ice cubes in a highball glass. Pour in the vodka and Kahlua and top up with cola.

BLACK RUSSIAN • 2

1¹/₂ oz (45 ml) vodka
1 oz (30 ml) Kahlua
2 oz (60 ml) freshly squeezed orange juice

Half fill a highball glass with ice cubes. Pour in the vodka, Kahlua, and orange juice. Stir gently.

BLACK MAGIC

1¹/₂ oz (45 ml) vodka
1 oz (30 ml) Kahlua
¹/₂ oz (15 ml) freshly squeezed lemon juice

Half fill a highball glass with ice cubes. Pour in the vodka, Kahlua, and lemon juice. Stir gently.

WHITE RUSSIAN

Fill a shaker two-thirds full with ice. Add the vodka, crème de cacao, and cream. Shake well and strain into a chilled martini glass.

- 2 oz (60 ml) vodka
- 1 oz (30 ml) white crème de cacao
- 3/4 oz (25 ml) heavy (double) cream

WHITE RUSSIAN • 1

2 oz (60 ml) vanilla vodka
1 oz (30 ml) Kahlua
1 oz (30 ml) light (single) cream

Place 2 ice cubes in a martini glass. Pour in the vodka and Kahlua and top up with the cream.

WHITE WITCH

2 oz (60 ml) vodka
1 oz (30 ml) white crème de cacao
1 scoop vanilla ice cream

Place the vodka, crème de cacao, and ice cream in a blender and blend until smooth. Pour into a chilled wine goblet.

REBEL RUSSIAN

$1^1/_2$ oz (45 ml) Southern Comfort
$1^1/_2$ oz (45 ml) Kahlua
3 oz (90 ml) light (single) cream

Fill a shaker two-thirds full with ice. Add the Southern Comfort, Kahlua, and cream. Shake well and pour into an old-fashioned glass over 4–5 ice cubes.

BLACK VELVET

Half fill a tall champagne flute
with stout. Tilt the glass and
pour in the champagne, trying to
create as little head as possible.

- **1 part Guinness stout**
- **1 part dry champagne**

■ ■ ■ *This old favorite was apparently thought up in 1861 in the*
Brooks Club in London where a group of gentlemen were gathered
to mark the passing of Queen Victoria's husband, Prince Albert.
Champagne was deemed too celebratory for the solemn occasion
so a little stout was added to tone things down. This is not a drink
to nurse; quaff it down—and have another!

BLACK PRINCE

1¹/₂ oz (45 ml) blackberry
brandy
Dash of lime juice
Dry champagne, well chilled,
to fill

Pour the brandy into a
champagne flute. Add the
lime juice and top up
with champagne.

PINK PRINCE

1¹/₂ oz (45 ml) Chambord
raspberry liqueur
Dry champagne, well chilled,
to fill

Pour the Chambord into a
champagne flute. Top up
with champagne.

RED PRINCE

¹/₂ oz (15 ml) Chambord
raspberry liqueur
¹/₂ oz (15 ml) crème
de cassis
Dry champagne, well chilled,
to fill

Pour the Chambord and
crème de cassis into a
champagne flute. Top
up with champagne.

MARTINI DRY

Fill a shaker two-thirds full with
ice. Add the gin and vermouth.
Shake well and strain into a
chilled martini glass.
Add the olive.

- **2 oz (60 ml) gin**
- **$1/3$ oz (10 ml) dry vermouth**
- **Stuffed or plain green cocktail olive**

FIFTY-FIFTY

$1^1/2$ oz (45 ml) gin
$1^1/2$ oz (45 ml) dry Vermouth
1 cocktail olive

Half fill a mixing glass with
ice cubes. Pour in the gin
and vermouth and stir well.
Strain into a chilled martini
glass. Add the olive.

IN AND OUT MARTINI

Splash of dry vermouth
3 oz (90 ml) gin
Twist of lemon peel,
to garnish

Fill a martini glass with ice
cubes and add the
vermouth. Swirl the ice in
the glass. Set aside. Fill a
shaker two-thirds full with
ice. Add the gin and shake
well. Throw out the ice and
vermouth in the martini
glass. Strain the gin into the
chilled glass. Garnish with
the lemon.

DIRTY MARTINI

2 oz (60 ml) gin
$1/2$ oz (15 ml) dry vermouth
$1/2$ oz (15 ml) brine
(from the olive jar)

Fill a shaker two-thirds full
with ice. Add the gin,
vermouth, and olive brine.
Shake well and strain into
a chilled martini glass.

VODKA MARTINI

Fill a shaker two-thirds full with ice. Add the vodka and vermouth. Shake well and strain into a chilled martini glass. Add the olive.

- **2 oz (60 ml) vodka**
- **Dash of dry vermouth**
- **Green olive**

VODKA MARTINI • 1

2 oz (60 ml) vodka
1 oz (30 ml) dry vermouth
2 drops Tabasco

Fill a shaker two-thirds full with ice. Add the vodka and vermouth. Shake well and strain into a chilled martini glass. Add the Tabasco.

FLAMING RUSSIAN

1 oz (30 ml) vodka
$1/3$ oz (10 ml) strong rum

Pour the vodka into a shot glass. Carefully layer the rum on top. Light the rum and serve at once.

EMERALD MARTINI

$1^1/_2$ oz (45 ml) vodka
$1/_2$ oz (15 ml) dry vermouth
Splash of green Chartreuse
Twist of lemon peel

Half fill a mixing glass with crushed ice. Pour in the vodka, vermouth, and Chartreuse and mix well. Strain into a chilled martini glass. Garnish with the lemon.

TEQUILA SUNRISE

Fill a shaker two-thirds full with ice. Add the tequila, orange juice, and lime juice. Shake well and strain into a collins glass over 4–5 ice cubes. Pour the grenadine slowly over the top. Do not stir. Garnish with the lime.

- 1¹/₂ oz (45 ml) white tequila
- 3 oz (90 ml) freshly squeezed orange juice
- ¹/₂ oz (15 ml) freshly squeezed lime juice
- ¹/₂ oz (15 ml) grenadine
- Slice of lime, to garnish

CAN CAN

1¹/₂ oz (45 ml) white tequila
¹/₂ oz (15 ml) dry vermouth
3 oz (90 ml) freshly squeezed grapefruit juice

Fill a shaker two-thirds full with ice. Add the tequila, vermouth, and grapefruit juice. Shake well and strain into an old-fashioned glass over 2–3 ice cubes.

PIERCED FUZZY NAVEL

1 oz (30 ml) white tequila
1¹/₂ oz (45 ml) peach schnapps
4 oz (120 ml) freshly squeezed orange juice

Half fill a collins glass with ice cubes, Pour in the tequila and peach schnapps. Top up with orange juice.

ARIZONA SUNRISE

1¹/₂ oz (45 ml) gold tequila
¹/₂ oz (15 ml) lime cordial
2 splashes of grenadine
4 oz (120 ml) freshly squeezed orange juice
Wedge of lime, to garnish

Half fill an old-fashioned glass with ice cubes. Pour in the grenadine and swirl around in the glass. Set aside. Fill a shaker two-thirds full with ice. Add the tequila, lime cordial, and orange juice. Shake well and strain into the glass. Garnish with the lime.

BETWEEN THE SHEETS

Fill a shaker two-thirds full with ice. Add the rum, brandy, Cointreau, and lemon or lime juice. Shake well and strain into a chilled martini glass.

- 1 oz (30 ml) white rum
- 3/4 oz (25 ml) brandy
- 3/4 oz (25 ml) Cointreau
- 3/4 oz (25 ml) freshly squeezed lemon or lime juice

336

X.Y.Z. COCKTAIL

1 oz (30 ml) gold rum
1/2 oz (15 ml) Cointreau
1/2 oz (15 ml) freshly squeezed lemon juice

Fill a shaker two-thirds full with ice. Add the rum, Cointreau, and lemon juice.

Shake well and strain into a chilled martini glass.

BOSTON SIDECAR

1 oz (30 ml) white rum
1/2 oz (15 ml) brandy
1/2 oz (15 ml) triple sec
1/2 oz (15 ml) freshly squeezed lemon juice

Fill a shaker two-thirds full with ice. Add the rum, brandy, triple sec, and lemon juice. Shake well and strain into a chilled martini glass.

FROZEN BERKELEY

1 1/2 oz (45 ml) white rum
1/2 oz (15 ml) brandy
1/2 oz (15 ml) passion fruit syrup
1/2 oz (15 ml) freshly squeezed lemon juice
1/2 cup (125 ml) crushed ice

Place the rum, brandy, passion fruit syrup, lemon juice, and ice in a blender and blend for a few seconds until just slushy. Pour into a wine goblet.

MOSCOW MULE

Place 4–6 cracked ice cubes in a 5 oz (150 ml) copper mug (use more ice if serving in an old fashioned or collins glass). Pour in the vodka and lime juice and stir gently. Top up with ginger beer. Float the slice of lemon or lime on top of the drink if serving in a mug, or garnish the rim if serving in a glass.

- **2 oz (60 ml) vodka**
- **3/4 oz (25 ml) freshly squeezed lime juice**
- **Ginger beer, to fill**
- **Slice or wedge of lemon or lime, to garnish**

■ ■ ■ *The 5 oz (150 ml) copper mug embossed with a kicking mule in which this drink is traditionally served was actually a clever marketing ploy. However, if you like the drink you may want to invest in a set of mugs which at least offers a talking point for guests. Make sure that all the ingredients, including the lime, are well chilled.*

RHETT BUTLER

Fill a shaker two-thirds full with ice. Add the Southern Comfort, orange curaçao, lime juice, lemon juice, and sugar syrup. Shake well and strain into a chilled martini glass. Garnish with the lemon or lime.

- 2 oz (60 ml) Southern Comfort
- 1/2 oz (15 ml) freshly squeezed lime juice
- 1 teaspoon orange curaçao
- 1 teaspoon freshly squeezed lemon juice
- 1 teaspoon sugar syrup
- Long thin sliver of lemon or lime peel, to garnish

'57 CHEVY

1 oz (30 ml) Southern Comfort
1/2 oz (15 ml) peach schnapps
1/2 oz (15 ml) amaretto
Splash of freshly squeezed orange juice
Splash of pineapple juice
Dash of grenadine

Fill a shaker two-thirds full with ice. Add the Southern Comfort, peach schnapps, amaretto, orange juice, pineapple juice, and grenadine. Shake well and strain into a hurricane glass.

ORANGE COMFORT

1 1/2 oz (45 ml) Southern Comfort
1 teaspoon anisette
1/2 oz (15 ml) freshly squeezed orange juice
1 teaspoon freshly squeezed lime juice

Fill a shaker two-thirds full with ice. Add the Southern Comfort, anisette, orange juice, and lime juice. Shake well and strain into an old-fashioned glass over 2–3 ice cubes.

YELLOW ALLIGATOR

1/2 oz (15 ml) Southern Comfort
1/2 oz (15 ml) peach schnapps
1/2 oz (15 ml) Midori melon liqueur
1/2 oz (15 ml) amaretto
1/2 oz (15 ml) freshly squeezed orange juice

Fill a shaker two-thirds full with ice. Add the Southern Comfort, peach schnapps, Midori, amaretto, and orange juice. Shake well. and strain into a chilled martini glass.

MAIDEN'S BLUSH

Fill a shaker two-thirds full with ice. Add the gin, Cointreau, lemon juice, and grenadine. Shake well and strain into a chilled martini glass or an old fashioned glass filled with ice.

- **2 oz (60 ml) gin**
- **1 teaspoon Cointreau**
- **1/2 teaspoon freshly squeezed lemon juice**
- **1/2 teaspoon grenadine**

MAIDEN'S BLUSH • 1

1¹/₂ oz (45 ml) gin
¹/₂ oz (15 ml) triple sec
1 teaspoon cherry brandy
1 oz (30 ml) freshly squeezed lemon juice
Maraschino cherry

Fill a shaker two-thirds full with ice. Add the gin, triple sec, cherry brandy, and lemon juice. Shake well and strain into a chilled martini glass. Garnish with the cherry.

CHELSEA BAR

1¹/₂ oz (45 ml) gin
²/₃ oz (20 ml) Cointreau
2 teaspoons freshly squeezed lemon juice

Fill a shaker two-thirds full with ice. Add the gin, Cointreau, and lemon juice.

Shake well and strain into a chilled martini glass.

CHANTICLEER

2 oz (60 ml) gin
1 oz (30 ml) freshly squeezed lemon juice
¹/₂ oz (15 ml) raspberry syrup
¹/₂ egg white

Fill a shaker two-thirds full with ice. Add the gin, lemon juice, raspberry syrup, and egg white. Shake well and strain into a chilled martini glass.

BRONX

Fill a shaker two-thirds full with ice. Add the gin, dry vermouth, sweet vermouth, and orange juice. Shake well and strain into a chilled martini glass. Garnish with the orange, if liked.

- 1$^1/_2$ oz (45 ml) gin
- $^1/_2$ oz (15 ml) dry vermouth
- $^1/_2$ oz (15 ml) sweet vermouth
- 1 oz (30 ml) freshly squeezed orange juice
- Slice of orange, to garnish (optional)

BRONX DRY

1 oz (30 ml) gin
1 oz (30 ml) dry vermouth
2 oz (60 ml) freshly squeezed orange juice
Slice of orange, to garnish

Fill a shaker two-thirds full with ice. Add the gin, vermouth, and orange juice. Shake well and strain into a chilled martini glass. Garnish with the orange.

GOLDEN BRONX

1$^1/_2$ oz (45 ml) gin
$^1/_2$ oz (15 ml) dry vermouth
$^1/_2$ oz (15 ml) sweet vermouth
2 oz (60 ml) freshly squeezed orange juice
1 egg yolk
Slice of orange, to garnish

Fill a shaker two-thirds full with ice. Add the gin, dry vermouth, sweet vermouth, orange juice, and egg yolk. Shake well and strain into an old-fashioned glass over 2–3 ice cubes. Garnish with the orange.

SILVER BRONX

1$^1/_2$ oz (45 ml) gin
$^1/_2$ oz (15 ml) dry vermouth
$^1/_2$ oz (15 ml) sweet vermouth
1 oz (30 ml) freshly squeezed orange juice
1 egg white

Fill a shaker two-thirds full with ice. Add the gin, dry vermouth, sweet vermouth, orange juice, and egg white. Shake well and strain into a chilled martini glass.

BLUE LAGOON

Place 4–6 ice cubes in a large wine goblet. Pour in the vodka, blue curaçao, and lime juice. Top up with lemon soda. Garnish with the cherries.

- **2 oz (60 ml) vodka**
- **1¹/₂ oz (45 ml) blue curaçao**
- **¹/₂ oz (15 ml) freshly squeezed lime juice**
- **Lemon soda, to fill**
- **Cocktail cherries (red or blue), to garnish**

346

BLACK AND BLUE

1¹/₂ oz (45 ml) vodka
1¹/₂ oz (45 ml) blue curaçao
1 oz (30 ml) blackberry schnapps

Fill a shaker two-thirds full with ice. Add the vodka, blue curaçao, and black-berry schnapps. Shake well and strain into a chilled martini glass

BLUE MOON

1¹/₂ oz (45 ml) vodka
¹/₂ oz (15 ml) dry vermouth
¹/₃ oz (10 ml) blue curaçao
Dash of Angostura bitters

Fill a shaker two-thirds full with ice. Add the vodka, vermouth, blue curaçao, and Angostura. Shake well and strain into a chilled martini glass.

BLUE SHARK

1 oz (30 ml) vodka
1 oz (30 ml) white tequila
¹/₂ oz (15 ml) blue curaçao

Fill a shaker two-thirds full with ice. Add the vodka, tequila, and blue curaçao. Shake well and strain into a chilled martini glass.

BLUE LADY

Fill a shaker two-thirds full with ice. Add the gin, blue curaçao, lemon juice, and egg white. Shake well and strain into a chilled martini glass.

- 1¹/₂ oz (45 ml) gin
- 1¹/₂ oz (45 ml) blue curaçao
- 1 oz (30 ml) freshly squeezed lemon juice
- 1 teaspoon egg white

348

BLUE MARTINI

1¹/₂ oz (45 ml) gin
¹/₂ oz (15 ml) dry vermouth
¹/₂ oz (15 ml) blue curaçao

Fill a shaker two-thirds full with ice. Add the gin, vermouth, and blue curaçao. Shake well and strain into a chilled martini glass.

BLUE DENIM

1 oz (30 ml) bourbon
¹/₂ oz (15 ml) dry vermouth
¹/₃ oz (10 ml) blue curaçao
2–3 dashes Angostura bitters
Wedge of lemon, to garnish

Fill a shaker two-thirds full with ice. Add the bourbon, vermouth, blue curaçao, and Angostura. Shake well and strain into an old-fashioned glass over 2–3 cubes of ice. Garnish with the lemon.

BLUE BAHAMAS

1 oz (30 ml) blue curaçao liqueur
¹/₂ oz (15 ml) gold rum
¹/₂ oz (15 ml) white rum
¹/₂ oz (15 ml) cream of coconut
1¹/₂ oz (45 ml) pineapple juice

Fill a shaker two-thirds full with ice. Add the blue curaçao, both types of rum, the cream of coconut, and pineapple juice. Shake well and strain into a collins glass half full with crushed ice.

CLASSIC OLD-FASHIONED

Place the slice of orange, cocktail cherry, and sugar in an old-fashioned glass and muddle. Add 4–5 ice cubes and pour in the bourbon, Angostura, and a dash of soda water. Swish gently in the glass before drinking.

- 3 oz (90 ml) bourbon
- 2–3 dashes Angostura bitters
- Slice of orange
- Cocktail cherry
- 1 teaspoon sugar
- Dash of soda water

NEW OLD-FASHIONED

2 oz (60 ml) blended whisky
1 teaspoon cherry syrup
1–2 dashes Angostura bitters
Slice of orange, to garnish
Maraschino cherry, to garnish

Place 4–5 ice cubes in an old-fashioned glass. Pour in the whisky, cherry syrup, and Angostura and stir well. Garnish with the orange and cherry.

FRUITY OLD-FASHIONED

1¹/₂ oz (45 ml) bourbon
1 teaspoon sugar syrup
2–3 dashes Angostura bitters
Fresh peach, cut in small cubes
Slice of orange, cut in 8
Strawberry, cut in half

Place 4–5 ice cubes in an old-fashioned glass. Pour in the whisky, sugar syrup, and Angostura and stir well. Add the fruit and stir gently.

CANADIAN OLD-FASH.

1¹/₂ oz (45 ml) Canadian whisky
1 teaspoon white curaçao
2 dashes Angostura bitters
2 dashes freshly squeezed lemon juice
Slice of orange, to garnish

Fill a shaker two-thirds full with ice. Add the whisky, curaçao, Angostura, and lemon juice. Shake well and strain into a chilled old-fashioned glass. Garnish with the orange over 2–3 ice cubes.

FROZEN COCKTAILS

FROZEN MARGARITA

Moisten the rim of a large wine goblet with lime juice. Dip into the salt to frost. Place the tequila, Cointreau, lime juice, and ice in a blender. Blend for a few seconds until just slushy (but not watery). Pour into the prepared glass and garnish with the lime.

354

- 1¹/₂ oz (45 ml) tequila
- ¹/₂ oz (15 ml) Cointreau
- 1 oz (30 ml) freshly squeezed lime juice
- ¹/₂ cup (125 ml) crushed ice
- Salt
- Slice of lime, to garnish

FROZEN MARGARITA •1

2¹/₂ oz (75 ml) white tequila
1 oz (30 ml) triple sec
2 oz (60 ml) freshly squeezed lime juice
¹/₂ cup (125 ml) crushed ice
Salt
1 lime wedge

Moisten the rim of a wine goblet with lime juice. Dip the glass into salt to frost. Place the tequila, triple sec, lime juice, and ice in a blender. Blend for a few seconds until just slushy. Pour into the glass.

PRADO

1¹/₂ oz (45 ml) white tequila
¹/₂ oz (15 ml) Maraschino liqueur
¹/₂ oz (15 ml) freshly squeezed lime juice
1 teaspoon grenadine
¹/₂ cup (125 ml) crushed ice

Place the tequila, Maraschino, lime juice, grenadine, and ice in a blender. Blend for a few seconds until just slushy. Pour into an old-fashioned glass.

PRICKLY PEAR MARG.

1¹/₂ oz (45 ml) white tequila
2 oz (60 ml) freshly squeezed lemon juice
2 teaspoons sugar syrup
1¹/₂ oz (45 ml) prickly pear juice
¹/₂ cup (125 ml) crushed ice
Slice of lime, to garnish

Place the tequila, lemon juice, sugar syrup, prickly pear juice, and ice in a blender. Blend for a few seconds until just slushy. Pour into a hurricane glass. Garnish with the lime.

FROZEN BANANA DAIQUIRI

Place the rum, banana liqueur, lime juice, banana, cream, and ice in a blender. Blend for a few seconds until just slushy. Pour into a chilled wine goblet. Garnish with the lime.

- 1^1/$_2$ oz (45 ml) white rum
- 1 oz (30 ml) banana liqueur
- 1 oz (30 ml) freshly squeezed lime juice
- ^{1}/$_2$ ripe banana
- 1 oz (30 ml) light (single) cream
- ^{1}/$_2$ cup (125 ml) crushed ice
- Slice of lime, to garnish

F. STRAWBERRY COLADA

1^1/$_2$ oz (45 ml) gold rum
2 oz (60 ml) cream of coconut
6–8 strawberries
1 medium banana
^{1}/$_2$ cup (125 ml) crushed ice

Place the rum, coconut cream, strawberries, banana, and ice in a blender. Blend for a few seconds until just slushy. Pour into a hurricane glass.

FROZEN BLUE DAIQUIRI

2 oz (60 ml) white rum
^{1}/$_2$ oz (15 ml) blue curaçao
^{1}/$_2$ oz (15 ml) freshly squeezed lime juice
^{1}/$_2$ cup (125 ml) crushed ice

Place the rum, blue curaçao, lime juice, and ice in a blender. Blend for a few seconds until just slushy. Pour into a wine goblet.

F. PINEAPPLE DAIQUIRI

1^1/$_2$ oz (45 ml) white rum
4 chunks pineapple
^{1}/$_2$ oz (15 ml) freshly squeezed lime juice
^{1}/$_2$ teaspoon sugar
^{1}/$_2$ cup (125 ml) crushed ice

Place the rum, pineapple, lime juice, sugar, and ice in a blender. Blend for a few seconds until just slushy. Pour into a wine goblet.

CHI CHI

Place the vodka, pineapple juice, cream of coconut, and ice in a blender. Blend for a few seconds until just slushy. Pour into a chilled collins glass. Garnish with the pineapple and cream, if liked.

- **2 oz (60 ml) vodka**
- **1¹/₂ oz (45 ml) pineapple juice**
- **1 oz (30 ml) cream of coconut**
- **³/₄ cup (200 ml) crushed ice**
- **Fresh pineapple, to garnish**
- **Whipped cream, to garnish (optional)**

PINEAPPLE CHI-CHI

1¹/₂ oz (45 ml) vodka
¹/₂ oz (15 ml) Cointreau
2 oz (60 ml) pineapple juice
1 oz (30 ml) cream of coconut
¹/₂ cup (125 ml) crushed ice

Place the vodka, Cointreau, pineapple juice, cream of coconut, and ice in a blender. Blend for a few seconds until just slushy. Pour into a wine goblet.

PASSION CHI-CHI

1¹/₂ oz (45 ml) vodka
1¹/₂ oz (45 ml) passion fruit juice
1 oz (30 ml) coconut milk
1 tablespoon sugar
¹/₂ cup (125 ml) crushed ice

Place the vodka, passion fruit juice, coconut milk, sugar, and ice in a blender. Blend for a few seconds until just slushy. Pour into a wine goblet.

PEACHY CHI-CHI

1¹/₂ oz (45 ml) vodka
1 oz (30 ml) peach schnapps
¹/₂ oz (15 ml) Cointreau
¹/₂ fresh peach, peeled and chopped
³/₄ cup (200 ml) crushed ice

Place the vodka, peach schnapps, Cointreau, peach, and ice in a blender. Blend for a few seconds until just slushy. Pour into a hurricane glass.

COOL STRAWBERRY DAIQUIRI

Place the rum, grapefruit juice, simple syrup, strawberries, and ice in a blender. Blend for a few seconds until just slushy. Pour into a large wine goblet. Garnish with the strawberry and cream, if liked.

- 1¹/₂ oz (45 ml) white rum
- 1 oz (30 ml) freshly squeezed grapefruit juice
- ¹/₂ oz (15 ml) sugar syrup
- 6–8 fresh strawberries
- ³/₄ cup (200 ml) crushed ice
- Strawberry, with green stalk, to garnish
- Whipped cream, to garnish (optional)

HURRICANE

1¹/₂ oz (45 ml) white rum
1 oz (30 ml) dark rum
1 oz (30 ml) freshly squeezed lime juice
1 oz (30 ml) passion fruit syrup
1 teaspoon sugar syrup
³/₄ cup (200 ml) crushed ice

Place both types of rum, the lime juice, passion fruit syrup, sugar syrup, and ice in a blender. Blend for a few seconds until just slushy. Pour into a hurricane glass.

HAVANA BUZZ

1¹/₂ oz (45 ml) white rum
2 oz (60 ml) pineapple juice
1 oz (30 ml) freshly squeezed lime juice
¹/₂ ripe banana
2 dashes orange bitters
¹/₂ cup (125 ml) crushed ice

Place the rum, pineapple juice, lime juice, banana, orange bitters, and ice in a blender. Blend for a few seconds until just slushy. Pour into a wine goblet.

HAVANA BANANA

2 oz (60 ml) white rum
1 oz (30 ml) banana liqueur
¹/₂ oz (15 ml) freshly squeezed lime juice
1 small ripe banana
³/₄ cup (200 ml) crushed ice

Place the rum, banana liqueur, lime juice, banana, and ice in a blender. Blend for a few seconds until just slushy. Pour into a hurricane glass.

CRANBERRY MARGARITA

Place the tequila, Grand Marnier, cranberry juice, cranberries, sugar, lime juice, and ice in a blender. Blend for a few seconds until just slushy. Serve in two chilled margarita glasses

- 4 oz (120 ml) white tequila
- 2 oz (60 ml) Grand Marnier
- 6 oz (180 ml) cranberry juice
- 5 oz (150 g) fresh or frozen cranberries
- 2 tablespoons sugar
- 2 oz (60 ml) freshly squeezed lime juice
- 1$1/2$ cups (375 ml) crushed ice

BLIZZARD

Place the Southern Comfort, cranberry juice, lemon juice, and ice in a blender. Blend for a few seconds until just slushy. Pour into a hurricane glass.

364

- 3 oz (90 ml) Southern Comfort
- 1 oz (30 ml) cranberry juice
- 1/2 oz (15 ml) freshly squeezed lemon juice
- 1/2 cup (125 ml) crushed ice

VANILLA BLIZZARD.

2 oz (60 ml) white crème de cacao
1 oz (30 ml) vanilla vodka
1 oz (30 ml) milk
2 scoops vanilla ice cream
11/2 oz (45 ml) whipped cream
Maraschino cherry, to garnish

Place the crème de cacao, vodka, milk, ice cream, and ice in a blender. Blend for a few seconds until smooth. Pour into a hurricane glass and top with the cream and cherry.

KENTUCKY BLIZZARD

11/2 oz (45 ml) bourbon
11/2 oz (45 ml) cranberry juice
1/2 oz (15 ml) freshly squeezed lime juice
1/2 oz (15 ml) grenadine
1 teaspoon sugar syrup
1/2 cup (125 ml) crushed ice

Place the bourbon, cranberry juice, lime juice, grenadine, sugar syrup, and ice in a blender. Blend for a few seconds until just slushy. Pour into a wine glass.

MOCHA BLIZZARD

1 oz (30 ml) brandy
1 oz (30 ml) Irish cream
1 oz (30 ml) coffee liqueur
1 oz (30 ml) white rum
2 scoops vanilla ice cream
Splash of light (single) cream
Grated nutmeg

Place the brandy, Irish cream, coffee liqueur, rum, ice cream, and cream in a blender. Blend until smooth. Pour into a large wine goblet. Dust with nutmeg.

FROZEN BLACK RUSSIAN

Place the Kahlua, vodka, and ice cream in a blender. Blend for a few seconds until smooth. Pour into a chilled wine goblet and garnish with the cherry.

- **2 oz (60 ml) Kahlua**
- **1 oz (30 ml) vodka**
- **2 scoops vanilla ice cream**
- **Cocktail cherry, to garnish**

VANILLA CREAM

3 oz (90 ml) vanilla vodka
2 oz (60 ml) Kahlua
2 oz (60 ml) Bailey's Irish cream
2 oz (60 ml) Barenjager
2 scoops vanilla ice cream
1 cup (250 ml) crushed ice

Place the vodka, Kahlua, Irish cream, ice cream, and ice in a blender. Blend until just slushy. Pour into two hurricane glasses.

CHOCOLATE RUSSIAN

$1^1/_2$ oz (45 ml) vodka
1 oz (30 ml) Kahlua
2 scoops chocolate ice cream

Place the vodka, Kahlua, and ice cream in a blender. Blend until smooth. Pour into a hurricane glass.

MOCHA RUSSIAN

$1^1/_2$ oz (45 ml) vodka
1 oz (30 ml) Kahlua
2 scoops coffee ice cream

Place the vodka, Kahlua, and ice cream in a blender. Blend until smooth. Pour into a hurricane glass.

FROZEN COLADA

Place the rum, Kahlua, pineapple juice, cream of coconut, and ice in a blender. Blend for a few seconds until just slushy. Pour into a hurricane glass and garnish with the orange.

- 2 oz (60 ml) dark rum
- 1 oz (30 ml) Kahlua
- 2 oz (60 ml) pineapple juice
- 1 oz (30 ml) cream of coconut
- $1/2$ cup (125 ml) crushed ice
- Slice of orange, to garnish

BANANA SPLIT

$1^1/2$ oz (45 ml) banana liqueur
$2/3$ oz (20 ml) white crème de cacao
$2/3$ oz (20 ml) caramel liqueur
$1/3$ cup (90 ml) crushed ice
2–3 splashes cherry brandy

Place the banana liqueur, crème de cacao, caramel liqueur, and ice in a blender. Blend for a few seconds until just slushy. Pour into a wine goblet and splash with the cherry brandy.

BANANA COCKTAIL

$1^1/2$ oz (45 ml) banana liqueur
$1/2$ oz (15 ml) white crème de cacao
$1/2$ oz (15 ml) Galliano
$1/2$ ripe banana
2 scoops vanilla ice cream
$1/2$ teaspoon vanilla extract (essence)
$1/4$ cup (60 ml) crushed ice

Place the banana liqueur, crème de cacao, Galliano, banana, ice cream, vanilla, and ice in a blender. Blend for a few seconds until just slushy. Pour into a hurricane glass.

FROZEN BANANA COLADA

$1^1/2$ oz (45 ml) dark rum
2 oz (60 ml) cream of coconut
1 ripe banana
$1/2$ cup (125 ml) crushed ice
Slices of banana, to garnish

Place the rum, cream of coconut, banana, and ice in a blender. Blend for a few seconds until just slushy. Pour into a wine goblet. Garnish with the slices of banana.

FROZEN DERBY SPECIAL

Place the rum, Cointreau, orange juice, lime juice, and ice in a blender. Blend for a few seconds until just slushy. Pour into a large wine goblet.

- **2 oz (60 ml) white rum**
- **$1/2$ oz (15 ml) Cointreau**
- **1 oz (30 ml) freshly squeezed orange juice**
- **$1/2$ oz (15 ml) freshly squeezed lime juice**
- **$1/2$ cup (125 ml) crushed ice**

FROZEN APPLE

$1^1/_2$ oz (45 ml) apple brandy
$1/2$ oz (15 ml) freshly squeezed lime juice
1 teaspoon sugar syrup
$1/2$ egg white
$1/2$ cup (125 ml) crushed ice

Place the apple brandy, lime juice, sugar syrup, egg white, and ice in a blender. Blend for a few seconds until just slushy. Pour into a wine goblet.

FROZEN MATADOR

$1^1/_2$ oz (45 ml) white tequila
2 oz (60 ml) pineapple juice
$1/2$ oz (15 ml) freshly squeezed lime juice
$3/4$ cup (200 ml) crushed ice
Wedge of fresh pineapple, to garnish

Place the tequila, pineapple juice, lime juice, and ice in a blender. Blend for a few seconds until just slushy. Pour into a hurricane glass. Garnish with the pineapple.

FROZEN DAZE

1 oz (30 ml) white rum
$1/2$ oz (15 ml) blackberry brandy
$1/2$ oz (15 ml) banana liqueur
$1/2$ oz (15 ml) grenadine
$1/2$ oz (15 ml) lime cordial
Splash of pineapple juice
$3/4$ cup (200 ml) crushed ice

Place the rum, blackberry brandy, banana liqueur, grenadine, lime cordial, pineapple juice, and ice in a blender. Blend for a few seconds until just slushy. Pour into a hurricane glass.

372

DOMINICAN COCO LOCO

Place the rum, amaretto, cream of coconut, pineapple juice, grenadine, cream, and ice in a blender. Blend for a few seconds until just slushy. Pour into a hurricane glass and garnish with the pineapple.

- **2 oz (60 ml) white rum**
- **$1/2$ oz (15 ml) amaretto**
- **1 oz (30 ml) cream of coconut**
- **$1/2$ oz (15 ml) pineapple juice**
- **2 dashes grenadine**
- **2 dashes heavy (double) cream**
- **$1/2$ cup (125 ml) crushed ice**
- **Small wedge of fresh pineapple, to garnish**

FROZEN COCO CABANA

$1^1/_2$ oz (45 ml) coconut liqueur
1 oz (30 ml) white rum
2 oz (60 ml) pineapple juice
$1/2$ cup (125 ml) crushed ice
Maraschino cherry, to garnish

Place the coconut liqueur, rum, pineapple juice, and ice in a blender. Blend for a few seconds until just slushy. Pour into a hurricane glass. Garnish with the cherry.

FROZEN FRUITY RUM

2 oz (60 ml) white rum
2 oz (60 ml) pineapple juice
$1/2$ oz (15 ml) freshly squeezed grapefruit juice
$1/2$ oz (15 ml) fresh mango, chopped
$1/2$ cup (125 ml) crushed ice

Place the rum, pineapple juice, grapefruit juice, mango, and ice in a blender. Blend for a few seconds until just slushy. Pour into a wine goblet.

TRADE WINDS

2 oz (60 ml) gold rum
$1/2$ oz (15 ml) sloe gin
$1/2$ oz (15 ml) freshly squeezed lime juice
2 teaspoons sugar syrup
$1/2$ cup (125 ml) crushed ice

Place the rum, sloe gin, lime juice, sugar syrup, and ice in a blender. Blend for a few seconds until just slushy. Pour into a wine goblet.

FROZEN BIKINI

Place the vodka, peach schnapps, peach juice, orange juice, lime juice, and ice in a blender. Blend for a few seconds until just slushy. Pour into a hurricane glass and top up with champagne. Garnish with the lemon and cherry.

- **2 oz (60 ml) vodka**
- **1 oz (30 ml) peach schnapps**
- **2 oz (60 ml) peach juice**
- **2 oz (60 ml) freshly squeezed orange juice**
- **1/2 oz (15 ml) freshly squeezed lime juice**
- **1/2 cup (125 ml) crushed ice**
- **Dry champagne, well chilled, to fill**
- **Wedge of lemon, to garnish**
- **Maraschino cherry, to garnish**

FROZEN PEACHES

1 oz (30 ml) vodka
1 oz (30 ml) peach schnapps
1/2 oz (15 ml) freshly squeezed lime juice
1 teaspoon sugar syrup
1/2 peach, peeled and chopped
1/2 cup (125 ml) crushed ice

Place the vodka, peach schnapps, lime juice, sugar syrup, peach, and ice in a blender. Blend for a few seconds until just slushy. Pour into a hurricane glass.

FROZEN ORANGE

3/4 oz (25 ml) brandy
3/4 oz (25 ml) sherry
3/4 oz (25 ml) Cointreau
3/4 oz (25 ml) freshly squeezed orange juice
3/4 oz (25 ml) heavy (double) cream
3/4 oz (25 ml) sugar syrup
1/2 cup (125 ml) crushed ice

Place the brandy, sherry, Cointreau, orange juice, cream, sugar syrup, and ice in a blender. Blend for a few seconds until just slushy. Pour into a hurricane glass.

FROZEN MINT

1/2 oz (15 ml) white crème de menthe
1/2 oz (15 ml) Kahlua
1/2 oz (15 ml) white crème de cacao
1/2 oz (15 ml) Bailey's Irish cream
11/2 oz (45 ml) cold milk
2 scoops vanilla ice cream

Place the crème de menthe, Kahlua, crème de cacao, Irish cream, milk, and ice cream in a blender. Blend for a few seconds until smooth. Pour into a hurricane glass.

FROZEN PEACH DAIQUIRI

Place the rum, cherry schnapps, honey, lime juice, cream, peach, and ice in a blender. Blend for a few seconds until just slushy. Pour into a hurricane glass. Garnish with the fruit.

- 2 oz (60 ml) white rum
- 1 oz (30 ml) cherry schnapps
- 1 tablespoon honey
- 1/2 oz (15 ml) freshly squeezed lime juice
- 1/2 oz (15 ml) heavy (double) cream
- 1 peach, peeled, pitted, and chopped
- 3/4 cup (200 ml) crushed ice
- Fresh fruit, to garnish

376

FROZEN DAIQUIRI

1 1/2 oz (45 ml) white rum
1/2 oz (15 ml) Cointreau
1 1/2 oz (45 ml) freshly squeezed lime juice
1 teaspoon sugar syrup
1/2 cup (125 ml) crushed ice

Place the rum, Cointreau, lime juice, sugar syrup, and ice in a blender. Blend for a few seconds until just slushy. Pour into a wine goblet.

FROZEN MINT DAIQUIRI

2 oz (60 ml) white rum
1/2 oz (15 ml) freshly squeezed lime juice
6 mint leaves
1 teaspoon sugar syrup
1/2 cup (125 ml) crushed ice

Place the rum, lime juice, mint leaves, sugar syrup, and ice in a blender. Blend for a few seconds until just slushy. Pour into a wine goblet.

FROZEN MINT JULEP

2 oz (60 ml) bourbon
1 oz (30 ml) freshly squeezed lemon juice
6–8 mint leaves
1 teaspoon sugar syrup
1/2 cup (125 ml) crushed ice

Place the bourbon, lemon juice, mint leaves, sugar syrup, and ice in a blender. Blend for a few seconds until just slushy. Pour into an old-fashioned glass.

KOALA BEAR

Place the crème de banana, crème de cacao, ice cream, and ice in a blender. Blend for a few seconds until just slushy.
Pour into a large wine goblet or hurricane glass. Dust with the nutmeg.

- 1 oz (30 ml) crème de banana
- 1 oz (30 ml) dark crème de cacao
- 2 small scoops vanilla ice cream
- $1/2$ cup (125 ml) crushed ice
- Freshly grated nutmeg, to dust

KIEV SUNDAE

Place the cinnamon vodka, crème de cacao, Irish cream, and ice cream in a blender. Blend for a few seconds until smooth. Pour into a hurricane glass. Float the raspberry vodka on top. Top with whipped cream.

- 1$^{1}/_{2}$ oz (45 ml) cinnamon vodka
- $^{3}/_{4}$ oz (25 ml) white crème de cacao
- $^{3}/_{4}$ oz (25 ml) Bailey's Irish cream
- 1 scoop vanilla ice cream
- 1–2 teaspoons raspberry vodka
- Whipped cream, to top

FROZEN FRUIT SUNDAE

2 oz (60 ml) banana liqueur
1 oz (30 ml) peach schnapps
3 oz (90 ml) freshly squeezed orange juice
$^{1}/_{2}$ cup (125 ml) crushed ice
Splash of grenadine

Place the banana liqueur, peach schnapps, orange juice, and ice in a blender. Blend for a few seconds until just slushy. Pour into a hurricane glass. Splash in the grenadine.

ADVOCAAT SUNDAE

2 oz (60 ml) advocaat
$^{1}/_{2}$ oz (15 ml) dark rum
2 oz (60 ml) freshly squeezed orange juice
$^{1}/_{2}$ ripe banana
$^{1}/_{2}$ cup (125 ml) crushed ice

Place the advocaat, rum, orange juice, banana, and ice in a blender. Blend for a few seconds until just slushy. Pour into an old-fashioned glass.

FROZEN WHISKY CREAM

1 oz (30 ml) Scotch whisky
1 oz (30 ml) Bailey's Irish cream
1 oz (30 ml) advocaat
$^{1}/_{2}$ cup (125 ml) crushed ice

Place the whisky, Irish cream, advocaat, and ice in a blender. Blend for a few seconds until just slushy. Pour into an old-fashioned glass.

BABY JANE

Place the cinnamon vodka, butterscotch schnapps, Irish cream, gin, ice cream, and ice in a blender. Blend for a few seconds until smooth. Pour into a hurricane glass.

- **1 oz (30 ml) cinnamon vodka**
- **1/2 oz (15 ml) butterscotch schnapps**
- **1/2 oz (15 ml) Bailey's Irish cream**
- **1/2 oz (15 ml) gin**
- **2 scoops vanilla ice cream**
- **1/2 cup (125 ml) crushed ice**

VANILLA VODKA CHILL

1 1/2 oz (45 ml) vanilla vodka
1/2 oz (15 ml) cinnamon schnapps
1/3 oz (10 ml) gin
1/3 oz (10 ml) triple sec
1/3 oz (10 ml) tequila
4 oz (120 ml) freshly squeezed orange juice
1 cup (250 ml) crushed ice

Place the vanilla vodka, cinnamon schnapps, gin, triple sec, tequila, orange juice, and ice in a blender. Blend for a few seconds until just slushy. Pour into a collins glass.

PLAIN JANE

1 1/2 oz (45 ml) vanilla vodka
3 oz (90 ml) cranberry juice
3 oz (90 ml) freshly squeezed orange juice

Fill an old-fashioned glass with crushed ice. Pour in the vodka, cranberry juice, and orange juice. Stir well.

BABY FRUIT CHILL

1 oz (30 ml) gin
1/2 oz (15 ml) coconut rum
4 oz (120 ml) freshly squeezed orange juice
2 oz (60 ml) cranberry juice

Fill an old-fashioned glass with crushed ice. Pour in the vodka, rum, orange juice, and cranberry juice, Stir well.

FROZEN SPRINGBOK

Place the Amarula cream, crème de menthe, ice cream, and ice in a blender. Blend for a few seconds until smooth. Pour into a hurricane glass. Garnish with the mint leaves.

- 1^1/$_2$ oz (45 ml) Amarula cream
- 1 oz (30 ml) green crème de menthe
- 2 scoops vanilla ice cream
- ^{1}/$_2$ cup (125 ml) crushed ice
- Fresh mint leaves, to garnish

FROZEN MUDSLIDE

1^1/$_2$ oz (45 ml) vodka
1^1/$_2$ oz (45 ml) Bailey's Irish cream
1^1/$_2$ oz (45 ml) Kahlua
1^1/$_2$ oz (45 ml) light (single) cream
1 scoop vanilla ice cream
2 scoops chocolate ice cream

Place the vodka, Irish cream, Kahlua, cream, and both types of ice cream in a blender. Blend for a few seconds until smooth. Pour into a highball glass.

FROZEN MUDSLIDE • 1

2 oz (60 ml) dark rum
2 oz (60 ml) Kahlua
2 oz (60 ml) Bailey's Irish cream
3 scoops vanilla ice cream
1 oz (30 ml) chocolate syrup

Place the rum, Kahlua, Irish cream, ice cream, and chocolate syrup in a blender. Blend for a few seconds until just smooth. Pour into a highball glass.

ALMOND MUDSLIDE

1 oz (30 ml) Kahlua
1 oz (30 ml) amaretto
2 scoops vanilla ice cream
1 oz (30 ml) chocolate syrup
Whipped cream, to top
Grated chocolate, to garnish

Place the Kahlua, amaretto, ice cream, and chocolate syrup in a blender. Blend for a few seconds until smooth. Pour into an old-fashioned glass. Top with the cream and garnish with chocolate.

BROWN COW

Place the rum, crème de menthe, crème de cacao, ice cream, and ice in a blender. Blend for a few seconds until smooth. Pour into a wine goblet. Garnish with the chocolate shavings.

- 1 oz (30 ml) white rum
- 1/2 oz (15 ml) green crème de menthe
- 1/2 oz (15 ml) dark crème de cacao
- 1 scoop chocolate ice cream
- 1/4 cup (60 ml) crushed ice
- Chocolate shavings, to garnish

BROWN COW • 1

3 oz (90 ml) Kahlua
1/2 cup (125 ml) crushed ice
Cold milk, to fill
Splash of chocolate syrup

Place the ice in an old-fashioned or highball glass. Pour in the Kahlua and top up with the milk. Splash in the chocolate syrup.

BROWN EYED SLUSHY

1 oz (30 ml) Bailey's Irish cream
1 oz (30 ml) Kahlua
1 oz (30 ml) amaretto
1 oz (30 ml) butterscotch schnapps
1/2 cup (125 ml) crushed ice

Place the Irish cream, Kahlua, amaretto, butterscotch schnapps, and ice in a blender. Blend for a few seconds until just slushy. Pour into an old-fashioned glass.

COWBOY'S SLUSHY

2 oz (60 ml) Southern Comfort
1 1/2 oz (45 ml) Canadian whisky
1/2 oz (15 ml) freshly squeezed lime juice
1/2 cup (125 ml) crushed ice
Cola, such as Pepsi or Coca-Cola, to fill

Place the ice in an old-fashioned or highball glass. Pour in the Southern Comfort, whisky, and lime juice. Top up with cola and stir well.

BLUE SKY

Place the Canadian mist, rum, blue curaçao, pineapple juice, and ice in a blender. Blend for a few seconds until just slushy. Pour into a highball glass. Garnish with the orange.

- 1$^1/_2$ oz (45 ml) Canadian mist
- $^3/_4$ oz (25 ml) white rum
- $^3/_4$ oz (25 ml) blue curaçao
- 4 oz (120 ml) pineapple juice
- $^3/_4$ cup (200 ml) crushed ice
- Slice of orange, to garnish

BLUE SLUSHY

1 oz (30 ml) white rum
$^1/_2$ oz (15 ml) blue curaçao
$^1/_2$ oz (15 ml) peach schnapps
$^1/_2$ oz (15 ml) freshly squeezed lime juice
$^1/_2$ oz (15 ml) white soda, such as 7-Up or Sprite
$^1/_2$ cup (125 ml) crushed ice

Place the rum, blue curaçao, peach schnapps, lemon juice, white soda, and ice in a blender. Blend for a few seconds until just slushy. Pour into a hurricane glass.

GREEN SLUSHY • 1

$^1/_2$ oz (15 ml) vodka
$^1/_2$ oz (15 ml) gin
$^1/_2$ oz (15 ml) white rum
$^1/_2$ oz (15 ml) white tequila
$^1/_2$ oz (15 ml) Cointreau
$^1/_2$ oz (15 ml) Chartreuse
$^1/_2$ oz (15 ml) blue curaçao
$^1/_2$ cup (125 ml) crushed ice

Place the vodka, gin, rum, tequila, Cointreau, Chartreuse, blue curaçao, and ice in a blender. Blend for a few seconds until just slushy. Pour into a hurricane glass.

BLUE BOHEMIAN

1 oz (30 ml) Becherovka herbal liqueur
1 oz (30 ml) white rum
$^1/_2$ oz (15 ml) blue curaçao
2 oz (60 ml) freshly squeezed orange juice
$^1/_2$ cup (125 ml) crushed ice
Slice of lemon, to garnish

Place the Becherovka, rum, blue curaçao, orange juice, and ice in a blender. Blend for a few seconds until just slushy. Pour into a wine goblet. Garnish with the lemon.

TABOO

Place the pineapple vodka, cranberry juice, grapefruit juice, Cointreau, and ice in a blender. Blend for a few seconds until just slushy. Pour into a wine goblet. Garnish with the pineapple.

- 1^1/$_2$ oz (45 ml) pineapple vodka
- ^{1}/$_2$ oz (15 ml) cranberry juice
- 2 oz (60 ml) freshly squeezed grapefruit juice
- Splash of Cointreau
- ^{1}/$_2$ cup (125 ml) crushed ice
- Wedge of fresh pineapple, to garnish

COSMOPOLITAN TABOO

1 oz (30 ml) vodka
1 oz (30 ml) Cointreau
^{1}/$_2$ oz (15 ml) cranberry juice
^{1}/$_2$ oz (15 ml) freshly squeezed lime juice
^{1}/$_2$ cup (125 ml) crushed ice

Place the vodka, Cointreau, cranberry juice, lime juice, and ice in a blender. Blend for a few seconds until just slushy. Pour into a martini glass.

PAPAYA SLUSHY

1 oz (30 ml) Southern Comfort
^{1}/$_2$ oz (15 ml) vodka
^{1}/$_2$ oz (15 ml) peach schnapps
^{1}/$_2$ oz (15 ml) freshly squeezed lime juice
2–3 tablespoons papaya, chopped
^{1}/$_2$ cup (125 ml) crushed ice
Slice of papaya, to garnish

Place the Southern Comfort, vodka, peach schnapps, lime juice, papaya, and ice in a blender. Blend for a few seconds until just slushy. Pour into a wine goblet. Garnish with the papaya.

VODKA SLUSHY

2 oz (60 ml) vodka
^{1}/$_2$ oz (15 ml) Cointreau
^{1}/$_2$ oz (15 ml) yellow Chartreuse
^{1}/$_2$ cup (125 ml) crushed ice
Twist of orange peel

Place the vodka, Cointreau, yellow Chartreuse, and ice in a blender. Blend for a few seconds until just slushy. Pour into a martini glass. Garnish with the orange.

SGROPPINO

Place the vodka, Midori, and lemon sorbet in a blender. Blend for a few seconds until smooth. Pour into two champagne flutes and top up with prosecco.

- **1 oz (30 ml) vodka**
- **1 oz (30 ml) Midori melon liqueur**
- **2 scoops lemon sorbet**
- **Prosecco (Italian dry sparkling wine), well chilled**

392

BLUE CHILL

1 oz (30 ml) vodka
1 oz (30 ml) blue curaçao
$1/2$ oz (15 ml) dry white wine
$1/2$ oz (15 ml) grenadine
$1/2$ cup (125 ml) crushed ice

Place the vodka, blue curaçao, wine, grenadine, and ice in a blender. Blend for a few seconds until just slushy. Pour into a wine goblet.

VODKA ORANGE CHILL

2 oz (60 ml) vodka
2 oz (60 ml) freshly squeezed orange juice
$1/2$ cup (125 ml) crushed ice
Slice of lime, to garnish

Place the vodka, orange juice, and ice in a blender. Blend for a few seconds until just slushy. Pour into a martini glass. Garnish with the lime.

COOL VODKA ORANGE

1 oz (30 ml) vodka
2 oz (60 ml) dry white wine
2 oz (60 ml) freshly squeezed orange juice
2 oz (60 ml) white soda, such as 7-Up or Sprite
1 cup (250 ml) crushed ice

Place the ice in a collins or highball glass. Pour in the vodka, wine, orange juice, and white soda. Stir well.

ICED RASPBERRY BELLINI

Place the raspberries, ice cream, and Chambord in a blender. Blend for a few seconds until smooth. Divide the mixture among six champagne flutes or martini glasses. Top up with champagne. Drop 1 or 2 whole raspberries into each glass so that they float on top.

- **2 cups fresh, ripe raspberries**
- **6 scoops vanilla ice cream, softened**
- **2 oz (60 ml) Chambord raspberry liqueur**
- **1 (750 ml) bottle dry champagne, well chilled**
- **Whole raspberries, to float or garnish (optional)**

395

FROZEN BANANA MAMA

Place the white rum, banana liqueur, dark rum, cream of coconut, pineapple juice, strawberries, and ice in a blender. Blend for a few seconds until just slushy. Pour into a hurricane glass. Garnish with the whole strawberry.

- 1$^1/_2$ oz (45 ml) white rum
- 1 oz (30 ml) banana liqueur
- $^3/_4$ oz (25 ml) dark rum
- 1 oz (30 ml) cream of coconut
- 2 oz (60 ml) pineapple juice
- 2–3 fresh ripe strawberries
- $^1/_2$ cup (125 ml) crushed ice
- Whole strawberry, to garnish

BANANA BOAT

2 oz (60 ml) Midori melon liqueur
1 oz (30 ml) banana liqueur
1 oz (30 ml) white curaçao
6 oz (180 ml) pineapple juice
1 ripe banana
1 cup (250 ml) crushed ice
Pineapple slice, to garnish

Place the Midori, banana liqueur, curaçao, pineapple juice, banana, and ice in a blender. Blend of a few seconds until just slushy, Pour into a collins or highball glass. Garnish with the pineapple.

PEACH COLADA

2 oz (60 ml) dark rum
1 oz (30 ml) cream of coconut
$^1/_2$ ripe banana
1 canned peach
1 oz (30 ml) canned peach juice
$^1/_2$ cup (125 ml) crushed ice

Place the rum, cream of coconut, banana, peach, peach juice, and ice in a blender. Blend for a few seconds until just slushy. Pour into a hurricane glass.

CARIBBEAN SMOOTHIE

2 oz (60 ml) dark rum
1 oz (30 ml) cream of coconut
1 oz (30 ml) pineapple juice
$^1/_2$ ripe banana
2 pineapple chunks
1 scoop vanilla ice-cream
1 cup (250 ml) crushed ice

Place the rum, cream of coconut, pineapple juice, banana, ice cream, and ice in a blender. Blend for a few seconds until just slushy. Pour into a collins glass.

ROAD RUNNER

Place the vodka, amaretto, coconut milk, cream, ice cream, and ice in a blender. Blend for a few seconds until just slushy. Pour into a chilled wine goblet. Dust with the nutmeg.

- **2 oz (60 ml) vodka**
- **1 oz (30 ml) amaretto**
- **1 oz (30 ml) coconut milk**
- **1 oz (30 ml) heavy (double) cream**
- **1 scoop vanilla ice cream**
- **$1/2$ cup (125 ml) crushed ice**
- **Freshly grated nutmeg, to dust**

BANANA ROAD RUNNER

$1^1/_2$ oz (45 ml) white rum
$1/_2$ oz (15 ml) banana liqueur
2 scoops vanilla ice cream
$1/_2$ cup (125 ml) crushed ice

Place the rum, banana liqueur, ice cream, and ice in a blender. Blend for a few seconds until just slushy. Pour into a hurricane glass.

MIXED ROAD RUNNER

1 oz (30 ml) dark rum
1 oz (30 ml) white rum
$1/_2$ oz (15 ml) blackberry brandy
$1/_2$ oz (15 ml) banana liqueur
Splash of grenadine
Splash of lime cordial
1 cup (250 ml) crushed ice

Place both types of rum, the blackberry brandy, banana liqueur, grenadine, lime cordial, and ice in a blender. Blend for a few seconds until just slushy. Pour into a collins glass.

FRUIT ROAD RUNNER

$1^1/_2$ oz (45 ml) rum
1 oz (30 ml) blackberry brandy
1 oz (30 ml) banana liqueur
$1/_2$ oz (15 ml) freshly squeezed lime juice
$1/_2$ oz (15 ml) grenadine
1 cup (250 ml) crushed ice

Place the rum, blackberry brandy, banana liqueur, lime juice, grenadine, and ice in a blender. Blend for a few seconds until just slushy. Pour into a collins glass.

STRAWBERRY DAWN

Place the gin, cream of coconut, strawberries, and ice in a blender. Blend for a few seconds until just slushy. Pour into a chilled wine goblet. Garnish with the mint and strawberry.

- **2 oz (60 ml) gin**
- **1¹/₂ oz (45 ml) cream of coconut**
- **5 large, very ripe strawberries, hulled**
- **¹/₂ cup (125 ml) crushed ice**
- **Sprig of mint, to garnish**
- **Strawberry, to garnish**

400

STRAWBERRY DREAM

1 oz (30 ml) strawberry schnapps
²/₃ oz (20 ml) dark rum
²/₃ oz (20 ml) light (single) cream
²/₃ oz (20 ml) pineapple juice
3 strawberries
2 scoops vanilla ice-cream

Place the strawberry schnapps, rum, cream, pineapple juice, strawberries, and ice cream in a blender. Blend until smooth. Pour into an old-fashioned glass.

STRAWBERRY DELIGHT

10-12 fresh strawberries
3 oz (90 ml) dark rum
2 oz (60 ml) freshly squeezed orange juice
³/₄ cup (200 ml) crushed ice
Sugar

Moisten the rim of a hurricane glass with orange juice and dip in the sugar to frost. Place the strawberries, half the rum, orange juice, and ice in a blender. Blend until just slushy. Pour into the glass and splash in the remaining rum.

STRAWBERRY KISS

1 oz (30 ml) strawberry schnapps
1 oz (30 ml) white rum
2 oz (60 ml) freshly squeezed orange juice
¹/₂ cup (125 ml) crushed ice

Place the strawberry schnapps, rum, orange juice, and ice in a blender. Blend until just slushy. Pour into a wine goblet.

SPECIAL
OCCASIONS

MULLED WINE WITH ANISE

Place the wine, orange juice, and brown sugar in a large saucepan over low heat. Wrap the cinnamon, star anise, cloves, and lemon peel in cheesecloth (muslim) and tie the top. Dangle the spice bag in the wine mixture and simmer very gently for 30 minutes. Stir from time to time. Serve in heatproof mugs or punch cups.

- **2 (750 ml) bottles dry red wine**
- **Freshly squeezed juice of 1 orange**
- **$1/4$ cup (50 g) firmly packed dark brown sugar**
- **2 sticks cinnamon**
- **4 star anise**
- **1 teaspoon whole cloves**
- **Short strips of lemon peel**

■ ■ ■ *You can keep this delicious brew over low heat for hours. It's perfect for Christmas get-togethers in northern climes and a great revivor in chilly après ski lodges the world over.*

WILD TURKEY THANKSGIVING

Fill a shaker two-thirds full with ice. Add the bourbon, apricot brandy, and orange juice. Shake well and strain into a chilled martini glass.

- 1¹/₂ oz (45 ml) Wild Turkey bourbon
- 1¹/₂ oz (45 ml) apricot brandy
- 1¹/₂ oz (45 ml) freshly squeezed orange juice

WILD TURKEY TEA

2 oz (60 ml) Wild Turkey bourbon
6 oz (180 ml) iced tea

Half fill a collins glass with ice cubes. Pour in the bourbon and tea and stir.

TURKEY TROT

8 oz (250 ml) Wild Turkey bourbon
16 oz (500 ml) cranberry juice
16 oz (500 ml) white soda, such as 7-Up or Sprite
1 cup (250 ml) crushed ice

Place the ice in a pitcher (jug). Pour in the bourbon, cranberry juice, and white soda. Stir well.

MEXICAN TURKEY

1¹/₂ oz (45 ml) Wild Turkey bourbon whiskey
1 can Mexican beer, well chilled

Pour the beer into a mug and splash in the bourbon.

407

4TH OF JULY

Layer the ingredients into a
chilled shot glass, taking care
to keep the colors separate.
Start with the grenadine, then
add the vodka, and finally
the blue curaçao.

- **1 oz (30 ml) grenadine**
- **1 oz (30 ml) vodka**
- **1 oz (30 ml) blue curaçao**

4TH OF JULY • 1

1/2 oz (15 ml) grenadine
1/2 oz (15 ml) light (single) cream
1/2 oz (15 ml) blue curaçao

Layer the ingredients into
a chilled shot glass, taking
care to keep the colors
separate. Start with the
grenadine, then add the
cream, and finally the
blue curaçao.

4TH OF JULY • 2

11/2 oz (45 ml) blue curaçao
11/2 oz (45 ml) sloe gin
Light (single) cream, to fill

Fill an old-fashioned glass
almost full with ice cubes.
Pour in the blue curaçao.
Carefully layer first the sloe
gin and then the cream in
on top. The drink will have
streaks of white shooting
through the blue and
red colors.

4TH OF JULY • 3

1/2 oz (15 ml) cinnamon schnapps
1/2 oz (15 ml) light (single) cream
1/2 oz (15 ml) blue curaçao

Layer the ingredients into
a chilled shot glass, taking
care to keep the colors
separate. Start with the
schnapps, then add the
cream, and finally the
blue curaçao on top.

BIRTHDAY COCKTAIL

Mash ten of the raspberries with the back of a fork. Fill a shaker two-thirds full with ice. Add the crushed raspberries, vodka, Cointreau, Chambord, lime juice, and sugar syrup. Shake well and strain into an old-fashioned glass half-filled with crushed ice. Garnish with the remaining raspberries.

- 12 fresh raspberries
- 2 oz (60 ml) raspberry vodka
- $1/2$ oz (15 ml) Cointreau
- $1/2$ oz (15 ml) Chambord raspberry liqueur
- 1 oz (30 ml) freshly squeezed lime juice
- $3/4$ oz (25 ml) sugar syrup

BIRTHDAY COCKTAIL • 1

1 oz (30 ml) vodka
$1/2$ oz (15 ml) Chambord raspberry liqueur
$1/2$ oz (15 ml) dark crème de cacao
1 oz (30 ml) milk

Fill a shaker two-thirds full with ice. Add the vodka, Chambord, crème de cacao, and milk. Shake well and strain into a martini glass.

BIRTHDAY COCKTAIL • 2

$1^1/2$ oz (45 ml) Kahlua
1 oz (30 ml) white crème de cacao
1 oz (30 ml) vodka
$1^1/2$ oz (45 ml) Chambord raspberry liqueur
$1^1/2$ oz (45 ml) cold milk

Fill a shaker two-thirds full with ice. Add the Kahlua, crème de cacao, vodka, Chambord, and milk. Shake well and strain into an old-fashioned glass over 3–4 ice cubes.

BIRTHDAY SHOT

2 oz (60 ml) vodka
1 oz (30 ml) Chambord raspberry liqueur
$1/2$ oz (15 ml) freshly squeezed lemon juice

Place 2 ice cubes in a shot glass and pour in the vodka, Chambord, and lime juice.

SNOWBALL

Fill a shaker two-thirds full with ice. Add the advocaat and lime juice. Shake well and strain into an old-fashioned glass over 2–3 ice cubes. Top up with lemonade.

- **2 oz (60 ml) advocaat**
- **1/2 oz (15 ml) freshly squeezed lime juice**
- **Lemonade, to fill**

SNOWBALL • 1

1/2 oz (15 ml) amaretto
1/2 oz (15 ml) coconut rum
1 1/2 oz (45 ml) white crème de cacao
2 oz (60 ml) milk

Fill a shaker two-thirds full with ice. Add the amaretto, rum, crème de cacao, and milk. Strain into a chilled old-fashioned glass.

SNOWBALL • 2

1 oz (30 ml) bourbon
1 oz (30 ml) peppermint schnapps

Place 1–2 ice cubes in a shot glass. Add the bourbon and schnapps and stir.

LEMON SNOWBALL

2 oz (60 ml) lemon vodka
Lemonade, to fill
Slice of lemon, to garnish

Half fill an old-fashioned glass with ice cubes. Pour in the vodka. Top up with the lemonade and garnish with the lemon.

BLUE FIZZ

Pour the blue curaçao into a chilled champagne flute. Top up with champagne and garnish with the cherry.

- **1 oz (30 ml) blue curaçao**
- **Dry champagne, well chilled, to fill**
- **Maraschino cherry, to garnish**

■ ■ ■ *Make sure that both the curaçao and champagne are well chilled before pouring this one. You may like to experiment with other very dry sparkling wines. For extra color, garnish the glass with bright red fruit, such as a strawberry, raspberry, or cherry.*

BLUEBERRY BUBBLES

1 oz (30 ml) blueberry schnapps
Dry champagne, well chilled, to fill

Pour the blueberry schnapps into a champagne flute. Top up with champagne.

VODKA BLUES

1 oz (30 ml) vodka
1/2 oz (15 ml) blue curaçao
1 oz (30 ml) dry champagne, well chilled
Maraschino cherry, to garnish

Place 2–3 ice cubes in a martini glass. Pour in the vodka and curaçao and top up with the champagne. Garnish with the cherry.

VODKA BLUES • 1

1 oz (30 ml) vodka
1/2 oz (15 ml) blue curaçao
3 oz (90 ml) chilled dry champagne

Place 1–2 ice cubes in a champagne flute. Pour in the vodka and curaçao and top up with the champagne.

HOT AND SPICY APPLE CIDER

Place the apple cider, cloves, cinnamon, and sugar over low heat and bring almost to a boil. Remove from heat and stir in the whisky. Strain into a heatproof glass mug.

- 1½ oz (45 ml) whisky
- 6 oz (180 ml) apple cider
- 4 whole cloves
- 1 stick cinnamon
- 1 teaspoon sugar

HOT APPLE PIE

½ oz (15 ml) sour apple schnapps
½ oz (15 ml) vanilla schnapps
½ oz (15 ml) cinnamon schnapps
Splash of cranberry juice

Fill a shaker two-thirds full with ice. Add the sour apple schnapps, vanilla schnapps, and cinnamon schnapps. Shake well and strain into a shot glass. Splash in the cranberry juice.

COLD APPLE PIE

1 oz (30 ml) Canadian whisky
½ oz (15 ml) cinnamon schnapps
Apple juice, well chilled, to fill

Half fill an old-fashioned glass with ice cubes. Pour in the whisky and cinnamon schnapps. Top up with apple juice.

ALMOND APPLE PIE

3 oz (90 ml) amaretto
½ oz (15 ml) cinnamon schnapps
Apple juice, well chilled, to fill

Half fill an old-fashioned glass with ice cubes. Pour in the amaretto and cinnamon schnapps. Top up with apple juice.

CHRISTMAS PARTY EGGNOG

Beat the egg yolks and sugar until pale and creamy. Pour in the milk and place over medium-low heat. Heat the mixture gently, stirring often, until it reaches 160°F (80°C) on an instant read thermometer, or lightly coats the back of a metal spoon. Remove from the heat and let cool. Stir in the rum, cognac, and cream. Chill in the refrigerator for at least 8 hours before serving. Serve in a punch bowl lightly dusted with the cinnamon (if liked).

- 12 fresh egg yolks
- 2 cups (400 g) sugar
- 1 1/2 quarts (1.5 liters) milk
- 16 oz (500 ml) dark rum
- 16 oz (500 ml) cognac
- 16 oz (500 ml) heavy (double) cream
- 1 teaspoon ground cinnamon (optional)

SPICY EGGNOG

Beat the eggs yolks, sugar, ginger, cinnamon, nutmeg, and salt until pale and creamy. Bring the milk to a boil in a small saucepan then beat it into the egg mixture. Return to low heat and cook, stirring constantly, until the mixture reaches 160°F (80°C) on an instant read thermometer, or lightly coats the back of a metal spoon. It should be like a very soft custard. Remove from the heat and let cool. Stir in the rum and food coloring, if liked. Refrigerate for at least 2 hours before serving. Just before serving, beat the cream with the confectioners' sugar and vanilla until thick. Spoon over the drinks.

■ ■ ■ *Chill a jug of this creamy, spicy eggnog and serve at Christmas time instead of dessert.*

- **3 egg yolks**
- **1/4 cup (50 g) sugar**
- **1/4 teaspoon ground ginger**
- **1/4 teaspoon ground cinnamon**
- **1/8 teaspoon ground nutmeg**
- **Pinch of salt**
- **16 oz (500 ml) milk**
- **1/2 teaspoon vanilla extract (essence)**
- **4 oz (120 ml) dark rum**
- **Few drops yellow food coloring (optional)**

Topping
- **6 oz (180 ml) heavy (double) cream**
- **1 tablespoon confectioners' (icing) sugar**
- **1/2 teaspoon vanilla extract (essence)**

TRADITIONAL WASSAIL

Preheat the oven to 350°F (180°C/gas 4). Peel and core two apples and cut in thick slices. Place in layers in a baking dish and sprinkle with the brown sugar. Drizzle with 2 oz (60 ml) of brown ale. Bake until the apples are very tender, about 45 minutes. Chop the apples and their cooking juices in a food processor until smooth. Place in a saucepan over medium-low heat and add the remaining ale, sherry, lemon peel, nutmeg, cinnamon, and ginger. Simmer gently for a few minutes. Peel and core the remaining apple and slice. Add the slices to the bowl and serve while still warm.

- 1 quart (1 liter) brown ale
- 8 oz (250 ml) dry sherry
- $1/2$ cup (100 g) dark brown sugar
- 3 apples
- Finely grated peel of $1/2$ lemon
- $1/2$ teaspoon each ground nutmeg, cinnamon, and ginger

■■■ *The Wassail Bowl or "Loving Cup" is an English tradition at Christmas, New Year, and Twelfth Night. The word "wassail" derives from Anglo-Saxon and means "Good health." There are many variations on the recipe but the rite is always the same. The wassail bowl is filled with a more or less alcoholic concoction then a cup is filled. The first drinker shouts Wassail!, takes a sip, and hands it along, with a kiss, to her neighbor. The rest of the group responds "Drinkhail," and so the cup makes its merry round.*

CINNAMON APPLE WASSAIL

Place the lemon juice, pineapple juice, orange juice, brown sugar, cinnamon sticks, nutmeg, and ginger in a large saucepan over medium-low heat and bring to a boil. Remove from the heat and pour in the sherry and apple cider. Return to low heat and stir gently until well warmed. Do not allow the mixture to boil. Add the studded lemon and serve hot.

- 12 oz (350 ml) freshly squeezed lemon juice
- 8 oz (250 ml) pineapple juice
- 4 oz (120 ml) freshly squeezed orange juice
- $1/2$ cup (100 g) firmly packed dark brown sugar
- 3 cinnamon sticks
- $1/2$ teaspoon ground nutmeg
- $1/2$ teaspoon ground ginger
- $11/2$ quarts (1.5 liters) dry sherry
- 2 quarts (2 liters) apple cider
- 1 lemon studded with 6 whole cloves

■ ■ ■ *There is another tradition attached to the wassail bowl which may explain why wassail recipes vary so much. At Christmas, a group of carolers would set out with a large wassail bowl of steaming brew. Moving from house to house, they would sing a carol or two, then knock on the door to offer the cup. Most times the householder would add a drop of two to the bowl to keep it full. A visit by the carolers with the wassail bowl was thought to auger well for the coming year. Apples are especially associated with the wassail tradition and it was not uncommon for people to take the wassail bowl and pour part of its contents onto the roots of apple trees as a blessing.*

EASTER BUNNY

Fill a shaker two-thirds full with ice. Add the crème de cacao and vodka and shake. Place 3–4 ice cubes in a chilled old-fashioned glass and strain the cocktail in over the top. Float the chocolate syrup and cherry brandy on top.

- 1½ oz (45 ml) white crème de cacao
- 1 oz (30 ml) vodka
- 2 teaspoons chocolate syrup
- 1 teaspoon cherry brandy

PAGAN BUNNY

2 oz (60 ml) tequila
1 oz (30 ml) apple brandy
3 dashes Cointreau
½ oz (15 ml) freshly squeezed lemon juice
½ teaspoon maple syrup
Slice of lemon, to garnish

Fill a shaker two-thirds full with ice. Add the tequila, apple brandy, Cointreau, lemon juice, and maple syrup. Shake well and strain into a chilled old-fashioned glass over 3–4 ice cubes. Garnish with the lemon.

CREAMY BUNNY

1 oz (30 ml) peach brandy
1 oz (30 ml) white crème de cacao
1 oz (30 ml) light (single) cream

Fill a shaker two-thirds full with ice. Add the peach brandy, crème de cacao, and cream. Shake well and strain into a martini glass.

DRUNKEN BUNNY

1 oz (30 ml) dark rum
1 oz (30 ml) blue curaçao
1 oz (30 ml) Midori melon liqueur
½ oz (15 ml) whipped cream

Pour the rum, blue curaçao, and Midori into a martini glass over 1–2 ice cubes. Top with the cream.

EASTER EGG

Layer the three ingredients into a shot glass in the order they appear.

- 1 oz (30 ml) Chambord raspberry liqueur
- 1 oz (30 ml) Tia Maria
- 1 oz (30 ml) heavy (double) cream

428

■ ■ ■ *This recipe produces an elegant little drink with the layers fading into each other. Serve it after lunch or dinner.*

EASTER EGG • 1

1 oz (30 ml) cognac
1 oz (30 ml) Cointreau
1 oz (30 ml) white crème de cacao
1 oz (30 ml) whipped cream
1 teaspoon egg yolk

Fill a shaker two-thirds full with ice. Add the cognac, Cointreau, crème de cacao, cream, and egg yolk. Shake well and strain into a wine goblet.

EASTER EGG • 2

1 oz (30 ml) Tia Maria
1 oz (30 ml) vodka
1 oz (30 ml) freshly squeezed lime juice

Fill an old-fashioned glass with ice cubes. Add the lime juice followed by the Tia Maria and vodka. Stir well.

EASTER COFFEE

1½ oz (45 ml) dark rum
½ oz (15 ml) Tia Maria
1 oz (30 ml) whipped cream
4 oz (120 ml) hot coffee

Place the coffee in a heatproof glass mug. Pour in the rum and Tia Maria. Top with the cream.

EASTER BONNET

Place 4–6 ice cubes in a chilled hurricane glass. Pour in the vodka, apricot brandy, and lime juice. Top up with champagne, stirring gently. Garnish with the fruit.

- **2 oz (60 ml) vodka**
- **1½ oz (45 ml) apricot brandy**
- **½ oz (15 ml) freshly squeezed lime juice**
- **Dry champagne, well chilled, to fill**
- **Slices of orange and pineapple, to garnish the glass**

ORANGE CHAMPERS

1 oz (30 ml) Grand Marnier
6 oz (180 ml) dry champagne, well chilled

Pour the Grand Marnier into a wine glass. Top up with the champagne.

COGNAC CHAMPERS

1½ oz (45 ml) cognac
1 oz (30 ml) freshly squeezed lemon juice
1 teaspoon sugar syrup
Dry champagne, well chilled, to fill
Twist of lemon peel, to garnish

Fill a shaker two-thirds full with ice. Add the cognac, lemon juice, and sugar syrup. Shake well and strain into a champagne flute. Top up with champagne. Garnish with the lemon.

GIN CHAMPERS

1½ oz (45 ml) gin
1½ oz (45 ml) freshly squeezed lemon juice
2 teaspoons sugar syrup
Dry champagne, well chilled, to fill
Slice of orange, to garnish

Fill a shaker two-thirds full with ice. Add the gin, lemon juice, and sugar syrup. Shake well and strain into an old-fashioned glass over 2–3 ice cubes. Top up with the champagne. Garnish with the orange.

TWELFTH NIGHT CHAMPAGNE

Moisten the rim of a champagne flute with Grand Marnier. Dip the rim into the sugar to frost. Fill the flute with champagne. Drop in 1–2 small pieces of orange.

- **Grand Marnier**
- **Granulated sugar**
- **Dry champagne, well chilled, to fill**
- **Small wedges of orange, with skin, dipped in Grand Marnier**

WITCHES BREW

2 oz (60 ml) Strega liqueur
2 oz (60 ml) dry champagne, well chilled

Pour the Strega into a chilled wine glass and top up with the champagne. Stir gently.

MIDNIGHT SPECIAL

1 oz (30 ml) vodka
3 oz (90 ml) dry champagne, well chilled
1 oz (30 ml) ginger ale

Half fill an old-fashioned glass with ice. Pour in the vodka and top up with the champagne and ginger ale. Stir gently.

SUMMER DAZE

1 oz (30 ml) peach schnapps
1 oz (30 ml) Midori melon liqueur
Dry champagne, well chilled, to fill

Fill a wine goblet with crushed ice. Pour in the peach schnapps and Midori and top up with the champagne.

CHRISTMAS SPARKLE PUNCH

Place the wine, rum, pineapple juice, lime juice, Cointreau, and grenadine in a punch bowl. Place in the refrigerator until well chilled. Just before serving, add the ice cubes and champagne.

- 1 (750 ml) bottle fruity white wine
- 8 oz (250 ml) white rum
- 4 oz (120 ml) pineapple juice
- 4 oz (120 ml) freshly squeezed lime juice
- 4 oz (120 ml) Cointreau
- 3 oz (90 ml) grenadine
- 2 cups (500 ml) ice cubes
- 2 (750 ml) bottles dry champagne, well chilled

434

CHRISTMAS PUNCH

1 (750 ml) bottle raspberry vodka
1/2 (750 ml) bottle vodka
1 quart (1 liter) cranberry juice
8 oz (250 ml) white soda, such as 7-Up or Sprite
1 cup (250 ml) ice cubes

Chill all the ingredients in the refrigerator overnight. Place the ice cubes in a punch bowl and pour in both types of vodka, the cranberry juice, and soda. Stir gently.

CHRISTMAS ELF

2 oz (60 ml) white Sambuca
1 oz (30 ml) cinnamon schnapps
1 oz (30 ml) apple schnapps
1/2 oz (15 ml) ginger syrup
3 oz (90 ml) apple juice
Pinch of ground cinnamon

Fill a shaker two-thirds full with ice. Add the Sambuca, cinnamon schnapps, apple schnapps, ginger syrup, and apple juice. Shake well and strain into a highball glass half full of crushed ice. Dust with the cinnamon.

CHAMPAGNE COCKTAIL

1 oz (30 ml) brandy
1 lump sugar
3–4 drops Angostura bitters
Dry champagne, well chilled, to fill

Place the sugar cube in a champagne flute. Soak with the Angostura. Pour in the brandy and top up with the champagne.

THANKSGIVING COCKTAIL

Fill a shaker two-thirds full with ice. Add the gin, dry vermouth, and apricot brandy. Shake well and strain into a chilled martini glass. Garnish with the cherry.

- 1¹/₂ oz (45 ml) gin
- 1 oz (30 ml) dry vermouth
- 1 oz (30 ml) apricot brandy
- 1 teaspoon freshly squeezed lemon juice
- Maraschino cherry, to garnish

436

THANKSGIVING CT • 1

1¹/₂ oz (45 ml) bourbon
¹/₂ oz (15 ml) apple brandy
1 teaspoon freshly squeezed lime juice
4 oz (120 ml) cranberry juice
Wedge of lime, to garnish

Half fill a highball glass with ice cubes. Pour in the bourbon, apple brandy, lime juice, and cranberry juice. Stir gently and garnish with the lime.

SPECIAL DAZE

2 oz (60 ml) dark rum
3–4 dashes white curaçao
3–4 dashes Maraschino liqueur
¹/₂ oz (15 ml) grenadine

Fill a shaker two-thirds full with ice. Add the rum, white curaçao, Maraschino, and grenadine. Shake well and strain into a chilled martini glass.

SPECIAL DAZE • 1

1 oz (30 ml) dry vermouth
¹/₂ oz (15 ml) gin
¹/₂ oz (15 ml) apricot brandy
1 teaspoon freshly squeezed lemon juice

Fill a shaker two-thirds full with ice. Add the vermouth, gin, apricot brandy, and lemon juice. Shake well and strain into a chilled martini glass.

437

IRISH SHILLELAGH

Half fill a wine goblet with cracked ice cubes. Add the finely chopped peach. Fill a shaker two-thirds full with ice. Add the whiskey, sloe gin, white rum, and sugar syrup. Shake well and strain into the glass. Garnish with the raspberries.

- 2 oz (60 ml) Irish whiskey
- 1/2 oz (15 ml) sloe gin
- 1/2 oz (15 ml) white rum
- 1 teaspoon sugar syrup
- 2 slices fresh peach, peeled and finely chopped
- Raspberries, to garnish

EMERALD ISLE

1 oz (30 ml) vodka
1/2 oz (15 ml) green crème de menthe
2 dashes orange bitters

Fill a shaker two-thirds full with ice. Add the vodka, crème de menthe, and bitters. Shake well and strain into a chilled martini glass.

IRISH ROSE

1 oz (30 ml) tequila
1 oz (30 ml) Bailey's Irish cream
1 oz (30 ml) dark crème de cacao

Fill a shaker two-thirds full with ice. Add the tequila, Irish cream, and crème de cacao. Shake well and strain into a chilled martini glass.

COLLEEN'S EYES

1 oz (30 ml) Irish whiskey
1/2 oz (15 ml) green crème de menthe
2 oz (60 ml) heavy (double) cream

Fill a shaker two-thirds full with ice. Add the whiskey, crème de menthe, and cream. Shake well and strain into a chilled martini glass.

SEX ON THE BEACH

Fill a shaker two-thirds full with ice. Add the vodka, peach schnapps, Chambord, orange juice, and cranberry juice. Shake well and strain into an old-fashioned glass half filled with ice. Skewer pieces of fresh fruit (peach, strawberry, pineapple, raspberries, grapes) on a toothpick to garnish the drink.

- 1 oz (30 ml) vodka
- 1 oz (30 ml) peach schnapps
- 1/2 oz (15 ml) Chambord raspberry liqueur
- 2 oz (60 ml) freshly squeezed orange juice
- 2 oz (60 ml) cranberry juice
- Fresh fruit, to garnish

HOT TODDY

Place the honey, whisky, and lemon juice in a heatproof glass mug. Fill the mug with boiling water. Stir gently to dissolve the honey. Stud the lemon with the cloves and drop into the drink. Garnish with the cinnamon stick.

- 1¹/₂ oz (45 ml) Scotch whisky
- 1–2 teaspoons honey
- Boiling water
- Wedge of lemon
- 3 cloves
- 1 stick cinnamon

■ ■ ■ *Serve this one on that special occasion we'd all rather avoid—the onset of a cold or influenza.*

CARIBBEAN CHAMPAGNE

Pour the rum and banana liqueur into a chilled champagne flute. Top up with champagne. Garnish with slices of banana.

- $1/2$ oz (15 ml) white rum
- $1/2$ oz (15 ml) banana liqueur
- Dry champagne, well chilled, to fill
- Banana, to garnish

TROPICAL CHAMPAGNE

$11/2$ oz (45 ml) mango, finely chopped

4 oz (120 ml) dry champagne, well chilled

1 oz (30 ml) Maraschino liqueur

Place the mango in a champagne flute. Slowly pour in the champagne, stirring very gently. Float the Maraschino on top.

APRICOT CHAMPERS

1 oz (30 ml) apricot brandy

4 oz (120 ml) dry champagne, well chilled

Pour the brandy into a champagne flute. Top up with the champagne.

CHAMPAGNE PASSION

$11/2$ oz (45 ml) passion fruit flesh, strained

1 teaspoon sugar syrup

4 oz (120 ml) dry champagne, well chilled

$1/2$ oz (15 ml) passion fruit liqueur

Place the passion fruit flesh in a champagne flute with the sugar syrup. Slowly pour in the champagne, stirring very gently. Float the passion fruit liqueur on top.

445

PUNCH

CITRUS SANGRIA

Place the wine, orange juice, lemon juice, lime juice, and sugar in a punch bowl or pitcher (jug) and stir well. Refrigerate overnight. Add the ginger ale and ice cubes just before serving. Pour into wine goblets and garnish with the orange, if liked.

- **1 (750 ml) bottle dry red wine**
- **Freshly squeezed juice of 2 oranges**
- **Freshly squeezed juice of 2 lemons**
- **Freshly squeezed juice of 2 limes**
- **2 tablespoons dark brown sugar**
- **16 oz (500 ml) ginger ale**
- **Wedges of orange, to garnish (optional)**

RUM 'N' VODKA PUNCH

5 oz (150 ml) vodka
8 oz (250 ml) dark rum
4 oz (120 ml) freshly squeezed lemon juice
1 quart (1 liter) ginger ale
1 peach, peeled and chopped
Slices of lime, lemon, or orange

Place the vodka, rum, and lemon juice in a large pitcher (jug). Stir well and refrigerate. Add the ginger ale, ice cubes, the peach, and slices of lime, lemon, or orange just before serving.

SANGRIA • 1

1 (750 ml) bottle dry red wine
1/2 cup (100 g) sugar
8 oz (250 ml) freshly squeezed orange juice
8 oz (250 ml) freshly squeezed lemon juice
1 teaspoon cloves
5 cinnamon sticks

Place the wine, sugar, orange juice, lemon juice, cloves, and cinnamon in a large pitcher (jug) and refrigerate until well chilled. Add ice cubes just before serving.

SANGRIA • 2

1 quart (1 liter) dry red wine
1 (750 ml) bottle sweet sherry
8 oz (250 ml) watermelon schnapps
8 oz (250 ml) blackcurrant schnapps
8 oz (250 ml) grapefruit schnapps
8 oz (250 ml) brandy
1 quart (1 liter) orange juice
16 oz (500 ml) lemon soda

Place all the ingredients in a punch bowl. Stir well and refrigerate until well chilled.

MRS BEETON'S NEGUS

As this beverage is more usually drunk at children's parties than at any other, the wine need not be very old or expensive for the purpose, a new fruity wine answering very well for it. Put the wine into a jug, rub some lumps of sugar (4 oz/125 g) on the lemon rind until all the yellow part of the skin is absorbed, then squeeze the juice, and strain it. Add the sugar and lemon-juice to the port wine, with the grated nutmeg; pour over it the boiling water, cover the jug, and, when the beverage has cooled a little, it will be fit for use. Negus may also be made of sherry, or any other sweet white wine, but is more usually made of port than of any other beverage.

- **16 oz (500 ml) port wine**
- **1 quart (1 liter) boiling water**
- **4 oz (125 g) sugar**
- **1 lemon**
- **Grated nutmeg**

■ ■ ■ *This recipe comes straight from Mrs Beeton's Book of Household Management, published in 1861. Children's parties have certainly changed in the last 150 years or so!*

TEA PUNCH WITH CUCUMBER

Peel the cucumber, cut it in half and scoop out the seeds. Chop in small cubes and place in a punch bowl. Add the port wine, brandy, tea, and lemon. Chill in the refrigerator for at least 2 hours. Add ice cubes just before straining into punch cups garnished with the mint.

- 1 cucumber
- 1 (750 ml) bottle port wine
- 3 oz (90 ml) brandy
- 1 quart (1 liter) strong black tea, chilled
- 1/2 lemon, cut in wedges
- Mint leaves, to garnish

VODKA COLA PUNCH

14 oz (400 ml) vodka, chilled
1 quart (1 liter) cola, such as Pepsi or Coca-Cola
16 oz (500 ml) black tea, chilled
Slices of lemon

Place the vodka, cola, and tea in a punch bowl. Refrigerate until well chilled. Add the lemon and ice cubes just before serving.

PORT CUPS

2 oz (60 ml) cognac
3 oz (90 ml) ruby port
2 egg yolks
3 oz (90 ml) heavy (double) cream
Freshly grated nutmeg, to dust

Beat the egg yolks and cream. Gradually mix in port and cognac. Heat in a saucepan over low heat; do not boil. Serve in 2 warmed wine goblets or mugs. Dust with nutmeg.

CLARET PUNCH

16 oz (500 ml) freshly squeezed lemon juice
1 cup (200 g) sugar
3 (750 ml) bottles claret
12 oz (300 ml) brandy
4 oz (120 ml) apricot brandy
4 oz (120 ml) bourbon
8 oz (250 ml) Cointreau
16 oz (500 ml) cold black tea
1 quart (1 liter) soda water
3 sliced oranges

Place all the ingredients (except soda water and orange) in a punch bowl. Refrigerate until well chilled. Add the soda water, oranges, and ice cubes just before serving.

453

APPLE CIDER PUNCH

Place the apple cider, orange juice, pineapple juice, and honey in a punch bowl. Stir gently. Refrigerate until well chilled. Add ginger ale, lime, and ice cubes just before serving. This is a fairly light punch. Add 4 oz (120 ml) of dark rum to liven it up.

- 1$^1/_2$ quarts (1.5 liters) apple cider
- 1$^1/_2$ quarts (1.5 liters) freshly squeezed orange juice
- 8 oz (250 ml) pineapple juice
- 2 tablespoons honey
- 1$^1/_2$ quarts (1.5 liters) ginger ale
- 1 lime, sliced

INSTANT CELEBRATION PUNCH

Place the ice cubes in a punch bowl and add the wine, champagne, ginger ale, and grapes.

- **2 (750 ml) bottles Sauternes wine, chilled**
- **2 (750 ml) bottles very dry champagne, chilled**
- **2 (750 ml) bottles ginger ale, chilled**
- **Bunch of plump seedless white grapes**
- **2 cups ice cubes**

SAUTERNES PUNCH

2 (750 ml) bottles Sauternes wine

2 oz (60 ml) Grand Marnier

2 oz (60 ml) white curaçao

2 oz (60 ml) Maraschino liqueur

$1/2$ cup (100 g) sugar

Sliced fresh fruit (optional)

Place the wine, Grand Marnier, curaçao, Maraschino, and sugar in a punch bowl or pitcher (jug). Add the sugar and stir until it has dissolved. Refrigerate until well chilled. Add fresh fruit and ice cubes just before serving.

PUNCH WITH A PUNCH

4 (750 ml) bottles dry white wine

2 (750 ml) bottles prosecco wine

1 (750 ml) bottle vodka

1 (750 ml) bottle gin

1 quart (1 liter) pineapple juice

2 quarts (2 liters) orange juice

Fresh fruit (optional)

Place all the ingredients in a large punch bowl and refrigerate until well chilled. Add fresh fruit and ice cubes just before serving.

MELON PUNCH

4 (750 ml) bottles chilled Sauternes wine

2 (750 ml) bottles chilled prosecco or champagne

1 (750 ml) bottle gold tequila

8 oz (250 ml freshly squeezed lemon juice

$1/2$ cup (100 g) sugar

1 large honeydew melon, made into balls

Place all the ingredients in a large punch bowl and refrigerate until well chilled. Add ice cubes just before serving.

KENTUCKY FRUIT PUNCH

Pour the bourbon, lemon juice, sugar, and tea into a punch bowl. Stir gently to dissolve the sugar. Refrigerate until well chilled. Pour in the club soda and add the fruit and ice cubes just before serving.

- 2 (750 ml) bottles bourbon
- Freshly squeezed juice of 12 lemons
- 1 cup (200 g) sugar
- 16 oz (500 ml) very strong black tea
- 2 (1 quart/1 liter) bottles soda water, chilled
- 2 sliced oranges
- 1 pineapple, peeled and cut in bite-sized chunks
- 2–4 cups ice cubes

BOURBON PUNCH

1 quart (1 liter) bourbon

1 (750 ml) bottle apple schnapps

12 oz (350 ml) bottle cinnamon schnapps

2 quarts (2 liters) lemon soda

Place all the ingredients in a large punch bowl. Refrigerate until well chilled. Add ice cubes just before serving.

KENTUCKY TEA

16 oz (500 ml) bourbon

16 oz (500 ml) Cointreau

16 oz (500 ml) sweet-and-sour mix

1 quart (1 liter) cola, such as Pepsi or Coca-Cola

Place the bourbon, Cointreau, and sweet-and-sour mix in a punch bowl. Refrigerate until well chilled. Add the cola and ice cubes just before serving.

CIDER PUNCH

1½ quarts (1.5 liters) apple cider

4 oz (120 ml) Scotch whisky

4 oz (120 ml) dry sherry

2 oz (60 ml) freshly squeezed lemon juice

8 oz (250 ml) soda water

3 cored, thinly sliced apples

Place the cider, whisky, sherry, and lemon juice in a punch bowl. Refrigerate until well chilled. Add the soda water, apples, and ice cubes just before serving.

FLAMING CHRISTMAS PUNCH

Heat the wine, tea, orange juice, lemon juice, and cinnamon in a large saucepan. Bring almost to the boil then remove from the heat. Pour into a heatproof punch bowl. Place the sugar in a large ladle and drench with rum. Pour the rest of the rum into the punch bowl. Ignite the rum in the ladle and pour it blazing into the punch. Add the slices of lemon and stir well, extinguishing the flames.

- 2 (750 ml) bottles dry red wine
- 16 oz (500 ml) strong black tea
- 4 oz (120 ml) freshly squeezed orange juice
- 4 oz (120 ml) freshly squeezed lemon juice
- 2 cinnamon sticks
- 1 cup (200 g) sugar
- 1 (750 ml) bottle dark rum
- 1 lemon, sliced (with skin)

■ ■ ■ *You can entertain family and friends with your flame-throwing abilities when preparing this one. Do make sure that your punch bowl is heatproof before you start! Be sure to extinguish the flames quickly too, as they will burn away the alcohol. Use a lid to cover the punch bowl to extinguish the flames. If your punch bowl doesn't have a lid, make one out of heavy aluminum foil.*

MEXICAN SUNRISE PUNCH

Place the tequila, Maraschino, brandy, and pineapple in a punch bowl. Refrigerate until well chilled. Just before serving, add the lemon soda, champagne, lime, and plenty of ice cubes. Stir gently but well.

462

- 1 quart (1 liter) white tequila
- 4 oz (120 ml) Maraschino liqueur
- 4 oz (120 ml) apricot brandy
- 1 (16-oz/450-g) can pineapple chunks
- 2 quarts (2 liters) lemon soda, well chilled
- 1 (750 ml) bottle dry champagne, well chilled
- 1 sliced lime

SOUTH OF THE BORDER

1 (750 ml) bottle white tequila
1 (750 ml) bottle white rum
2 quarts (2 liters) red wine
3 cans Red Bull energy drink
8 oz (250 ml) lime cordial
1 quart (1 liter) tonic water
4 sliced limes, with skin

Place tequila, rum, wine, Red Bull, and lime cordial in a punch bowl. Refrigerate until well chilled. Add the tonic water, limes, and ice cubes just before serving.

MIXED PUNCH

3 oz (90 ml) gin
3 oz (90 ml) white rum
3 oz (90 ml) vodka
3 oz (90 ml) white tequila
3 oz (90 ml) Cointreau
3 oz (90 ml) Midori melon liqueur
3 oz (90 ml) peach schnapps
3 oz (90 ml) cherry brandy
12 oz (350 ml) tonic water
12 oz (350 ml) freshly squeezed orange juice
14 oz (400 ml) ginger ale

Place all the ingredients in a punch bowl. Refrigerate until well chilled.

THREE RUM PUNCH

8 oz (250 ml) white rum
4 oz (120 ml) dark rum
3 oz (90 ml) coconut rum
16 oz (500 ml) pineapple juice
16 oz (500 ml) orange juice
2 oz (60 ml) freshly squeezed lime juice
1½ oz (45 ml) grenadine

Place all the ingredients in a punch bowl. Refrigerate until well chilled.

LIME SHERBET AND WHISKY PUNCH

Place the whisky, orange juice, pineapple juice, sugar, and lime juice in a punch bowl. Stir gently until the sugar has dissolved. Refrigerate until well chilled. Just before serving, pour in the ginger ale and drop in tiny scoops of sherbert. Add the orange and pineapple slices and serve.

- **1 quart (1 liter) Scotch whisky**
- **16 oz (500 ml) freshly squeezed orange juice**
- **8 oz (250 ml) pineapple juice**
- **1 cup (200 g) brown sugar**
- **4 oz (120 ml) freshly squeezed lime juice**
- **2 quarts (2 liters) ginger ale, chilled**
- **1 pound (500 g) lime sherbert**
- **Slices of orange and pineapple, to garnish**

REGGAE PUNCH

1 (750 ml) bottle white rum
12 oz (350 ml) frozen lime cordial
2 quarts (2 liters) ginger ale
2 quarts (2 liters) lime sherbet

Place all the ingredients in a punch bowl. Stir well.

BOURBON MILK PUNCH

8 oz (250 ml) bourbon
1 tablespoon sugar
12 oz (350 ml) cold milk
1/2 teaspoon ground cinnamon

Place the bourbon and sugar in a pitcher (jug). Stir until the sugar has dissolved. Add the milk and ice cubes. Dust with the cinnamon.

BOURBON EGGNOG

1 quart (1 liter) bourbon
1 quart (1 liter) milk
1 quart (1 liter) heavy (double) cream
24 pasteurized eggs, separated
1 1/2 cups (300 g) sugar
1 tablespoon ground nutmeg

Beat the egg yolks and 1 cup (200 g) of sugar until creamy. Beat the whites, and remaining sugar. Stir the bourbon into the yolks and whites. Beat the cream, milk, and nutmeg into the mixture.

CARIBBEAN PUNCH

Place the red wine, bourbon, rum, peach brandy, Grand Marnier, Benedictine, orange juice, and lemon juice in a large punch bowl. Stir gently to mix then refrigerate until well chilled. Just before serving, add the peach, lime, and ice cubes.

- 2 (750 ml) bottles dry red wine
- 1 (750 ml) bottle bourbon
- 16 oz (500 ml) dark rum
- 4 oz (120 ml) peach brandy
- 4 oz (120 ml) Grand Marnier
- 3 oz (90 ml) Benedictine
- 24 oz (750 ml) freshly squeezed orange juice
- 16 oz (500 ml) freshly squeezed lemon juice
- 1 large ripe peach, peeled and diced
- 1 sliced lime

BANANA SLUSH

Bring the sugar and water to a boil in a large saucepan. Remove from heat and let cool completely. Place the bananas in a food processor with $1/2$ cup (120 ml) of pineapple juice and chop until smooth. Stir in the cooled sugar mixture, the remaining pineapple juice, orange juice, and lemon juice. Stir well then transfer to a 5-quart (5-liter) freezer container and freeze. Stir once during the freezing process. About 30 minutes before serving, place the mixture in a punch bowl. Just before serving, pour in the ginger ale and rum. Stir well and ladle into glasses. The mixture should have a semi-frozen "slushy" consistency.

- **1 quart (1 liter) water**
- **1 cup (200 g) sugar**
- **5 very ripe bananas**
- **$1^1/_4$ quarts (1.25 liters) pineapple juice**
- **16 oz (500 ml) freshly squeezed orange juice**
- **8 oz (250 ml) freshly squeezed lemon juice**
- **2 quarts (2 liters) ginger ale**
- **1 (750 ml) bottle white rum**

469

WHITE SANGRIA

Place the wine, grapefruit, Cointreau, and lemon juice in a punch bowl. Refrigerate until well chilled. Just before serving, add the champagne and plenty of ice cubes. Garnish with the mint.

- 1 (750 ml) bottle chablis wine
- 1 large grapefruit, cut in small cubes, with peel
- 16 oz (500 ml) Cointreau
- 8 oz (250 ml) freshly squeezed lemon juice
- 2 (750 ml) bottles dry champagne, well chilled
- Fresh mint leaves, to garnish

TROPICAL PUNCH

1 quart (1 liter) cranberry juice
1 quart (1 liter) orange juice
1 bottle (750 ml) champagne, well chilled
Splash of pineapple juice

Place all the ingredients in a large punch bowl with plenty of ice cubes.

GLOGG

2 (750 ml) bottles Cabernet Sauvignon red wine
1 (750 ml) bottle vodka
20 cardamom pods
10 cloves
2 cinnamon sticks
1 orange, sliced
1 1/2 cups (125 g) blanched almonds
1 1/2 cups (125 g) raisins
10 dried figs
3 cups (600 g) sugar

Place all the ingredients in a large saucepan over low heat. Bring almost to a boil then remove from the heat. Serve in heatproof glass mugs.

PINEAPPLE SANGRIA

1 (750 ml) dry white wine
1 cup (200 g) sugar
16 oz (500 ml) apple juice
16 oz (500 ml) pineapple juice
8 oz (250 g) pineapple chunks
1 oz (30 ml) freshly squeezed lemon juice
1 (750 ml) bottle ginger ale

Place the wine, sugar, apple juice, pineapple juice, pineapple chunks, and lemon juice in a punch bowl. Stir until the sugar has dissolved. Refrigerate until well chilled. Add the ginger ale and plenty of ice just before serving.

SOUTHERN COMFORT PUNCH

Pour the Southern Comfort, rum, orange juice, and lemon juice into a punch bowl. Refrigerate until well chilled. Frozen fruit ring: Place the sliced fruit in a freezerproof mold about 10 inches (25 cm) in diameter. Pour the lemonade in over the top. Freeze until solid, about 4 hours. Place the fruit ring in the punch bowl and pour in the ginger ale.

- 1 bottle (750 ml) Southern Comfort
- 8 oz (250 ml) dark rum
- 16 oz (500 ml) freshly squeezed orange juice
- 4 oz (120 ml) freshly squeezed lemon juice
- 1¹/₂ quarts (1.5 liters) ginger ale, chilled

Frozen fruit ring
- 2 sliced lemons
- 1 sliced orange
- 2 sliced limes
- 6 maraschino cherries
- 1 quart (1 liter) lemonade

JUST PUNCH

1 quart (1 liter) dark rum
1 quart (1 liter) vodka
16 oz (500 ml) freshly squeezed orange juice
4 oz (120 ml) freshly squeezed lemon juice
3 quarts (3 liters) soda water, well chilled
Slices of lemon and orange

Pour the rum, vodka, orange juice, and lemon juice into a large punch bowl. Refrigerate until well chilled. Add the soda water, fruit, and ice cubes just before serving.

FULMINATOR

1 (750 ml) bottle gold tequila
1 (750 ml) bottle cachaça
8 oz (250 ml) bourbon
8 oz (250 ml) vodka
2 quarts (2 liters) freshly squeezed orange juice
6 lemons
1¹/₄ cups (250 g) sugar

Pour the tequila, cachaça, bourbon, vodka, orange juice, and sugar into a punch bowl. Stir well to dissolve the sugar. Refrigerate until well chilled. Add ice cubes just before serving.

FAMILY PUNCH

16 oz (500 ml) vodka
16 oz (500 ml) white rum
6 oz (180 ml) frozen orange juice
6 oz (180 ml) frozen lemonade
2 quarts (2 liters) cold water
2 cups (400 g) sugar
2 quarts (2 liters) ginger ale
1 (750 ml) bottle champagne, well chilled

Pour the vodka, rum, orange juice, lemonade, water, and sugar into a punch bowl. Stir to dissolve the sugar. Refrigerate until well chilled. Add the ginger ale and ice cubes just before serving.

CHAMPAGNE PUNCH

Pour the rum, brandy, pineapple juice, lemon juice, and cherry juice into a punch bowl. Stir gently and refrigerate until well chilled. Add the champagne and ice cubes just before serving.

- 12 oz (350 ml) dark rum
- 12 oz (350 ml) brandy
- 16 oz (500 ml) pineapple juice
- 8 oz (250 ml) freshly squeezed lemon juice
- 8 oz (250 ml) cherry juice
- 2 (750 ml) bottles dry champagne, well chilled

474

CHAMPAGNE PUNCH • 1

4 oz (120 ml) brandy
4 oz (120 ml) Cointreau
1 (750 ml) bottle champagne, well chilled
8 oz (250 ml) soda water, well chilled

Pour the brandy, Cointreau, champagne, and soda water into a large pitcher (jug). Stir gently.

CHAMPAGNE PUNCH • 2

16 oz (500 ml) brandy
2 cups (400 g) sugar
5 (750 ml) bottles dry champagne, well chilled
3 sliced oranges
3 sliced lemons
3 sliced limes
1 pineapple, peeled and cut in chunks

Place the brandy, sugar, 4 bottles of champagne, and the fruit into a large punch bowl. Stir gently to dissolve the sugar. Pour in the remaining bottle of champagne and ice cubes and serve.

CHAMPAGNE PUNCH • 3

1 quart (1 liter) white rum
1 quart (1 liter) dark rum
1 (750 ml) bottle sweet vermouth
1 (750 ml) bottle dry champagne
1 quart (1 liter) freshly squeezed orange juice
8 oz (250 ml) cranberry juice
2 sliced oranges

Chill all the ingredients separately for at least 2 hours. Place all the ingredients in a punch bowl. Add ice cubes just before serving.

PARADISE PUNCH

Peel the pineapple and coarsely chop. Remove the tough, pithy center. Place the pineapple pieces, sugar, and 4 oz (120 ml) of rum in a blender or food processor and chop until smooth. Transfer to a punch bowl and add the remaining rum, crème de cacao, orange juice, lemon juice, and passion fruit juice. Stir gently and refrigerate until well chilled. Add the soda water and ice cubes just before serving.

- 1 juicy ripe pineapple
- 1/4 cup (50 g) firmly packed light brown sugar
- 1 (750 ml) bottle dark rum
- 16 oz (500 ml) white crème de cacao
- 16 oz (500 ml) freshly squeezed orange juice
- 8 oz (250 ml) freshly squeezed lemon juice
- 4 oz (120 ml) passion fruit juice
- 1 quart (1 liter) soda water, well chilled

RASPBERRY CHAMPAGNE PUNCH

Pour the brandy, Cointreau, Chambord, and pineapple juice into a punch bowl. Stir gently and refrigerate until well chilled. Add the ginger ale, ice cubes, and champagne just before serving.

- 8 oz (250 ml) brandy
- 8 oz (250 ml) Cointreau
- 4 oz (120 ml) Chambord raspberry liqueur
- 16 oz (500 ml) pineapple juice
- 1¹/₂ quarts (1.5 liters) ginger ale, chilled
- 2 cups (500 ml) ice cubes
- 2 (750 ml each) bottles very dry champagne, chilled

RASPBERRY PUNCH

1¹/₂ quarts (1.5 liters) vodka
5 oz (150 ml) banana liqueur
5 oz (150 ml) peach schnapps
3 quarts (3 liters) raspberry juice
16 oz (500 ml) lemonade
2 sliced oranges
20 cherries

Place the vodka, banana liqueur, peach schnapps, and raspberry juice in a punch bowl. Refrigerate until well chilled. Add the lemonade, fruit, and ice cubes just before serving.

ITALIAN PUNCH

12 oz (350 ml) white rum
2 (750 ml) bottles prosecco
1 quart (1 liter) lemonade
12 oz (350 ml) white grape juice
8 oz (250 ml) freshly squeezed orange juice
10 strawberries

Chill all the ingredients separately for at least 2 hours. Place all the ingredients in a punch bowl with ice cubes. Serve in wine glasses.

LIME CHAMPAGNE

1 (750 ml) bottle champagne, well chilled
4 tablespoons clear honey
4 oz (120 ml) crème de cassis
1¹/₂ oz (45 ml) freshly squeezed lime juice
1 quart (1 liter) cranberry juice
1 quart (1 liter) soda water
1 sliced lime

Dissolve the honey in the lime and cranberry juice in a punch bowl. Add all the remaining ingredients and ice cubes and stir well.

ORANGE VODKA PUNCH

Pour the vodka, Cointreau, orange juice, pineapple juice, and lemon juice into a punch bowl. Stir gently and refrigerate until well chilled. Add the soda water and ice cubes just before serving. Garnish with the orange and lime.

- 1 (750 ml) bottle vodka
- 1 (750 ml) bottle Cointreau
- 16 oz (500 ml) freshly squeezed orange juice
- 16 oz (500 ml) pineapple juice
- 8 oz (250 ml) freshly squeezed lemon juice
- 2 quarts (2 liters) soda water
- Orange and lime slices, to garnish

PARTY PUNCH

8 oz (250 ml) gin
8 oz (250 ml) dark rum
8 oz (250 ml) gold tequila
8 oz (250 ml) vodka
8 oz (250 ml) bourbon
1 can pineapple chunks, with juice
16 oz (500 ml) cola, such as Pepsi or Coca-Cola

Chill all the ingredients separately for at least 2 hours. Place them all in a punch bowl with ice cubes.

FRUIT PUNCH

8 oz (250 ml) gold rum
8 oz (250 ml) gold tequila
8 oz (250 ml) vodka
8 oz (250 ml) bourbon
1 cup each chunks of fresh peach and pineapple
1 sliced orange
1 sliced lime
16 oz (500 ml) white soda, such as 7-Up or Sprite

Chill all the ingredients separately for at least 2 hours. Place them all in a punch bowl with ice cubes.

LITE FRUIT PUNCH

8 oz (250 ml) vodka
4 oz (120 ml) coconut rum
1 quart (1 liter) pineapple juice
1 quart (1 liter) freshly squeezed orange juice
1 quart (1 liter) white grape juice
2 sliced apples
2 sliced oranges

Chill all the ingredients separately for at least 2 hours. Place them all in a punch bowl with ice cubes.

481

GINGER APPLE PUNCH

Place the green ginger wine, apple brandy, cherry brandy, grapefruit juice, and pineapple juice in a punch bowl. Stir gently and refrigerate until well chilled. Add the ginger ale and plenty of ice just before serving. To garnish, drizzle the cored and sliced apples with lemon juice then drop them into the punch.

- 1 (750 ml) bottle green ginger wine
- 16 oz (500 ml) apple brandy
- 4 oz (120 ml) cherry brandy
- 16 oz (500 ml) freshly squeezed grapefruit juice
- 16 oz (500 ml) pineapple juice
- 1 quart (1 liter) ginger ale
- 1 red apple, cored and sliced
- 1 green apple, cored and sliced
- 1 yellow apple, cored and sliced
- Freshly squeezed lemon juice

HOT CHOCOLATE PUNCH

Place the hot chocolate in a heatproof bowl or pitcher. Pour in the tequila, Kahlua, and Tia Maria and stir gently. Pour into heatproof cups. Top with the cream (run it down a swizzle stick so that it floats on top of the chocolate). Dust with the cocoa powder.

- 16 oz (500 ml) tequila
- 8 oz (250 ml) Kahlua
- 4 oz (120 ml) Tia Maria
- 1 quart (1 liter) hot chocolate (strong brew)
- 8 oz (250 ml) heavy (double) cream
- Unsweetened cocoa powder, to dust

484

COOL CHOCOLATE

8 oz (250 ml) white rum
12 oz (350 ml) cold milk
12 oz (350 ml) coconut milk
3 scoops chocolate ice cream
1 tablespoon vanilla extract (essence)
1 teaspoon ground cinnamon

Place the rum, milk, coconut milk, ice cream, vanilla, and cinnamon in a pitcher (jug). Stir gently and refrigerate for 1 hour. Serve in shot glasses.

BOURBON CHOCOLATE

1 1/2 oz (45 ml) bourbon
1/2 oz (15 ml) dark crème de cacao
8 oz (250 ml) hot chocolate
2 tablespoons whipped cream
Unsweetened cocoa powder, to dust

Pour the bourbon and crème de cacao into the hot chocolate and stir gently. Top with the cream and dust with the cocoa powder.

KAHLUA CHOCOLATE

1 oz (30 ml) Kahlua
8 oz (250 ml) hot chocolate
2 tablespoons whipped cream
Chocolate shavings

Pour the Kahlua into the hot chocolate and stir gently. Top with the cream and chocolate shavings.

COCONUT AND BANANA RUM PUNCH

Place the bananas, coconut milk, cream of coconut, and milk in a blender. Blend for a few seconds until smooth. Transfer to a heavy saucepan and pour in the rum and banana liqueur. Place over low heat and heat until very warm; do not boil. Serve in heatproof glasses or cups garnished with slices of banana and dusted with nutmeg.

- **2 large ripe bananas**
- **16 oz (500 ml) coconut milk**
- **8 oz (250 ml) cream of coconut**
- **8 oz (250 ml) milk**
- **4 oz (120 ml) golden rum**
- **2 oz (60 ml) banana liqueur**
- **Slices of banana, to garnish**
- **Freshly grated nutmeg, to garnish**

SAILORS' PUNCH • 1

1 (750 ml) bottle dark rum
1 (750 ml) bottle brandy
4 oz (120 ml) peach brandy
24 oz (750 ml) lemon juice
1 cup (200 g) sugar
1 quart (1 liter) cold water

Place the rum, brandy, peach brandy, lemon juice, sugar, and water in a punch bowl. Stir to dissolve the sugar. Refrigerate until well chilled. Add ice cubes just before serving.

SAILORS' PUNCH • 2

2 quarts (2 liters) dark rum
8 oz (250 ml) brandy
2 quarts (2 liters) water
2 quarts (2 liters) black tea
3 tablespoons honey
4 oz (120 ml) sugar syrup
5 oz (150 ml) freshly squeezed lime juice
Peel of 3 limes

Heat the water in a pot. Stir in the sugar, tea, and honey, and bring to a boil. Add the rum, brandy, and lime juice and peel and simmer for 5 minutes. Serve hot in heatproof mugs or glasses.

PINEAPPLE CUPS

3 oz (90 ml) white rum
8 oz (250 ml) pineapple juice
4 oz (120 ml) cream of coconut
1 cup (250 ml) crushed ice

Place the rum, pineapple juice, cream of coconut, and ice in a blender. Blend for a few seconds until just slushy. Pour into 2 hurricane glasses.

SHOOTERS

ALABAMA SLAMMER

Fill a shaker two-thirds full with ice. Add the amaretto, Southern Comfort, sloe gin, and orange juice. Shake well and strain into two shot glasses.

- 1 oz (30 ml) amaretto
- 1 oz (30 ml) Southern Comfort
- 3/4 oz (25 ml) sloe gin
- 3/4 oz (25 ml) freshly squeezed orange juice

490

ALABAMA SLAMMER • 1

1 oz (30 ml) Southern Comfort
1 oz (30 ml) amaretto
1/2 oz (15 ml) sloe gin
Splash of freshly squeezed lemon juice

Place 2–3 ice cubes in an old-fashioned glass. Pour in the Southern Comfort, amaretto, and sloe gin. Stir gently then splash in the lemon juice.

ALABAMA FREEDOM

2 oz (60 ml) Southern Comfort
1 oz (30 ml) peppermint schnapps
1 oz (30 ml) vodka
2 oz (60 ml) freshly squeezed orange juice

Place 3–4 ice cubes in an old-fashioned glass. Pour in the Southern Comfort, peppermint schnapps, vodka, and orange juice and stir gently.

WHAM BAM

1 oz (30 ml) bourbon
1 oz (30 ml) amaretto
1 oz (30 ml) sloe gin
1 oz (30 ml) Southern Comfort
1 oz (30 ml) freshly squeezed orange juice

Pour the bourbon, amaretto, sloe gin, Southern Comfort, and orange juice into a shot glass. Stir gently.

SHOOTERS

FIFTH AVENUE

Carefully layer the ingredients into a shot glass in the order they are given. Start with the crème de cacao and finish with the cream.

- 1/2 oz (15 ml) dark crème de cacao
- 1/2 oz (15 ml) cherry brandy
- 1/2 oz (15 ml) heavy (double) cream

492

■ ■ ■ *This striking layered shooter, or pousse-café, is surprisingly easy to make.*

FIFTH AVENUE • 1

1/2 oz (15 ml) crème de cacao
1/2 oz (15 ml) apricot brandy
1/2 oz (15 ml) light (single) cream

Carefully layer the ingredients into a shot glass in the order they are given.

ANTHRAX

1/2 oz (15 ml) spiced rum
1/2 oz (15 ml) white rum
1/2 oz (15 ml) bourbon

Pour the spiced rum, white rum, and bourbon into a shot glass. Stir gently.

ANGEL'S WING

1/2 oz (15 ml) white crème de cacao
1/2 oz (15 ml) brandy
1/2 oz (15 ml) light (single) cream

Carefully layer the ingredients into a shot glass in the order they are given.

FRENCH CONNECTION

Pour the cognac and Grand
Marnier into a shot glass
and stir gently.

- $^1/_2$ oz (15 ml) cognac
- $^1/_2$ oz (15 ml) Grand
  Marnier

494

■ ■ ■ *This shot can also be served in an
old-fashioned glass over 2–3 cubes of ice.*

PURPLE HAZE

Fill a shaker two-thirds full with ice. Add the vodka, lime juice, and sugar syrup. Shake well and strain into a chilled shot glass. Pour in the Chambord.

- 1 oz (30 ml) vodka
- 1/2 oz (15 ml) freshly squeezed lime juice
- 1/2 teaspoon sugar syrup
- 1 oz (30 ml) Chambord raspberry liqueur

PURPLE HAZE • 1

1/2 oz (15 ml) vodka
1/2 oz (15 ml) gin
1/2 oz (15 ml) Chambord raspberry liqueur

Pour the vodka, gin, and Chambord into a shot glass. Stir gently.

PURPLE HAZE • 2

2 oz (60 ml) vodka
1 oz (30 ml) blackberry schnapps
1 oz (30 ml) freshly squeezed orange juice

Pour the vodka, blackberry schnapps, and orange juice into a shot glass. Stir gently.

PURPLE HAZE • 3

1/2 oz (15 ml) bourbon
1/2 oz (15 ml) blue curaçao
2 dashes grenadine
1 teaspoon freshly squeezed lime juice

Half fill a mixing glass with ice cubes. Add the bourbon, blue curaçao, grenadine, and lime juice and stir gently. Strain into a shot glass.

APPLE CAR

Fill a shaker two-thirds full with ice. Add the apple brandy, Cointreau, and lemon juice. Shake well and strain into a chilled old-fashioned glass.

- 1¹⁄₂ oz (45 ml) apple brandy
- ¹⁄₃ oz (10 ml) Cointreau
- ³⁄₄ oz (25 ml) freshly squeezed lemon juice

■ ■ ■ *Use Calvados, an apple brandy from Normandy, in this recipe.*

KEY LIME SHOOTER

Fill a shaker two-thirds full with ice. Add the Licor 43, rum, cream, lime juice, and sugar. Shake well and strain into two chilled shot glasses.

- 1 oz (30 ml) Licor 43 liqueur
- 1/2 oz (15 ml) white rum
- 1/2 oz (15 ml) heavy (double) cream
- 1/3 oz (10 ml) freshly squeezed lime juice
- 1 teaspoon sugar

KEY LIME PIE

3/4 oz (25 ml) Licor 43
Splash of vodka
1/3 oz (10 ml) lime cordial
1/2 oz (15 ml) milk

Half fill a mixing glass with ice cubes. Pour in the Licor 43, vodka, lime cordial, and milk and stir well. Strain into a shot glass.

ALLEY CAT

1/2 oz (15 ml) vodka
1/2 oz (15 ml) Bailey's Irish cream
1/2 oz (15 ml) Kahlua
1/2 oz (15 ml) Frangelico
1/2 oz (15 ml) amaretto

Half fill a mixing glass with ice cubes. Pour in the vodka, Irish cream, Kahlua, Frangelico, and amaretto and stir well. Strain into a shot glass.

COMFORT SHOOTER

1/2 oz (15 ml) Southern Comfort
1/2 oz (15 ml) amaretto
1/2 oz (15 ml) sweet-and-sour mix
Splash of grenadine

Half fill a mixing glass with ice cubes. Pour in the Southern Comfort, amaretto, sweet-and-sour mix and grenadine and stir well. Strain into a shot glass.

RUSSIAN ROULETTE

Fill a shaker two-thirds full with
ice. Add the gin and shake.
Strain into a shot glass with ice.
Pour the kahlua in on top.
When the Kahlua sinks to
the bottom, drink up.

- **2 oz (60 ml) gin**
- **1 oz (30 ml) Kahlua**

502

AFTER EIGHT

Carefully layer the ingredients into a shot glass in the order they are given.

- **1/2 oz (15 ml) Kahlua**
- **1/2 oz (15 ml) Bailey's Irish cream**
- **1/2 oz (15 ml) white crème de menthe**

504

AFTER EIGHTEEN

2 oz (60 ml) Kahlua
2 oz (60 ml) white crème de menthe
Splash of chocolate milk

Pour the kahlua and crème de menthe into an old-fashioned glass over 2–3 ice cubes. Splash in the chocolate milk.

AFTER DARK

1/2 oz (15 ml) Kahlua
1/2 oz (15 ml) Bailey's Irish cream
1/2 oz (15 ml) Licor 43

Carefully layer the ingredients into a shot glass in the order they are given.

AFTER THE CRIME

1/2 oz (15 ml) raspberry schnapps
1/2 oz (15 ml) Bailey's Irish cream
1/2 oz (15 ml) grenadine

Pour the raspberry schnapps and grenadine into a shot glass. Pour the Bailey's cream into the center and let it curdle.

CEMENT MIXER

Pour the Irish cream into a shot glass. Add the lime juice and wait five seconds while it curdles.

- 1 oz (30 ml) Bailey's Irish cream
- $1/3$ oz (10 ml) freshly squeezed lime juice

CEMENT MIXER • 1

2 oz (60 ml) Bailey's Irish cream

2 or 3 splashes lemon or lime juice

Pour the Irish cream into a shot glass and add the lemon juice.

TWO UP

2 oz (60 ml) Bailey's Irish cream

1 oz (30 ml) rum

1 oz (30 ml) freshly squeezed lime juice

Pour the Irish cream into a shot glass. Pour the rum and lime juice into a second shot glass. To drink, take a sip of Irish cream and a sip of rum and lime and mix in your mouth.

VODKA SHOOTER

1 oz (30 ml) lemon vodka

1 oz (30 ml) pepper vodka

1 oz (30 ml) blackcurrant vodka

1 oz (30 ml) vodka

1 oz (30 ml) freshly squeezed orange juice

Fill a shaker two-thirds full with ice. Add the four types of vodka and the orange juice. Shake well and strain into a martini glass.

B52

Carefully layer the ingredients into a shot glass in the order they are given.

- 1/2 oz (15 ml) Kahlua
- 1/2 oz (15 ml) Bailey's Irish Cream
- 1/2 oz (15 ml) Grand Marnier

B-52 • 1

1/2 oz (15 ml) Kahlua
1/2 oz (15 ml) amaretto
1/2 oz (15 ml) Bailey's Irish cream

Carefully layer the ingredients into a shot glass in the order they are given.

B-52 • 2

3/4 oz (25 ml) Tia Maria
3/4 oz (25 ml) Bailey's Irish cream
3/4 oz (25 ml) Cointreau Maria

Carefully layer the ingredients into a shot glass in the order they are given.

B-52 • 3

1/2 oz (15 ml) Bailey's Irish cream
1/2 oz (15 ml) Tia Maria
1/3 oz (10 ml) absinthe

Carefully layer the ingredients into a shot glass in the order they are given.

KAMAKAZI

Fill a shaker two-thirds full with ice. Add the vodka, Cointreau, and lime cordial. Shake well and strain into a chilled shot glass

- **1 oz (30 ml) vodka**
- **¹/₂ oz (15 ml) Cointreau**
- **¹/₃ oz (10 ml) lime cordial**

510

KAMAKAZI DELUXE

¹/₂ oz (15 ml) vodka
¹/₂ oz (15 ml) Cointreau
¹/₂ oz (15 ml) amaretto
¹/₂ oz (15 ml) freshly squeezed lime juice

Fill a shaker two-thirds full with ice. Add the vodka, Cointreau, amaretto, and lime juice. Shake well and strain into a shot glass.

KAMAKAZI • 1

³/₄ oz (25 ml) vodka
³/₄ oz (25 ml) Cointreau
¹/₃ oz (10 ml) freshly squeezed orange juice

Fill a shaker two-thirds full with ice. Add the vodka, Cointreau, and orange juice. Shake well and strain into a shot glass.

RASPBERRY KAMAKAZI

1 oz (30 ml) Chambord raspberry liqueur
¹/₂ oz (15 ml) vodka
¹/₂ oz (15 ml) Cointreau
¹/₂ oz (15 ml) freshly squeezed lime juice
¹/₂ teaspoon sugar syrup

Half fill a mixing glass with ice cubes. Pour in the Chambord, vodka, Cointreau, lime juice, and sugar syrup and stir well. Strain into a shot glass.

BRAIN HEMORRHAGE

Layer the Kahlua, schnapps, and Bailey's in a shot glass. Dribble in the grenadine.

- **1 oz (30 ml) Kahlua**
- **1 oz (30 ml) peach schnapps**
- **1 oz (30 ml) Bailey's Irish Cream**
- **1/2 teaspoon grenadine**

BRAIN HEMORRHAGE • 1

1 oz (30 ml) peach schnapps
1 teaspoon Bailey's Irish cream
1/2 teaspoon grenadine

Pour the schnapps into a shot glass. Dribble in the Irish cream. Do not stir. Splash in the grenadine.

BLOODY BRAIN

1 oz (30 ml) peach schnapps
1 oz (30 ml) Bailey's Irish cream
1/2 teaspoon grenadine

Pour the schnapps into a shot glass. Carefully float the Irish cream on top. Drip the grenadine in one drop at a time.

NO-BRAIN COCKTAIL

1 1/2 oz (45 ml) peach schnapps
1/2 oz (15 ml) Bailey's Irish cream
Splash of grenadine
Splash of cherry brandy

Pour the schnapps into a shot glass. Carefully float the Irish cream on top. Splash in the grenadine and then the cherry brandy.

HOT SHOTS

Pour the vodka and peppermint schnapps into a shot glass. Add the Tabasco.

- **3/4 oz (25 ml) vodka**
- **1/2 oz (15 ml) peppermint schnapps**
- **Dash of Tabasco**

PEPPERMINT PATTY

1 oz (30 ml) white crème de cacao
1/2 oz (15 ml) peppermint schnapps

Pour the crème de cacao into a shot glass. Drizzle in the peppermint schnapps.

BEST SHOT

3/4 oz (25 ml) cognac
3/4 oz (25 ml) root beer schnapps
1 teaspoon whipped cream

Pour the cognac and root beer schnapps into a shot glass and top with the cream.

FOREST FIRE

1 oz (30 ml) vodka
10 drops Tabasco
1 slice kiwi

Pour the vodka into a shot glass and add the Tabasco. Garnish with the kiwi.

CHOCOLATE CHERRY SHOOTER

Layer the Kahlua, amaretto, and crème de menthe in a shot glass. Drizzle with the grenadine.

- 1/2 oz (15 ml) Kahlua
- 1/2 oz (15 ml) amaretto
- 1/2 oz (15 ml) white crème de menthe
- 2–3 drops grenadine

516

CHOCOLATE SHOT

1 oz (30 ml) amaretto
1/2 oz (15 ml) vodka
2 oz (60 ml) chocolate milk
1 teaspoon grenadine

Fill a shaker two-thirds full with ice. Add the amaretto, vodka, chocolate milk, and grenadine. Shake well and strain into a chilled martini glass.

CHERRY SHOOTER

1/2 oz (15 ml) Kahlua
1/2 oz (15 ml) amaretto
1/2 oz (15 ml) white crème de cacao
3–4 drops cherry brandy

Carefully layer the Kahlua, amaretto, and crème de menthe into a shot glass. Dribble with the cherry brandy.

CHERRY BOMB

1 oz (30 ml) vodka
11/2 oz (45 ml) white crème de cacao
3/4 oz (25 ml) grenadine

Fill a shaker two-thirds full with ice. Add the vodka, crème de cacao, and grenadine. Shake well and strain into a chilled martini glass.

SICILIAN KISS

Fill a shaker two-thirds full with ice. Add the Southern Comfort and amaretto. Shake well and strain into a chilled shot glass.

- 1 oz (30 ml) Southern Comfort
- 3/4 oz (25 ml) amaretto

RAINBOW SHOOTER

1/3 oz (10 ml) white crème de cacao
1/3 oz (10 ml) sloe gin
1/3 oz (10 ml) brandy
1/3 oz (10 ml) light (single) cream

Carefully layer the ingredients into a shot glass in the order they are given.

SICILIAN KILLER

1 oz (30 ml) Frangelico
1 oz (30 ml) Bailey's Irish cream
1 oz (30 ml) Southern Comfort
1 oz (30 ml) amaretto
1 oz (30 ml) Kahlua
1 oz (30 ml) cold milk

Half fill a mixing glass with ice cubes. Add the Frangelico, Irish cream, Southern Comfort, amaretto, Kahlua, and milk and stir. Strain into an old-fashioned glass over 2–3 ice cubes.

KISS AND TELL

3/4 oz (25 ml) cherry brandy
3/4 oz (25 ml) dry vermouth
3/4 oz (25 ml) gin

Half fill a mixing glass with ice cubes. Add the cherry brandy, vermouth, and gin and stir well. Strain into a martini glass.

WATERMELON SHOOTER

Fill a shaker two-thirds full with ice. Add the hazelnut liqueur, amaretto, Southern Comfort, and pineapple juice. Shake well and strain into a shot glass.

- 1/2 oz (15 ml) hazelnut liqueur
- 1/2 oz (15 ml) amaretto
- 1/2 oz (15 ml) Southern Comfort
- 1/2 oz (15 ml) pineapple juice

520

W. SHOOTER • 1

1 oz (30 ml) bourbon
1 oz (30 ml) pineapple juice
Splash of grenadine

Half fill a mixing glass with ice cubes. Add the bourbon, pineapple juice, and grenadine and stir well. Strain into a shot glass.

W. SHOOTER • 2

1½ oz (45 ml) vodka
1½ oz (45 ml) Midori melon liqueur
Splash of grenadine

Half fill a mixing glass with ice cubes. Add the vodka, Midori, and grenadine and stir well. Strain into a chilled shot glass.

W. SHOOTER • 3

1 oz (30 ml) vodka
1 oz (30 ml) Midori
1 oz (30 ml) sweet-and-sour mix

Place 2 ice cubes in a martini glass. Pour in the vodka, Midori, and sweet-and-sour mix. Stir gently.

VOODOO SHOT

Pour the vodka and peppermint schnapps into a shot glass.

- 1/2 oz (15 ml) vodka
- 1/2 oz (15 ml) peppermint schnapps

CANADIAN COFFEE

2 oz (60 ml) Canadian whisky
1 oz (30 ml) Kahlua

Pour the whisky and Kahlua into a chilled shot glass.

RAMBO SHOT

1/2 oz (15 ml) Jägermeister
1/2 oz (15 ml) peppermint liqueur

Pour the Jägermeister and peppermint schnapps into a chilled shot glass.

TEX-MEX SHOT

1 1/2 oz (45 ml) vodka
Tabasco to taste

Pour the vodka into a shot glass and finish with a generous splash of Tabasco.

URBAN COWBOY

Pour the tequila, bourbon, and Southern Comfort into a shot glass.

- **1/2 oz (15 ml) tequila**
- **1/2 oz (15 ml) bourbon**
- **1/2 oz (15 ml) Southern Comfort**

BABY COWBOY

1/2 oz (15 ml) rum
1/2 oz (15 ml) bourbon

Pour the rum and bourbon into a shot glass.

MIDNIGHT COWBOY

2 oz (60 ml) bourbon
1 oz (30 ml) dark rum
1/2 oz (15 ml) heavy (double) cream

Fill a shaker two-thirds full with ice. Add the bourbon, rum, and cream. Shake well and strain into a chilled martini glass.

OLDTIMER

1/2 oz (15 ml) bourbon
1/2 oz (15 ml) rum
1/2 oz (15 ml) Jägermeister

Fill a shaker two-thirds full with ice. Add the bourbon, rum, and Jagermeister. Shake well and strain into a shot glass.

UNDERTAKER

Carefully layer the ingredients into a shot glass in the order they are given.

- 1/2 oz (15 ml) Jägermeister
- 1/2 oz (15 ml) white rum
- 1/2 oz (15 ml) Cointreau

526

FOUR SQUARE

1/2 oz (15 ml) Goldschlager
1/2 oz (15 ml) Jägermeister
1/2 oz (15 ml) peppermint schnapps
1/2 oz (15 ml) rum

Fill a shaker two-thirds full with ice. Add the Goldschlager, Jägermeister, peppermint schnapps, and rum. Shake well and strain into a shot glass.

LITTLE GREEN MAN

1/2 oz (15 ml) Jägermeister
1/2 oz (15 ml) peppermint schnapps
Green maraschino cherry

Place the cherry in a shot glass. Pour in the Jägermeister and peppermint schnapps.

DESERT LANDSCAPE

1 oz (30 ml) Goldschlager
1 oz (30 ml) Jägermeister
1 oz (30 ml) tequila

Carefully layer the ingredients into a shot glass in the order they are given.

TRAFFIC LIGHT

Carefully layer the ingredients into a shot glass in the order they are given.

- 1/2 oz (15 ml) green crème de menthe
- 1/2 oz (15 ml) banana cream liqueur
- 1/2 oz (15 ml) sloe gin

528

BACK2FRONT

1 oz (30 ml) peach schnapps

1 oz (30 ml) freshly squeezed orange juice

1/2 oz (15 ml) grenadine

1/2 oz (15 ml) blue curaçao

1/2 oz (15 ml) vodka

Place 2 ice cubes in a martini glass. Pour in the peach schnapps and orange juice and stir. Slowly add the grenadine and let sink. Mix the vodka and curaçao in a mixing glass. Pour over the surface of the drink.

BLINDED BY THE LIGHT

1 oz (30 ml) absinthe

2 oz (60 ml) Pernod

2 oz (60 ml) Sambuca

2 oz (60 ml) vodka

Fill a shaker two-thirds full with ice. Add the absinthe, Pernod, Sambuca, and vodka. Shake well and strain into 3 shot glasses.

ANNIE'S SPECIAL

1 1/2 oz (45 ml) apricot brandy

1 teaspoon gin

1/2 oz (15 ml) light (single) cream

Fill a shaker two-thirds full with ice. Add the apricot brandy, gin, and cream. Shake well and strain into a chilled martini glass.

TEQUILA BLUES

Carefully layer the ingredients into a shot glass in the order they are given.

- **1 oz (30 ml) blue curaçao**
- **1 oz (30 ml) white tequila**

530

BASIC BLUE

¹/₃ oz (10 ml) blue curaçao
¹/₃ oz (10 ml) blueberry schnapps
¹/₃ oz (10 ml) vodka
¹/₃ oz (10 ml) sweet-and-sour mix
¹/₃ oz (10 ml) white soda, such as 7-Up or Sprite

Place an ice cube a shot glass and pour the ingredients in over the top. Stir gently.

8 IRON

¹/₃ oz (10 ml) blue curaçao
¹/₃ oz (10 ml) Ouzo
¹/₃ oz (10 ml) banana liqueur

Place an ice cube a shot glass and pour the ingredients in over the top. Stir gently.

AWAY WITH THE GODS

1 oz (30 ml) vodka
1 oz (30 ml) gin
1 oz (30 ml) white rum
1 oz (30 ml) blue curaçao

Fill a shaker two-thirds full with ice. Add the vodka, gin, rum, and blue curaçao. Shake well and pour into a chilled martini glass.

SPRINGBOK

Pour the green crème de menthe in a shot glass and carefully layer with the Amarula cream.

- **1 oz (30 ml) green crème de menthe**
- **1 oz (30 ml) Amarula cream**

FALLEN ANGEL

1¹/₂ oz (45 ml) white crème de menthe

2 oz (60 ml) heavy (double) cream

1 oz (30 ml) spiced rum

Pour the crème de menthe into a chilled martini glass. Pour in the cream. Stir well and carefully float the rum on the top.

MIDNIGHT MINT

1 oz (30 ml) Bailey's Irish cream

³/₄ oz (25 ml) white crème de menthe

³/₄ oz (25 ml) heavy (double) cream

Sugar syrup

Unsweetened cocoa powder

Moisten the rim of a martini glass with sugar syrup and dip into the cocoa. Fill a shaker two-thirds full with ice. Add the Irish cream, crème de menthe, and cream. Shake well and strain into the glass.

AFRICAN CREAM

³/₄ oz (25 ml) white crème de menthe

¹/₃ oz (10 ml) Amarula cream

Dash of light (single) cream

Pour the crème de menthe into a shot glass. Carefully layer with the Amarula, then add a thin layer of cream.

ZAMBODIAN

Fill a shaker two-thirds full with ice. Add the vodka, blackberry brandy, and pineapple juice. Shake well and strain into a chilled martini glass.

- **3/4 oz (25 ml) vodka**
- **3/4 oz (25 ml) blackberry brandy**
- **3/4 oz (25 ml) pineapple juice**

534

WARPATH

1/2 oz (15 ml) vodka
1/2 oz (15 ml) brandy
1/2 oz (15 ml) Kahlua
1/2 oz (15 ml) Bailey's Irish cream

Fill a shaker two-thirds full with ice. Add the vodka, brandy, Kahlua, and Irish cream. Shake well and strain into a shot glass.

HAMLET

3/4 oz (25 ml) vodka
3/4 oz (25 ml) apricot brandy
1/3 oz (10 ml) freshly squeezed lime juice
White soda, such as 7-Up or Sprite, to fill

Fill a shaker two-thirds full with ice. Add the vodka, apricot brandy, and lime juice. Shake well and strain into a chilled martini glass.

APRICOT SHOT

2 oz (60 ml) vodka
1/2 oz (15 ml) apricot brandy
1 oz (30 ml) pineapple juice

Fill a shaker two-thirds full with ice. Add the vodka, apricot brandy, and pineapple juice. Shake well and strain into a chilled martini glass.

RATTLESNAKE

Carefully layer the ingredients into a shot glass in the order they are given.

- 3/4 oz (25 ml) Kahlua
- 3/4 oz (25 ml) amaretto
- 3/4 oz (25 ml) single (light) cream

536

■ ■ ■ *Another delicious layered shot. These drinks are not easy to make; you'll need a steady hand and a little bit of practice. Remember that the densest —usually the sweetest—liqueur should always go on the bottom. It should be followed by the next densest and topped by the lightest. Part of the problem with successful layering is that different brands of liqueurs are often of different densities.*

PEACHES AND CREAM

Carefully layer the peach schnapps and cream into a shot glass. Splash in the rum.

- **3/4 oz (25 ml) peach schnapps**
- **3/4 oz (25 ml) single (light) cream**
- **Dash of 151 rum**

538

TEQUILA CHAMPAGNE SLAMMER

Pour the tequila and champagne into an old fashioned glass. Slam down on the bar and quaff while the drink is still fizzing.

- 1¹/₂ oz (45 ml) tequila
- 1¹/₂ oz (45 ml) very dry champagne, chilled

540

MAYA GOLD

3 oz (90 ml) dry champagne, well chilled
³/₄ oz (25 ml) watermelon schnapps
¹/₂ oz (15 ml) gold tequila

Pour the ingredients into a champagne flute in the order they are given.

HOTEL CALIFORNIA

1 oz (30 ml) gold tequila
2 oz (60 ml) mandarin juice
2 oz (60 ml) pineapple juice
4 oz (120 ml) dry champagne, well chilled

Fill a shaker two-thirds full with ice. Add the tequila, mandarin juice, and pineapple juice. Shake well and strain into two champagne flutes. Top up with the champagne.

BLUE TAHOE

1 oz (30 ml) tequila
1 oz (30 ml) blue curaçao liqueur
1 oz (30 ml) freshly squeezed lime juice
Dry champagne, well chilled to fill

Fill a shaker two-thirds full with ice. Add the tequila, blue curaçao, and lime juice. Shake well and strain into two champagne flutes. Top up with champagne.

APPLE CIDER SLAMMER

Pour the Southern Comfort, peach schnaaps, and apple cider into a shot glass. Slam down on the bar and quaff while the drink is still fizzing.

- 1 oz (30 ml) apple cider
- 1/2 oz (15 ml) Southern Comfort
- 1/2 oz (15 ml) peach schnapps

542

CORE BUSINESS

1 oz (30 ml) spiced rum
3/4 oz (25 ml) apple schnapps
3/4 oz (25 ml) cinnamon schnapps
Dash of white soda, such as 7-Up or Sprite

Fill a shaker two-thirds full with ice. Add the rum, both types of schnapps, and the white soda. Shake well and strain into a shot glass.

CINNAMON SHOT

1 oz (30 ml) Canadian whisky
1/3 oz (10 ml) cinnamon schnapps
Dash of apple juice

Place 2–3 ice cubes in an old-fashioned glass. Add the whisky and cinnamon schnapps together and stir gently. Splash in the apple juice.

SOUR APPLE SHOT

11/2 oz (45 ml) sour apple schnapps
11/2 oz (45 ml) Cointreau
11/2 oz (45 ml) green apple vodka

Fill a shaker two-thirds full with ice. Add the sour apple schnapps, Cointreau, and green apple vodka. Shake well and strain into a chilled martini glass.

GREEN APPLE SHOOTER

Moisten the rim of a shot glass and dip in the salt to frost. Pour in the schnaaps and lime juice.

- 1¹/₂ oz (45 ml) green apple schnapps
- 1 teaspoon freshly squeezed lime juice
- Salt

544

APPLE BLOSSOM

1 oz (30 ml) brandy
1 oz (30 ml) vodka
2 oz (60 ml) apple juice
1 teaspoon freshly squeezed lemon juice

Half fill a mixing glass with ice cubes. Add the brandy, vodka, apple juice, and lemon juice. Strain into an old-fashioned glass over 2–3 ice cubes.

CINNAMON JOY

1 oz (30 ml) apple schnapps
¹/₃ oz (10 ml) Goldschlager

Pour the apple schnapps and Goldschlager into a shot glass and stir gently.

BACKSTOPPER

1 oz (30 ml) apple schnapps
1 oz (30 ml) citrus vodka
Dash of white soda, such as 7-Up or Sprite

Pour the apple schnapps and vodka into a chilled shot glass and top up with soda.

545

HARBOR LIGHTS

Carefully layer the ingredients into a shot glass in the order they are given.

- **1 oz (30 ml) Kahlua**
- **1 oz (30 ml) tequila**
- **1 oz (30 ml) 151 Rum**

LIGHTHOUSE

¹/₂ oz (15 ml) Bailey's Irish cream

¹/₂ oz (15 ml) butterscotch schnapps

1 oz (30 ml) honey Canadian whisky

Pour the Irish cream and butterscotch schnapps into a shot glass. Float the whisky on top. Ignite the whisky and serve with a straw to sip from the bottom of the glass while the top is still burning.

CORNFIELD

¹/₂ oz (15 ml) butterscotch schnapps

¹/₂ oz (15 ml) Bailey's irish cream

¹/₃ oz (10 ml) Midori melon liqueur

Carefully layer the ingredients into a shot glass in the order they are given.

KLONDIKE

1¹/₂ oz (45 ml) Bailey's Irish cream

1¹/₂ oz (45 ml) honey Canadian whisky

Place 2 ice cubes in a martini glass. Pour in the Irish cream and then the whisky. Stir gently.

HALLOWEEN SPIDER

Layer the liqueurs into a shot glass in the order given.

- **1 oz (30 ml) white crème de menthe**
- **1 oz (30 ml) crème de cacao**

548

GREEN SPIDER

1 oz (30 ml) rum
1/2 oz (15 ml) green crème de menthe

Pour the rum and crème de menthe into a shot glass and stir gently.

WHITE SPIDER • 1

1 oz (30 ml) vodka
1 oz (30 ml) white crème de menthe

Pour the vodka and crème de menthe into an old-fashioned glass over 2–3 ice cubes and stir gently.

ORANGE SPIDER

1 oz (30 ml) gin
1/2 oz (15 ml) Cointreau
1 oz (30 ml) sweet-and-sour mix

Fill a shaker two-thirds full with ice. Add the gin, Cointreau, and sweet-and-sour mix. Shake well and strain into a chilled martini glass.

AFTER DINNER

KAHLUA CUP

Place the crème de cacao,
Kahlua, and ice cream in a
blender. Blend until smooth.
Pour into a chilled martini glass
and dust with the cocoa.

- **2 oz (60 ml) crème de cacao**
- **2 oz (60 ml) Kahlua**
- **1 scoop vanilla ice cream**
- **Unsweetened cocoa powder, to dust**

552

TEX-MEX KAHLUA

1/2 oz (15 ml) tequila
1/2 oz (15 ml) Kahlua
5 oz (150 ml) cola, such as Pepsi or Coca-Cola

Half fill a collins glass with
ice cubes. Add the kahlua
and tequila and stir well.
Top up with cola.

KAHLUA COGNAC

1 oz (30 ml) cognac
1 oz (30 ml) Kahlua

Pour the cognac and Kahlua
into a cognac ballon. Swish
gently in the glass.

KAHLUA SNAP

1 oz (30 ml) vodka
1 oz (30 ml) Kahlua
1 oz (30 ml) peppermint schnapps
Cold milk, to fill

Place 2–3 ice cubes in an
old-fashioned glass. Pour
in the vodka, Kahlua, and
peppermint schnapps.
Top up with the milk.

AFTER DINNER HOT CHOCOLATE

In a large saucepan, stir together the cream, milk, orange juice, orange peel, and a pinch of salt and bring to a boil over medium heat. In a small heatproof bowl, whisk together the chocolate and about 4 oz (120 ml) of the hot milk mixture until smooth. Whisk the chocolate mixture into the remaining milk mixture. Place the hot chocolate over low heat and whisk for 2 minutes. Remove from the heat and stir in the Grand Marnier. Divide the hot chocolate between two heatproof Irish coffee glasses. Top with the whipped cream and either dust with the cocoa or sprinkle with the orange zest.

- 4 oz (120 ml) heavy (double) cream
- 8 oz (250 ml) milk
- 3 oz (90 ml) freshly squeezed orange juice
- 2 long strips orange peel
- Salt
- 4 oz (120 g) bittersweet (dark) chocolate, grated
- 3 oz (90 ml) Grand Marnier
- 4–6 tablespoons whipped cream
- Unsweetened cocoa powder, to dust (optional)
- Finely grated orange zest, to garnish (optional)

554

X-RATED HOT CHOCOLATE

Melt the chocolate chips in a double boiler over barely simmering water. Place the milk, cream, and sugar in a saucepan and bring to a boil. Very slowly add about 1 cup (250 ml) of the milk mixture to the melted chocolate and whisk until well mixed. Pour the chocolate mixture back into the remaining milk mixture. Remove from the heat and stir in rum and almond liqueur. Divide the hot chocolate among four heatproof Irish coffee glasses. Top with the whipped cream and add a cinnamon stick to each drink.

- **4 oz (120 g) semisweet (dark) chocolate chips**
- **16 oz (500 ml) milk**
- **4 oz (120 ml) heavy (double) cream**
- **1/4 cup (50 g) sugar**
- **3 oz (90 ml) rum**
- **2 oz (60 ml) almond liqueur**
- **4 oz (120 ml) heavy (double) cream**
- **Cinnamon sticks**

557

NUTTY IRISHMAN

Pour the Irish cream and
Frangelico into a heated Irish
coffee glass. Top up with
the coffee.

- 1 oz (30 ml) Bailey's
  Irish cream
- 1 oz (30 ml) Frangelico
- 4 oz (120 ml) hot
  strong black coffee

558

NUTTY IRISHMAN • 1

1 oz (30 ml) Irish whiskey
1 oz (30 ml) Frangelico

Fill a shaker two-thirds full
with ice. Add the whiskey
and Frangelico. Shake well
and strain into an old-
fashioned glass over
2–3 ice cubes.

NUTTY IRISHMAN • 2

1 oz (30 ml) vodka
1 oz (30 ml) Bailey's Irish
cream
1 oz (30 ml) Frangelico
1/2 oz (15 ml) dark crème de
cacao
Ground nutmeg, to dust

Fill a shaker two-thirds full
with ice. Add the vodka,
Irish cream, Frangelico, and
crème de cacao. Shake well
and strain into a chilled
martini glass. Dust with
the nutmeg.

NUTTY BARMAN

11/2 oz (45 ml) vodka
11/2 oz (45 ml) amaretto
1/2 oz (15 ml) cognac
2 oz (60 ml) dry red wine
2 oz (60 ml) dry white wine
Ginger ale, to fill
Splash of Grand Marnier

Fill a shaker two-thirds full
with ice. Add the vodka,
amaretto, cognac, red wine,
and white wine. Shake well
and strain into a collins
glass half-filled with ice
cubes. Top up with ginger
ale and splash in the
Grand Marnier.

ALEXANDER

Fill a shaker two-thirds full with ice. Add the gin, crème de cacao, and cream. Shake well and strain into a chilled martini glass. Dust with nutmeg, if liked.

- 1 oz (30 ml) gin
- 1 oz (30 ml) white crème de cacao
- 1 oz (30 ml) heavy (double) cream
- Ground nutmeg, to dust (optional)

BLUE GIN ALEXANDER

1 oz (30 ml) gin
1/2 oz (15 ml) blue curaçao
1/2 oz (15 ml) cream

Fill a shaker two-thirds full with ice. Add the gin, blue curaçao, and cream. Shake well and strain into a chilled martini glass.

RUM ALEXANDER

1 1/2 oz (45 ml) white rum
1/2 oz (15 ml) dark crème de cacao
1 oz (30 ml) light (single) cream
Ground nutmeg, to dust

Fill a shaker two-thirds full with ice. Add the rum, crème de cacao, and cream. Shake well and strain into a chilled martini glass. Dust with the nutmeg.

MOCHA ALEXANDER

1 oz (30 ml) brandy
1 oz (30 ml) Kahlua
1 oz (30 ml) light (single) cream
Grated chocolate, to top

Fill a shaker two-thirds full with ice. Add the brandy, Kahlua, and cream. Shake well and strain into a chilled martini glass. Top with grated chocolate.

ALEXANDER'S SISTER

Fill a shaker two-thirds full with ice. Add the gin, crème de menthe, crème de cacao, and cream. Shake well and strain into a chilled martini glass. Dust with nutmeg, if liked.

- 1 oz (30 ml) gin
- 1 oz (30 ml) crème de menthe
- 1/2 oz (15 ml) dark crème de cacao
- 1 oz (30 ml) heavy (double) cream
- Ground nutmeg, to dust (optional)

562

SKY BLUE ALEXANDER

2 oz (60 ml) vodka
1/2 oz (15 ml) blue curaçao
1/2 oz (15 ml) heavy (double) cream

Fill a shaker two-thirds full with ice. Add the vodka, blue curaçao, and cream. Shake well and strain into a chilled martini glass.

PRINCESS ALEX

1 1/2 oz (45 ml) vanilla vodka
1 oz (30 ml) white crème de cacao
1 oz (30 ml) light (single) cream
Ground nutmeg, to dust

Fill a shaker two-thirds full with ice. Add the vodka, crème de cacao, and cream. Shake well and strain into a chilled martini glass. Dust with the nutmeg.

ALEXANDRA

2/3 oz (20 ml) rum
2/3 oz (20 ml) Tia Maria
2/3 oz (20 ml) white crème de cacao
2/3 oz (20 ml) light (single) cream

Fill a shaker two-thirds full with ice. Add the rum, Tia Maria, crème de cacao, and cream. Shake well and strain into a chilled martini glass.

CHOCOLATE VODKA MARTINI

Fill a shaker two-thirds full with ice. Add the chocolate liqueur and vodka. Shake well and strain into a chilled martini glass. Sprinkle with the chocolate.

- **2 oz (60 ml) chocolate liqueur**
- **1 1/2 oz (45 ml) vodka**
- **Coarsely grated bittersweet (dark) chocolate, to garnish**

FRENCH CONNEX

Half fill an old-fashioned glass with ice cubes. Pour in the brandy and amaretto and stir gently.

- 2 oz (60 ml) cognac
- 1 oz (30 ml) amaretto

566

FRENCH CONNEX • 1

1 oz (30 ml) cognac
1 oz (30 ml) Grand Marnier

Place 2 ice cubes in an old-fashioned glass. Pour in the cognac and Grand Marnier. Swish in the glass to mix.

AFTER DINNER A.B.C.

$1/2$ oz (15 ml) amaretto
$1/2$ oz (15 ml) Bailey's Irish cream
$1/2$ oz (15 ml) cognac

Carefully layer ingredients into a shot glass in the order they are given.

IRISH CONNECTION

$1/2$ oz (15 ml) rum
1 oz (30 ml) amaretto
$1/3$ oz (10 ml) Bailey's Irish cream

Fill a shaker two-thirds full with ice. Add the rum and amaretto. Shake well and strain into a chilled martini glass and add Irish cream.

AMARETTO COFFEE

Pour the cognac and amaretto into a small heatproof glass. Add the hot coffee and sugar and stir well. Drop a single dollop of whipped cream in the middle and dust with cocoa.

- **1/2 oz (15 ml) cognac**
- **1/2 oz (15 ml) amaretto**
- **Double espresso**
- **1 teaspoon sugar**
- **Whipped cream**
- **Unsweetened cocoa powder, to dust**

568

VANILLA COFFEE

1/2 oz (15 ml) Xanath vanilla liqueur
4 oz (120 ml) hot black coffee
1 teaspoon sugar
2 tablespoons whipped cream
Ground nutmeg, to dust

Pour the hot coffee and Xanath into a heatproof glass mug. Add the sugar and top with the cream. Dust with nutmeg.

VIENNA COFFEE

1/2 oz (15 ml) peppermint schnapps
1/2 oz (15 ml) Kahlua
5 oz (150 ml) hot black coffee
1 teaspoon sugar
2 tablespoons whipped cream
Grated chocolate, to garnish

Pour the hot coffee, peppermint schnapps, and Kahlua into a heatproof glass mug. Add the sugar and top with the cream. Sprinkle with the chocolate.

CELTIC COFFEE

11/2 oz (45 ml) dark crème de cacao
1/2 oz (15 ml) Irish whiskey
1/2 oz (15 ml) Irish cream
5 oz (150 ml) hot black coffee
2 oz (60 ml) hot milk
2 tablespoons whipped cream
Splash of green crème de menthe

Pour the crème de cacao, whiskey, Irish cream, coffee, and milk into a heatproof glass mug. Top with the cream and splash with the crème de menthe.

GENTLE BULL

Fill a shaker two-thirds full with ice. Add the tequila, coffee liqueur, and cream. Shake well and strain into a small chilled wine goblet. Top with whipped cream and sprinkle lightly with coffee granules.

- **2 oz (60 ml) white tequila**
- **1 oz (30 ml) coffee liqueur**
- **1 oz (30 ml) heavy (double) cream**
- **Whipped cream**
- **Coffee granules, to garnish**

TEXAS BULL

1 oz (30 ml) white tequila
1/2 oz (15 ml) white crème de cacao
1/2 oz (15 ml) Kahlua

Fill a shaker two-thirds full with ice. Add the tequila, crème de menthe, and Kahlua. Shake well and strain into a chilled martini glass.

GENTLE BEAR

1 1/2 oz (45 ml) bourbon
3/4 oz (25 ml) orange curaçao
3/4 oz (25 ml) freshly squeezed lime juice
1/2 oz (15 ml) grenadine

Fill a shaker two-thirds full with ice. Add the bourbon, orange curaçao, lime juice, and grenadine. Shake well and strain into a chilled martini glass.

JAMAICAN CREAM

1 1/2 oz (45 ml) Jamaican dark rum
1/2 oz (15 ml) Kahlua
Dash of heavy (double) cream

Place 4–5 ice cubes in an old-fashioned glass. Pour in the rum and Kahlua and stir gently. Splash in the cream.

WHISKY SOUR

Fill a shaker two-thirds full with ice. Add the bourbon, lemon juice, and sugar syrup. Shake well and strain into a chilled whisky glass either straight up or over ice. Garnish with the lemon or orange.

- 2 oz (60 ml) bourbon
- 1/2 oz (15 ml) freshly squeezed lemon juice
- 1 teaspoon sugar syrup
- Slice of orange

WHISKEY SOUR • 1

1 1/2 oz (45 ml) Scotch whisky
1/2 oz (15 ml) Maraschino cherry juice
2 dashes orange bitters
4 oz (120 ml) sweet-and-sour mix

Place 3–4 ice cubes in an old-fashioned glass. Add the whisky, cherry juice, and bitters. Top up with sweet-and-sour mix.

WHISKY COCKTAIL

2 oz (60 ml) blended whisky
1 teaspoon sugar syrup
Dash of orange bitters
Maraschino cherry, to garnish

Half fill a mixing glass with ice cubes. Add the whisky, sugar syrup, and orange bitters and stir well. Strain into a chilled martini glass and garnish with the cherry.

WHISKY COCKTAIL • 1

2 oz (60 ml) blended whisky
1/2 teaspoon freshly squeezed lemon juice
Dash of orange bitters

Half fill a mixing glass with ice cubes. Add the whisky and lemon juice and stir well. Strain into a chilled martini glass.

SOMBRERO

Fill a shaker two-thirds full with ice. Add the coffee liqueur and cream and shake. Strain into a chilled snifter.

- 1$^{1}/_{2}$ oz (45 ml) Kahlua or other coffee liqueur
- 1 oz (30 ml) heavy (double) cream

EL SOMBRERO

$^{1}/_{2}$ oz (15 ml) brandy
$^{1}/_{2}$ oz (15 ml) bourbon
$^{1}/_{2}$ oz (15 ml) gold tequila

Fill a shaker two-thirds full with ice. Add the brandy, bourbon, and tequila. Shake well and strain into a chilled shot glass.

SIMPLE SOMBRERO

1$^{1}/_{2}$ oz (45 ml) Bailey's Irish cream
1$^{1}/_{2}$ oz (45 ml) amaretto

Place 3–4 ice cubes in an old-fashioned glass. Add the amaretto and Irish cream and stir well.

RUSSIAN SOMBRERO

1$^{1}/_{2}$ oz (45 ml) vodka
1 oz (30 ml) Bailey's Irish cream
2 oz (60 ml) light (single) cream

Half fill a mixing glass with ice cubes. Add the vodka, Irish cream, and cream and stir well. Strain into a chilled martini glass.

CREAMY AMARETTO SOMBRERO

Fill a shaker two-thirds full with ice. Add the amaretto and cream. Shake well and strain into a chilled champagne flute.

- 2 oz (60 ml) amaretto
- 2 oz (60 ml) heavy (double) cream

576

ORANGE SOMBRERO

1 oz (30 ml) amaretto
1¹/₂ oz (45 ml) light (single) cream
¹/₂ oz (15 ml) freshly squeezed orange juice
Maraschino cherry, to garnish

Fill a shaker two-thirds full with ice. Add the amaretto, cream and orange juice. Shake well and strain into a chilled martini glass. Garnish with the cherry.

DARK LADY

1 oz (30 ml) pepper vodka
¹/₂ oz (15 ml) Kahlua
1 oz (30 ml) light (single) cream

Fill a shaker two-thirds full with ice. Add the vodka, Kahlua, and cream. Shake well and strain into a chilled martini glass.

LITE SOMBRERO

1 oz (30 ml) amaretto
2 oz (60 ml) light (single) cream

Fill a shaker two-thirds full with ice. Add the amaretto and cream. Shake well and strain into a chilled champagne flute.

A TASTE OF THE CARIBBEAN

Place the coconut on a small plate. Moisten the rim of a chilled martini glass with water and dip in the coconut. Shake off the excess. Fill a shaker two-thirds full with ice. Add the rum and cream of coconut and shake well. Drizzle the chocolate syrup into a chilled martini glass and strain in the cocktail.

- Shredded coconut, to garnish the glass
- 2 oz (60 ml) white rum
- 1 oz (30 ml) cream of coconut
- 1/2 oz (15 ml) chocolate syrup

GIANDUIA VODKA MARTINI

Fill a shaker two-thirds full with ice. Add the vodka, hazelnut liqueur, and crème de cacao. Shake well and strain into a chilled martini glass.

- 1 oz (30 ml) vodka
- $1/2$ oz (15 ml) hazelnut liqueur
- $1/2$ oz (15 ml) white crème de cacao

580

■ ■ ■ *Substitute the hazelnut liqueur with almond, orange, or mint liqueur for a dramatic change of flavor.*

CHOC-ORANGE MARTINI

2 oz (60 ml) vodka
1 oz (30 ml) Cointreau
1 oz (30 ml) chocolate liqueur

Fill a shaker two-thirds full with ice. Add the vodka, Cointreau, and chocolate liqueur. Shake well and strain into a chilled martini glass.

CHOCOLATE PIRATE

$1^1/2$ oz (45 ml) rum
1 oz (30 ml) Kahlua
1 oz (30 ml) cold milk
2 scoops chocolate ice cream
2 tablespoons whipped cream (optional)

Place the rum, Kahlua, milk, and ice cream in a blender. Blend for a few seconds until smooth. Pour into a hurricane glass. Top with the cream, if liked.

BIG 'N' SWEET

2 oz (60 ml) vanilla vodka
2 oz (60 ml) amaretto
2 oz (60 ml) Bailey's Irish cream
2 oz (60 ml) Kahlua
2 oz (60 ml) chocolate syrup

Fill a shaker two-thirds full with ice. Add the vodka, amaretto, Irish cream, Kahlua, and chocolate syrup. Shake well and strain into a chilled old-fashioned glass.

TALL DARK RUSSIAN

Place the crème de cacao, cinnamon schnapps, vodka, milk, and ice cream in a blender. Blend for a few seconds until smooth. Pour into a chilled highball or collins glass over 3–4 ice cubes. Garnish with the slices of banana. Serve with a long-handled dessert spoon.

- 1 oz (30 ml) dark crème de cacao
- $1/2$ oz (15 ml) cinnamon schnapps
- $1/2$ oz (15 ml) vodka
- 2 oz (60 ml) milk
- 2 scoops chocolate ice cream
- Slices of fresh banana

■ ■ ■ *Serve this drink instead of dessert.*

CELTIC CREAM

2 oz (60 ml) vodka
1 oz (30 ml) Kahlua
1 oz (30 ml) Irish cream
1 oz (30 ml) light (single) cream

Place 6–8 ice cubes in an old-fashioned glass. Add the vodka and Kahlua and stir. Top up with the Irish cream and cream.

QUARTET

2 oz (60 ml) vodka
1 oz (30 ml) Bailey's Irish cream
1 oz (30 ml) crème de cacao
1 oz (30 ml) Frangelico

Fill a shaker two-thirds full with ice. Add the vodka, Irish cream, crème de cacao, and Frangelico. Shake well and strain into an old-fashioned glass over 2–3 ice cubes.

LIZA'S QUARTET

$1^1/2$ oz (45 ml) vodka
1 oz (30 ml) Kahlua
1 oz (30 ml) Bailey's Irish cream
$1/2$ oz (15 ml) Frangelico

Fill a shaker two-thirds full with ice. Add the vodka, Kahlua, Irish cream, and Frangelico. Shake well and strain into a chilled martini glass.

MINT CHOCOLATE CREAM

Place the crème de menthe, milk, and ice cream in a blender. Blend for a few seconds until smooth. Add a little more milk if the drink is not liquid enough. Pour into a chilled collins glass and garnish with the mint.

- 2 oz (60 ml) green crème de menthe
- Dash of milk
- 2 scoops chocolate ice cream
- Mint leaves, to garnish

■ ■ ■ *This is another delicious drink that can be served in place of dessert.*

CHOCOLATE RUM

1 oz (30 ml) dark rum
1/2 oz (15 ml) gold rum
1/2 oz (15 ml) dark crème de cacao
1/3 oz (10 ml) white crème de menthe
1/2 oz (15 ml) light (single) cream
Mint leaves, to garnish

Fill a shaker two-thirds full with ice. Add both types of rum, the crème de cacao, crème de menthe, and cream. Shake well and strain into a chilled martini glass. Garnish with mint.

COCO-MINT CREAM

1 oz (30 ml) vodka
1 oz (30 ml) Bailey's Irish cream
1/2 oz (15 ml) white crème de cacao
1/2 oz (15 ml) peppermint liqueur
1/3 oz (10 ml) green crème de menthe
4 oz (120 ml) light (single) cream
Mint leaves, to garnish

Half fill a hurricane glass with crushed ice. Pour in all the ingredients and stir well. Garnish with mint.

TOP CHOCOLATE

1 oz (30 ml) Bailey's Irish cream
1 oz (30 ml) white crème de menthe
5 oz (150 ml) hot chocolate
2 tablespoons whipped cream
Grated chocolate

Pour the chocolate into a heatproof glass mug. Pour in the Irish cream and crème de menthe and stir. Top with the whipped cream and chocolate.

COOL IRISH COFFEE

Place the whiskey, chocolate liqueur, coffee, Kahlua, and both types of ice cream in a blender. Blend for a few seconds until smooth. Pour into a chilled hurricane glass. Dust with cocoa.

586

- **1 oz (30 ml) Irish whiskey**
- **1 oz (30 ml) chocolate cream liqueur**
- **1 espresso coffee**
- **1/2 oz (15 ml) Kahlua**
- **1 scoop chocolate ice cream**
- **1 scoop coffee ice cream**
- **Unsweetened cocoa powder, to dust**

CHILLED IRISH COFFEE

1 oz (30 ml) Bailey's Irish cream
8 oz (250 ml) cold milk
1 oz (30 ml) water
2 teaspoons instant coffee
1 teaspoon sugar
1 scoop chocolate ice cream

Pour the water into a shaker. Add the coffee and sugar and shake until the coffee has dissolved. Add the milk and shake again. Pour into an Irish coffee cup. Add the Irish cream and ice cream.

CUBAN COFFEE

1 oz (30 ml) rum
1 oz (30 ml) strong sweet black coffee
1 1/2 oz (45 ml) cold water
2 tablespoons whipped cream
Coffee granules

Pour the rum, coffee, and water into a champagne flute and stir. Top with the cream and garnish with the coffee.

COFFEE COMFORT

3/4 oz (25 ml) dark rum
3/4 oz (25 ml) Southern Comfort
1/2 oz (15 ml) dark crème de cacao
4 oz (120 ml) cold black coffee, sweetened, if liked

Fill a shaker two-thirds full with ice. Add the rum, Southern Comfort, crème de cacao, and coffee. Shake well and strain into a hurricane glass half full with crushed ice.

587

APPLEROSE

Fill a shaker two-thirds full with ice. Add the Calvados, vanilla, and rose syrup and shake. Strain into a chilled martini glass. Garnish with the rose petals.

- **1¹/₂ oz (45 ml) Calvados**
- **2–3 drops vanilla extract (essence)**
- **Dash of rose syrup**
- **Rose petals, to garnish**

ARC DE TRIOMPHE

1¹/₂ oz (45 ml) Calvados
¹/₂ oz (15 ml) freshly squeezed lemon juice
1 teaspoon sugar syrup

Half fill a mixing glass with ice cubes. Add the Calvados, lemon juice, and sugar syrup and stir well. Strain into a chilled martini glass.

CALVADOS COCKTAIL

1¹/₂ oz (45 ml) Calvados
¹/₂ teaspoon sugar syrup
¹/₂ oz (15 ml) freshly squeezed lemon juice
2–3 dashes grenadine

Fill a shaker two-thirds full with ice. Add the Calvados, sugar syrup, lemon juice, and grenadine. Shake well and strain into a chilled martini glass.

LIME COCKTAIL

³/₄ oz (25 ml) white rum
³/₄ oz (25 ml) Calvados
1 sugar cube
Wedge of lime

Place the sugar cube in an old-fashioned glass. Drizzle with lime juice and break up with a bar spoon. Add the Calvados and rum and stir well. Add 3–4 ice cubes and stir again.

CHOCOLATE LEMON CREAM

Fill a shaker two-thirds full with ice. Add the lemon vodka, chocolate schnapps, and lemon juice. Shake well and strain into a chilled martini glass.

- 2 oz (60 ml) lemon vodka
- 1 oz (30 ml) chocolate schnapps
- 1/2 oz (15 ml) freshly squeezed lemon juice

590

RED SOLDIER

1 1/2 oz (45 ml) gin
3/4 oz (25 ml) Dubonnet rouge
1 oz (30 ml) freshly squeezed lime juice

Fill a shaker two-thirds full with ice. Add the gin, Dubonnet, and lime juice. Shake well and strain into a chilled martini glass.

CHOCOLATE RED SPOT

1 oz (30 ml) amaretto
1/2 oz (15 ml) vodka
2 oz (60 ml) chocolate milk
1 teaspoon grenadine

Fill a shaker two-thirds full with ice. Add the amaretto, vodka, and milk. Shake well and strain into a chilled martini glass. Splash in the grenadine.

KGB CHOCOLATE

1 oz (30 ml) vodka
2 oz (60 ml) Kahlua
1 oz (30 ml) amaretto
5 oz (150 ml) chocolate milk

Half fill a hurricane glass with crushed ice and stir. Pour in the vodka, Kahlua, amaretto, and chocolate milk. Stir gently.

CARAMEL CREAM

Place the crème de cacao, caramel liqueur, and ice cream in a blender. Blend for a few seconds until smooth. Pour into a chilled hurricane glass and garnish with the nuts.

- 1$\frac{1}{2}$ oz (45 ml) white crème de cacao
- 1 oz (30 ml) caramel liqueur
- 1 scoop vanilla ice cream
- **Chopped nuts, to garnish**

CARAMEL SPLIT

1 oz (30 ml) white crème de cacao

1 oz (30 ml) caramel liqueur

2 scoops vanilla ice-cream

2 tablespoons whipped cream

1 teaspoon chopped nuts

Place the crème de cacao, caramel liqueur, and ice-cream in a blender. Blend for a few seconds until smooth. Pour into a small wine goblet and top with whipped cream and chopped nuts.

CARAMEL APPLE

1 oz (30 ml) Goldschlager schnapps

2 oz (60 ml) apple cider, well chilled

1 oz (30 ml) caramel liqueur

Pour the schnapps into a chilled martini glass. Top with the apple cider and finish with the caramel liqueur.

CARAMEL APPLE • 1

1 oz (30 ml) chilled caramel liqueur

1 oz (30 ml) apple schnapps

1 oz (30 ml) hot milk

5 oz (150 ml) hot strong black coffee

2 tablespoons whipped cream

Place the caramel liqueur in a heatproof glass mug and carefully pour the schnapps over the top. Slowly add the hot milk and carefully pour the coffee over the top. Top with the cream.

RASPBERRY SLUSHY

Set a few raspberries apart to garnish. Place the rest in a small bowl and add the gin. Stir well and marinate for 1 hour. Place the ice in a blender. Add the raspberry mixture, wine, and kirsch and blend for a few seconds until just slushy. Pour into two chilled wine glasses and top with the whole raspberries.

- **1 cup fresh raspberries**
- **2 oz (60 ml) gin**
- **5 oz (150 ml) full-bodied white wine**
- **2 oz (60 ml) kirsch**
- **1 cup (250 ml) crushed ice**

CHERRY SLUSHY

2 oz (60 ml) cherry brandy
1/2 oz (15 ml) freshly squeezed lemon juice
4 oz (120 ml) white soda, such as 7-Up or Sprite

Fill a shaker two-thirds full with ice. Add the cherry brandy and lemon juice. Shake well and strain into a collins glass half full with crushed ice. Top up with white soda.

RASPBERRY CREAM

1 1/2 oz (45 ml) raspberry vodka
1 1/2 oz (45 ml) Bailey's Irish cream
1 1/2 oz (45 ml) dark crème de cacao
2–3 Maraschino cherries

Pour the vodka, Irish cream, and crème de cacao into a warmed old-fashioned glass and stir. Garnish with the cherries.

SOUTHERN TART

1 oz (30 ml) Southern Comfort
1 oz (30 ml) Chambord raspberry liqueur
1 oz (30 ml) amaretto
1 oz (30 ml) sweet-and-sour mix

Half fill a mixing glass with ice cubes. Add the Southern Comfort, Chambord, amaretto, and sweet-and-sour mix and stir well. Pour into an old-fashioned glass over 2–3 ice cubes.

CHILLY RUM SODA

Place the ice cream in a soda cup and drizzle with the rum. Pour the cola carefully over the top. Top with the whipped cream and sprinkle with a little shredded coconut, if liked. Serve with a long-handled dessert spoon.

- 2 scoops vanilla ice cream
- 2 oz (60 ml) dark rum
- 4 oz (120 ml) cola, such as Pepsi or Coca-Cola
- 2–4 tablespoons whipped cream
- Shredded coconut, to garnish (optional)

SPICED RUM SODA

1 oz (30 ml) spiced rum
1/2 oz (15 ml) butterscotch liqueur
1/2 oz (15 ml) vanilla vodka
5 oz (150 ml) white soda, such as 7-Up or Sprite

Half fill a collins glass with ice cubes. Pour in the rum, butterscotch liqueur, and vodka. Top up with the white soda.

RUM FLOATER

1 1/2 oz (45 ml) white rum
1/2 oz (15 ml) blackberry brandy
1/2 oz (15 ml) banana liqueur
1/2 oz (15 ml) grenadine
1 1/2 oz (45 ml) freshly squeezed orange juice
1 1/2 oz (45 ml) pineapple juice
1 oz (30 ml) dark rum

Half fill a hurricane glass with ice cubes. Pour in the white rum, blackberry brandy, banana liqueur, grenadine, orange juice, and pineapple juice and stir well. Float the dark rum on top.

LEMON RUM

1 1/2 oz (45 ml) gold rum
1 oz (30 ml) freshly squeezed lemon juice

Fill a shaker two-thirds full with ice. Add the rum and lemon juice. Shake well and strain into a chilled martini glass over 2 ice cubes.

FRIAR TUCK

Fill a shaker two-thirds full with ice. Add the Frangelico, crème de cacao, and cream. Shake well and strain into a chilled martini glass. Dust with the cinnamon.

- **1 oz (30 ml) Frangelico**
- **1 oz (30 ml) dark crème de cacao**
- **2 oz (60 ml) heavy (double) cream**
- **Ground cinnamon, to dust**

598

FRIAR TUCK • 1

1¹/₂ oz (45 ml) Frangelico
¹/₂ oz (15 ml) brandy
1 oz (30 ml) freshly squeezed lemon juice
1 teaspoon grenadine
Maraschino cherry

Fill a shaker two-thirds full with ice. Add the Frangelico, brandy, lemon juice, and grenadine. Shake well and strain into a chilled martini glass. Garnish with the cherry.

MAID MARION

1¹/₂ oz (45 ml) vodka
¹/₂ oz (15 ml) white crème de cacao
¹/₂ oz (15 ml) heavy (double) cream

Fill a shaker two-thirds full with ice. Add the vodka, crème de cacao, and cream. Shake well and strain into a chilled martini glass.

MAID MARION • 1

1¹/₂ oz (45 ml) rum
¹/₂ oz (15 ml) dark crème de cacao
¹/₂ oz (15 ml) light (single) cream

Fill a shaker two-thirds full with ice. Add the rum, crème de cacao, and cream. Shake well and strain into a chilled martini glass.

MILANO

Drizzle a little extra lemon juice on the banana garnish so that it doesn't discolor. Fill a shaker two-thirds full with ice. Add the gin, Galliano, and lemon juice. Shake well and strain into a chilled martini glass. Garnish with the banana.

- **1 oz (30 ml) gin**
- **1 oz (30 ml) Galliano**
- **1 oz (30 ml) freshly squeezed lemon juice**
- **Slice or two of banana, to garnish**

MARTINI MILANO

2 oz (60 ml) gin
1/2 oz (15 ml) dry vermouth
1/2 oz (15 ml) dry white wine
1 teaspoon Campari

Fill a shaker two-thirds full with ice. Add the gin, vermouth, white wine, and Campari. Shake well and strain into a chilled martini glass.

FALL OF ROME

2 oz (60 ml) dry vermouth
1 oz (30 ml) brandy
Splash of sherry
Splash of freshly squeezed lime juice
Orange juice, to fill

Place 3–4 ice cubes in a highball glass. Pour in the vermouth, brandy, sherry, and lime juice. Top up with orange juice.

MIDNIGHT MARTINI

1 oz (30 ml) gin
1 oz (30 ml) dry vermouth
Black olive

Fill a shaker two-thirds full with ice. Add the gin and vermouth, Shake well and strain into a chilled martini glass. Add the olive.

COOL COFFEE CHANTILLY

Fill a shaker two-thirds full with ice. Add the coffee schnapps, vodka, cream, and Cointreau and shake. Strain into a chilled wine goblet.

- 1¹/₂ oz (45 ml) coffee schnapps
- 1 oz (30 ml) vodka
- 3 oz (90 ml) heavy (double) cream
- ¹/₂ oz (15 ml) Cointreau

602

COOL COFFEE KAHLUA

6 oz (180 ml) cold black coffee
1-2 teaspoons sugar
4 oz (120 ml) cold milk
¹/₂ cup (125 ml) crushed ice
2 oz (60 ml) Kahlua

Place the coffee, sugar, milk, and ice in a blender. Blend for a few seconds until just slushy. Pour into an old-fashioned glass and add the Kahlua. Mix gently.

SPANISH COFFEE

2 oz (60 ml) cognac
2 oz (60 ml) Kahlua
4 oz (120 ml) hot black coffee, sweetened, if liked
Whipped cream, to top

Pour the coffee into a heatproof glass mug. Pour in the cognac and Kahlua. Top with cream.

COFFEE SLUSH

2 oz (60 ml) Bailey's Irish cream
2 oz (60 ml) Kahlua
1 oz (30 ml) Frangelico
6 oz (180 ml) cold black coffee
¹/₂ cup (125 ml) crushed ice

Place the Irish cream, Kahlua, Frangelico, black coffee, and ice in a blender. Blend until just slushy. Pour into an old-fashioned glass.

COFFEE COOLER

Place the ice cream in a soda cup or highball glass. Fill a shaker two-thirds full with ice. Add the Kahlua, vodka, coffee, and cream. Shake well and strain into the cup or glass over the ice cream. Sprinkle with a few coffee beans.

- **1–2 scoops coffee ice cream**
- **1¹/₂ oz (45 ml) Kahlua**
- **1 oz (30 ml) vodka**
- **3 oz (90 ml) strong black coffee**
- **2 oz (60 ml) heavy (double) cream**
- **Coffee beans, to garnish**

BARBADOS COFFEE

1¹/₂ oz (45 ml) dark rum
1 cup (250 ml) cold coffee
1–2 teaspoons sugar

Place 4–6 ice cubes in a highball glass. Pour in the rum. Top up with coffee and add the sugar. Stir well.

CAFFÈ CORRETTO

1 oz (30 ml) Kahlua
¹/₂ oz (15 ml) cognac
¹/₂ oz (15 ml) Strega
¹/₂ oz (15 ml) white rum
1 oz (30 ml) cold coffee

Fill a shaker two-thirds full with ice. Add the Kahlua, cognac, Strega, rum, and coffee. Shake well and strain into a hurricane glass half full with crushed ice.

FROZEN IRISH COFFEE

1¹/₂ oz (45 ml) Irish whiskey
5 oz (150 ml) hot black coffee
2 tablespoons vanilla ice cream
Grated chocolate

Half fill a collins glass with crushed ice. Pour in the whiskey and coffee and stir gently. Top with the ice cream and chocolate.

CHOCOLATE MARTINI

Fill a shaker two-thirds full with ice. Add the crème de menthe, vodka, white crème de menthe, and cream. Shake well and strain into the glass. Top with the shavings of chocolate.

- **1¹/₂ oz (45 ml) dark crème de menthe**
- **1 oz (30 ml) vodka**
- **¹/₂ oz (15 ml) white crème de menthe**
- **2 oz (60 ml) heavy (double) cream**
- **Shavings of bittersweet (dark) chocolate**

CHOCOLATE MARTINI • 1

1 oz (30 ml) vodka
1 oz (30 ml) dark crème de cacao

Fill a shaker two-thirds full with ice. Add the vodka and crème de cacao. Shake well and strain into a chilled martini glass.

CHOCOLATE MARTINI • 2

1 oz (30 ml) light crème de cacao
¹/₂ oz (15 ml) vodka
¹/₂ oz (15 ml) blackberry brandy
Shavings of chocolate

Fill a shaker two-thirds full with ice. Add the crème de cacao, vodka and blackberry brandy. Shake well and strain into a chilled martini glass. Top with the shavings of chocolate.

CHOCOLATE MARTINI • 3

2 oz (60 ml) vodka
1 oz (30 ml) Cointreau
1 oz (30 ml) chocolate liqueur

Fill a shaker two-thirds full with ice. Add the vodka, Cointreau, and chocolate liqueur. Shake well and strain into a chilled martini glass.

HOMEMADE IRISH CREAM

Place the condensed milk, cream, and eggs in a double boiler over low heat and stir until the mixture measures 160°F (80°C) on an instant-read thermometer (or until it coats the back of a metal spoon). Remove from the heat and let cool to room temperature. Add the whiskey, coffee, chocolate syrup, vanilla, and almond extract and stir well.

- 1 can (14 oz/400 g) sweet and condensed milk
- 8 oz (250 ml) heavy (double) cream
- 4 eggs
- 16 oz (500 ml) Irish whiskey
- 2 oz (60 ml) espresso (very strong black) coffee
- 1 oz (30 ml) chocolate syrup
- 1 teaspoon vanilla extract (essence)
- 1/4 teaspoon almond extract

■ ■ ■ *This homemade liqueur is simple to make and will keep for up to a month in the refrigerator. For an authentic Irish cream, be sure to use good quality Irish whiskey rather than Scotch or American whisky. This recipe makes about 1$^{1}/_{4}$ quarts (1.25 liters). Serve after dinner in shot glasses or over ice cubes in old-fashioned glasses.*

ALMOND JOY

Fill a shaker two-thirds full with ice. Add the amaretto, crème de cacao, cream of coconut, and cream. Shake well and strain into a chilled martini glass.

- 1¹/2 oz (45 ml) amaretto
- 1 oz (30 ml) dark crème de cacao
- 1 oz (30 ml) cream of coconut
- 2 oz (60 ml) heavy (double) cream

ALMOND JOY • 1

1/2 oz (15 ml) coconut rum
1 oz (30 ml) amaretto
1 oz (30 ml) white crème de cacao
2 oz (60 ml) light (single) cream

Fill a shaker two-thirds full with ice. Add the coconut rum, amaretto, crème de cacao, and cream. Shake well and strain into a chilled martini glass.

ALMOND JOY • 2

2 oz (60 ml) amaretto
1 oz (30 ml) heavy (double) cream
Freshly grated nutmeg, to dust

Fill a shaker two-thirds full with ice. Add the amaretto and cream. Shake well and strain into a chilled martini glass. Dust with the nutmeg.

ALMOND GROVE

1¹/2 oz (45 ml) amaretto
1 oz (30 ml) cream of coconut
Unsweetened cocoa powder, to dust

Fill a shaker two-thirds full with ice. Add the amaretto and cream of coconut. Shake well and strain into a chilled martini glass. Dust with the nutmeg.

AFTER DINNER COOKIE

Place the raisins in a chilled martini glass and pour in the Jägermeister. Refrigerate for 10 minutes. Fill a shaker two-thirds full with ice. Add the butterscotch schnapps, Irish cream, and cinnamon schnapps. Shake well and strain into the martini glass over the raisins.

- **1 oz (30 ml) butterscotch schnapps**
- **3/4 oz (25 ml) Bailey's Irish cream**
- **1/2 oz (15 ml) cinnamon schnapps**
- **1/3 oz (10 ml) Jägermeister**
- **6–8 raisins**

■ ■ ■ *Serve this one with a cocktail spoon or cocktail skewers so that the delicious soaked raisins can be savored too.*

ALMOND CREAM COFFEE

Pour the cognac and amaretto into a heatproof glass or mug. Add the sugar and top up with coffee. Stir gently. Spoon the cream over the top and dust with the cocoa.

- 1/2 oz (15 ml) cognac
- 1/2 oz (15 ml) amaretto
- 3 oz (90 ml) very strong, hot black coffee
- 1–2 teaspoons sugar
- 2–3 tablespoons whipped cream
- Unsweetened cocoa powder, to dust

KAHLUA SMOOTHIE

2 oz (30 ml) Kahlua
1 oz (30 ml) amaretto
2 scoops coffee ice cream
Coffee beans, to garnish

Place the Kahlua, amaretto, and ice cream in a blender. Blend for a few seconds until smooth. Pour into a chilled hurricane glass. Top with the coffee beans.

RED SPOT SHOT

1 oz (30 ml) white crème de cacao
1 oz (30 ml) amaretto
1 oz (30 ml) Bailey's Irish cream
Dash of grenadine

Pour the crème de cacao and amaretto into a shot glass. Float the Irish cream on top. Splash in the grenadine. Do not stir.

AMARETTO SMOOTHIE

2 oz (60 ml) brandy
2 oz (60 ml) amaretto
2 scoops chocolate ice-cream
Shavings of chocolate

Place the brandy, amaretto, and ice cream in a blender. Blend for a few seconds until smooth. Pour into a chilled old-fashioned glass. Top with the chocolate.

CHOCOLATE MUDSLIDE

Place the Kahlua, Irish cream, vodka, chocolate ice cream, and cream in a blender. Blend for a few seconds until smooth. Pour into a martini glass or wine goblet. Drop the maraschino cherries in on top.

- **2 oz (60 ml) Kahlua**
- **1 oz (30 ml) Irish cream**
- **1 oz (30 ml) vodka**
- **1 scoop chocolate ice cream**
- **2 oz (60 ml) heavy (double) cream**
- **2–3 canned Maraschino cherries, drained**

CHOCOLATE FIRE

1 oz (30 ml) Kahlua
1 oz (30 ml) Bailey's Irish cream
1 oz (30 ml) rum

Pour the Kahlua, Irish cream, and rum into a shot glass. Light the rum and serve will still burning.

CHOCOLATE RUM

1/2 oz (15 ml) crème de cacao
1/2 oz (15 ml) white crème de menthe
1 teaspoon dark rum
1/2 oz (15 ml) light (single) cream

Fill a shaker two-thirds full with ice. Add the crème de cacao, crème de menthe, rum, and cream. Shake well and strain into a chilled martini glass.

CHOCOLATE MILK

1 oz (30 ml) Kahlua
1 oz (30 ml) amaretto
6 oz (180 ml) cold milk
1 oz (30 ml) chocolate syrup

Half fill a mixing glass with ice cubes. Add the Kahlua, amaretto, milk, and chocolate syrup and stir well. Strain into a collins glass over ice cubes.

CALVADOS TODDY

Place the honey in a heatproof cup or glass and pour in the apple brandy. Top up with boiling water.

- **2 oz (60 ml) apple brandy (Calvados or applejack)**
- **1–2 teaspoons honey**
- **Boiling water**

HOT TEA TODDY

4 oz (120 ml) hot black tea
4 oz (120 ml) Bailey's Irish cream
1 oz (30 ml) Scotch whisky

Place the tea in a heatproof glass mug. Add the Irish cream and finish with the whisky.

BRANDY TODDY

2 oz (60 ml) brandy
6 oz (180 ml) boiling water
1 teaspoon sugar
Slice of lemon, to garnish
Freshly grated nutmeg, to dust

Place the boiling water and sugar in a heatproof glass mug. Add the brandy and stir well. Garnish with the lemon slice and dust with the nutmeg.

SCOTCH TEA TODDY

1 oz (30 ml) Scotch whisky
1 tablespoon honey
1 tea bag
Boiling water

Place the whisky, honey, and tea bag in a heatproof glass mug. Pour in enough boiling water to fill the glass. Steep for 1–2 minutes, then remove the tea bag.

LATE NIGHT SPECIAL

Fill a shaker two-thirds full with ice. Add the kirsch, pineapple juice, and Maraschino and shake. Half fill an old-fashioned glass with ice and strain the drink in over the top.

- 1$^1/_2$ oz (45 ml) kirsch
- 1$^1/_2$ oz (45 ml) pineapple juice
- $^1/_2$ oz (15 ml) Maraschino liqueur

MANDALAY GOLD

1 oz (30 ml) white rum
1 oz (30 ml) gold rum
1 oz (30 ml) freshly squeezed orange juice
$^1/_2$ oz (15 ml) freshly squeezed lemon juice
3 oz (90 ml) ginger ale
Twist of lemon peel

Fill a shaker two-thirds full with ice. Add both types of rum, the orange juice, and lemon juice. Shake well and strain into a collins glass over 6–8 ice cubes. Top up with ginger ale and garnish with the lemon.

DUSK

$^1/_2$ oz (15 ml) vodka
$^1/_2$ oz (15 ml) rum
1 oz (30 ml) pineapple juice
Splash of grenadine

Place 1–2 ice cubes in a shot glass. Pour in the vodka, rum, and pineapple juice. Splash with grenadine.

SPANISH MARTINI

1$^1/_2$ oz (45 ml) gin
$^1/_2$ oz (15 ml) cherry brandy
$^1/_2$ oz (15 ml) Madeira
1 teaspoon freshly squeezed orange juice

Fill a shaker two-thirds full with ice. Add the gin, cherry brandy, Madeira, and orange juice. Shake well and strain into a chilled martini glass.

JIM JAMS FIZZ

Place the Calvados, brandy, and apricot brandy in a small, heavy-bottomed saucepan over low heat. Heat until warm; do not boil. Pour into two heatproof glass mugs. Dust with nutmeg.

- **4 oz (120 ml) Calvados**
- **2 oz (60 ml) brandy**
- **4 oz (120 ml) apricot brandy**
- **4 oz (120 ml) heavy (double) cream**
- **Freshly grated nutmeg, to dust**

CREAMY GIN FIZZ

2 oz (60 ml) gin
1 oz (30 ml) freshly squeezed lemon juice
1 teaspoon sugar syrup
1 teaspoon light (single) cream
Soda water, to fill

Fill a shaker two-thirds full with ice. Add the gin, lemon juice, sugar syrup, and cream. Shake well and strain into an old-fashioned glass over 4–5 ice cubes. Top up with soda and stir gently.

LADIES FIZZ

2 oz (60 ml) gin
1 oz (30 ml) freshly squeezed lemon juice
1 teaspoon sugar syrup
2 teaspoons light (single) cream
1 egg white
Soda water, to fill

Fill a shaker two-thirds full with ice. Add the gin, lemon juice, sugar syrup, cream, and egg white. Shake well and strain into a collins glass half filled with ice cubes. Top up with soda water and stir gently.

SILVER FIZZ

1¹/₂ oz (45 ml) gin
¹/₂ oz (15 ml) dark rum
¹/₂ oz (15 ml) freshly squeezed lime juice
¹/₂ teaspoon sugar syrup
1 tablespoon milk
Soda water, to fill

Fill a shaker two-thirds full with ice. Add the gin, rum, lime juice, sugar syrup, and milk. Shake well and strain into a collins glass half filled with ice cubes. Top up with soda and stir gently.

GODFATHER

Place 4–6 ice cubes in an old-fashioned glass. Pour in the whisky and amaretto. Swish the drink gently in the glass.

- **2 oz (60 ml) Scotch whisky**
- **1 oz (30 ml) amaretto**

J.P. SPECIAL

2 oz (60 ml) bourbon
1/2 oz (15 ml) amaretto

Half fill an old-fashioned glass with ice cubes. Pour in the bourbon and amaretto and stir well.

FANCY SCOTCH

2 oz (60 ml) Scotch whisky
1/2 teaspoon Cointreau
1/2 teaspoon sugar
Dash of orange bitters
Twist of lime peel

Fill a shaker two-thirds full with ice. Add the whisky, Cointreau, sugar, and orange bitters. Shake well and strain into a chilled martini glass. Garnish with the lime.

BALMORAL

1 1/2 oz (45 ml) Scotch whisky
1/2 oz (15 ml) sweet vermouth
1/2 oz (15 ml) dry vermouth
Dash of orange bitters

Half fill a mixing glass with ice cubes. Add the whisky, sweet vermouth, dry vermouth and bitters and stir well. Strain into a chilled martini glass.

MOCKTAILS

CHOCOLATE PEANUT SHAKE

Place the peanut butter, chocolate syrup, and 2 oz (60 ml) of milk in a blender and blend until smooth. Add the rest of the milk and the ice cream and blend again until smooth and creamy. Pour into a chilled highball glass. Whip the cream and spoon over the top. Sprinkle with the chocolate.

- **2 oz (60 g) smooth peanut butter**
- **2 oz (60 ml) chocolate syrup**
- **1 cup (250 ml) milk**
- **2 scoops vanilla ice cream**
- **1/4 cup (60 ml) heavy (double) cream**
- **1–2 tablespoons grated milk chocolate, to garnish**

VIRGIN MARY

Fill a shaker two-thirds full with ice. Add all the ingredients and shake. Strain into a large chilled collins glass over 3–4 ice cubes. Garnish with a grind or two of black pepper.

- 8 oz (250 ml) tomato juice
- 1 oz (30 ml) freshly squeezed lime juice
- 2–3 dashes Tabasco
- 2–3 dashes Worcestershire sauce
- 1 teaspoon finely chopped fresh dill
- Freshly ground black pepper
- Celery salt

VIRGIN MARY • 1

5 oz (150 ml) clam-tomato juice
1/2 teaspoon Worcestershire sauce
2–3 drops Tabasco
1 teaspoon freshly squeezed lemon juice
Salt
Freshly ground black pepper
Slice of lime

Fill a shaker two-thirds full with ice. Add the clam-tomato juice, Worcestershire sauce, Tabasco, and lemon juice. Shake well and strain into an old-fashioned glass. Season with salt and pepper and garnish with the lime.

TJ TANG

4 oz (120 ml) chilled tomato juice
1 oz (30 ml) freshly squeezed lemon juice
1/2 cup (125 ml) crushed ice
2–3 drops Tabasco
Salt
Freshly ground black pepper

Place the tomato juice, lemon juice, and ice in a blender. Blend until just slushy. Season with Tabasco, salt, and pepper to taste.

TOMATO COOLER

5 oz (150 ml) tomato juice
1 oz (30 g) peeled cucumber
2 dashes Worcestershire sauce
1 teaspoon freshly squeezed lemon juice
Salt
Freshly ground black pepper
1/2 cup (125 ml) crushed ice
Slice of cucumber, to garnish

Place all the ingredients in a blender. Blend until just slushy. Pour into an old-fashioned glass, and garnish with the cucumber.

SHIRLEY TEMPLE

Fill a collins glass with ice and pour in the ginger ale and grenadine. Garnish with the lemon slice and cherry.

- 5 oz (150 ml) ginger ale
- 1/2 oz (15 ml) grenadine
- Lemon slice, to garnish
- Maraschino cherry, to garnish

SHIRLEY TEMPLE • 1

4 oz (120 ml) white soda, such as 7-Up or Sprite

2 oz (60 ml) freshly squeezed lemon or lime juice

4 drops grenadine

Wedge of orange

Fill a shaker two-thirds full with ice. Add the white soda, lemon juice, and grenadine. Shake well and strain into a chilled old-fashioned glass. Garnish with the orange.

EASY SHIRLEY TEMPLE

8 oz (250 ml) white soda, such as 7-Up or Sprite

1 oz (30 ml) grenadine

Wedge of orange

Half fill a collins glass with ice. Pour in the white soda and grenadine and stir gently. Garnish with the orange.

FRUIT LULLABY

1 1/2 oz (45 ml) coconut milk

1 oz (30 ml) light (single) cream

2 oz (60 ml) pineapple juice

1 oz (30 ml) banana syrup

1 small, ripe banana, sliced

1/2 cup (125 ml) crushed ice

Place the coconut milk, cream, pineapple juice, banana syrup, banana, and ice in a blender. Blend until just slushy. Pour into an old-fashioned glass.

LIME AID

Fill a shaker two-thirds full with ice. Add lime juice and sugar syrup. Shake well and strain into a collins glass over a 5–6 ice cubes. Top up with soda water. Garnish with the lime.

- **2 oz (60 ml) freshly squeezed lime juice**
- **2 oz (60 ml) sugar syrup**
- **6 oz (180 ml) soda water**
- **Lime wedge, to garnish**

■ ■ ■ *A variation on an old classic. It can also be made with lemon juice, although in that case you may want to add a tad more syrup. Children will love it served with a brightly colored straw.*

LIMEADE

3 oz (90 ml) freshly squeezed lime juice
1/2 oz (15 ml) sugar syrup
Soda water, to fill
Lime peel, to garnish

Half fill a collins glass with ice cubes. Add the lime juice and sugar and stir well. Top up with soda water and garnish with the lime.

APPLE COBBLER

3 oz (90 ml) apple juice
8 wedges lime
2 teaspoons brown sugar
1 cup (250 ml) crushed Ice

Place the lime wedges and sugar in a mixing glass and muddle well. Place the ice in an old-fashioned glass. Pour in the lime mixture and apple juice and stir well.

FRUIT COCKTAIL

1 oz (30 ml) freshly squeezed orange juice
1 oz (30 ml) freshly squeezed grapefruit juice
1 oz (30 ml) passion fruit juice
1 oz (30 ml) mango juice
1 oz (30 ml) pineapple juice
1/3 oz (10 ml) freshly squeezed lime juice
1/2 oz (15 ml) kiwi syrup

Fill a shaker two-thirds full with ice. Add all the ingredients and shake well. Strain into a wine goblet.

RASPBERRY SODA

Place the raspberries in a blender with 4 tablespoons of the ice cream and blend until smooth. Place the remaining ice cream in a soda glass or glass dessert cup. Pour the raspberry mixture over the top. Fill up with soda. Beat the cream until stiff and spoon over the top. Garnish with the whole raspberries.

- 1/2 cup fresh raspberries
- 2 scoops vanilla ice cream
- White soda, such as 7-Up or Sprite, chilled
- 2 oz (60 ml) heavy (double) cream
- 2–3 whole raspberries, to garnish

■ ■ ■ This falls somewhere between a drink and a dessert. Serve with a long-handled spoon and a brightly colored straw.

FRUIT SHAKE

Place the yogurt, banana, passion fruit pulp, and honey in a blender and blend until smooth. Place a few ice cubes in a large chilled wine glass. Pour in the drink. Garnish with the banana and mint, if liked.

- **4 oz (120 ml) plain yogurt**
- **1 small ripe banana**
- **Strained pulp of 2 passion fruit**
- **1 teaspoon liquid honey**
- **Banana slices, with skin, to garnish**
- **Fresh mint, to dust (optional)**

■ ■ ■ *There are endless variations on this deliciously healthy drink. This is our favorite, but you can vary the fruit to suit your taste or the season.*

CRANBERRY COOLER

Fill a shaker two-thirds full with ice. Add the cranberry juice, orange juice, and lime juice. Shake well and strain into a large collins glass over a few ice cubes. Top up with soda water and garnish with the orange.

- **4 oz (120 ml) cranberry juice**
- **1 oz (30 ml) freshly squeezed orange juice**
- **$1/2$ oz (15 ml) freshly squeezed lime juice**
- **Soda water. to fill**
- **Slice of orange, to garnish**

CRANBERRY BLOG

4 oz (120 ml) cranberry juice
2 oz (60 ml) freshly squeezed orange juice

Fill a shaker two-thirds full with ice. Add the cranberry juice and orange juice. Shake well and strain into a chilled martini glass.

FRIENDLY MONSTER

5 oz (150 ml) freshly squeezed orange juice
5 oz (150 ml) cranberry juice
$1/2$ cup (125 ml) crushed ice

Place the orange juice, cranberry juice, and ice in a blender. Blend until just slushy and pour into a hurricane glass.

FRUIT GINGER COOLER

2 oz (60 ml) cranberry juice
2 oz (60 ml) freshly squeezed orange juice
2 oz (60 ml) pineapple juice
2 oz (60 ml) ginger ale

Half fill a collins glass with ice cubes. Pour in the cranberry juice, orange juice, pineapple juice, and ginger ale and stir well.

641

VIRGIN COLADA

Fill a shaker two-thirds full with ice. Add the pineapple juice, cream of coconut, cream, and lime juice, and shake. Place the crushed ice in a large chilled wine goblet or hurricane glass and strain the cocktail over the top. Garnish with the pineapple.

- 4 oz (120 ml) pineapple juice
- 2 oz (60 ml) cream of coconut
- 1 oz (30 ml) heavy (double) cream
- 1 oz (30 ml) freshly squeezed lime juice
- 2 tablespoons crushed ice
- Wedge of freshly sliced pineapple, to garnish

VIRGIN. BANANA COLADA

6 oz (180 ml) pineapple juice
1¹/₂ oz (45 ml) cream of coconut
1 very ripe banana
1 cup (250 ml) crushed ice
Fresh fruit, to garnish (optional)

Place the pineapple juice, cream of coconut, and banana in a blender. Blend for a few seconds until just slushy. Pour into a hurricane glass over 2–3 ice cubes. Garnish with fresh fruit, if liked.

VIRGIN PIÑA COLADA

6 oz (180 ml) pineapple juice
2 oz (60 ml) cream of coconut
¹/₂ cup (125 ml) crushed ice

Place the pineapple juice and cream of coconut, and banana in a blender. Blend for a few seconds until just slushy. Pour into a hurricane glass.

FRUIT MILK SHAKE

4 oz (120 ml) freshly squeezed orange juice
4 oz (120 ml) freshly squeezed grapefruit juice
4 oz (120 ml) milk
¹/₂ oz (15 g) sugar
2 drops vanilla extract (essence)
¹/₂ cup (125 ml) crushed ice

Place the orange juice, grapefruit juice, milk, sugar, vanilla, and ice in a blender. Blend for a few seconds until just slushy. Pour into a hurricane glass.

STRAWBERRY COLADA

Place the strawberries in a blender and blend until smooth. Fill a shaker two-thirds full with ice. Add the strawberries, cream of coconut, pineapple juice, and yogurt and shake well. Place the crushed ice in a large chilled wine goblet or hurricane glass and pour the cocktail over the top. Garnish with the strawberry.

- 3 oz (90 g) fresh strawberries, cleaned
- 3 oz (90 ml) cream of coconut
- 3 oz (90 ml) pineapple juice
- 2 tablespoons thick creamy plain yogurt (Greek yogurt)
- 1/4 cup (60 ml) crushed ice
- Fresh strawberry, with green stalk intact, to garnish

■ ■ ■ *Make a raspberry or blackberry colada by replacing the strawberries with the same amount of raspberries or blackberries.*

VIRGIN MANHATTAN

Fill a shaker two-thirds full with ice. Add the cranberry juice, orange juice, cherry juice, lemon juice, and bitters and shake well. Strain into a chilled old-fashioned glass over 2–3 ice cubes. Garnish with the cherry.

- **2 oz (60 ml) cranberry juice**
- **2 oz (60 ml) freshly squeezed orange juice**
- **1 teaspoon cherry juice**
- **1 teaspoon freshly squeezed lemon juice**
- **2 dashes orange bitters**
- **Maraschino cherry, to garnish**

VIRGIN ON THE BEACH

4 oz (120 ml) freshly squeezed orange juice
4 oz (120 ml) cranberry juice
1 oz (30 ml) peach juice
1 tablespoon grenadine

Half fill a collins glass with ice cubes. Add the orange juice, cranberry juice, and peach juice and stir well. Splash in the grenadine.

V. SEX ON THE BEACH

2 oz (60 ml) peach juice
1 oz (30 ml) mango juice
4 oz (120 ml) dry ginger ale
Wedges of pineapple, to garnish

Fill a hurricane glass with ice cubes. Pour in the peach juice and mango juice and stir well. Top up with ginger ale. Garnish with the pineapple.

ICE CREAM COCKTAIL

2 oz (60 ml) freshly squeezed orange juice
1 scoop vanilla ice cream

Fill a shaker two-thirds full with ice. Add the orange juice and ice cream and shake well. Strain into a hurricane glass.

VIRGIN RASPBERRY DAIQUIRI

Fill a shaker two-thirds full with ice. Add the raspberry purée, pineapple juice, lemon juice, sugar syrup, and raspberry syrup and shake well. Place the crushed ice in a chilled wine goblet and strain the cocktail into on top. Garnish with the raspberries, if liked

- 4 oz (120 ml) raspberry purée
- 2 oz (60 ml) pineapple juice
- 1 oz (30 ml) freshly squeezed lemon juice
- 1 teaspoon sugar syrup
- 1 oz (30 ml) raspberry syrup
- 1/2 cup (125 ml) crushed ice
- Fresh raspberries, to garnish (optional)

FRUITLOOPS

3 oz (90 ml) pineapple juice
1 1/2 oz (45 ml) freshly squeezed orange juice
1 oz (30 ml) cranberry juice
Splash of grenadine
Slice of orange, to garnish

Half fill a collins glass with ice. Add the pineapple juice, orange juice, cranberry juice, and grenadine and stir well. Garnish with the orange.

CRANBERRY SODA

4 oz (120 ml) cranberry juice
2 oz (60 ml) pineapple juice
1/2 oz (15 ml) freshly squeezed lemon juice
2 oz (60 ml) soda water
Wedge of lime, to garnish

Fill a shaker two-thirds full with ice. Add the cranberry juice, pineapple juice, and lemon juice. Shake well and strain into a highball glass over ice cubes. Garnish with the lime.

FRUIT CREAM

8 oz (250 ml) peach juice
2 scoops vanilla ice cream
1/2 sliced peach
3 oz (90 g) blackberries
3–4 fresh raspberries

Place the peach juice, ice cream, peach, and blackberries in a blender. Blend for a few seconds until smooth. Pour into a hurricane glass and garnish with raspberries.

APRÈS TENNIS

Half fill a chilled collins glass with ice cubes and pour in the orange juice. Top up with the ginger ale. Garnish with the lemon slice.

- **3 oz (90 ml) freshly squeezed orange juice**
- **6 oz (180 ml) ginger ale**
- **Slice of lemon, to garnish**

CLEAN COCKTAIL

$1/2$ oz (15 ml) freshly squeezed orange juice

$1/2$ oz (15 ml) freshly squeezed lemon juice

1 teaspoon sugar syrup

2 oz (60 ml) light (single) cream

Fill a shaker two-thirds full with ice. Add the orange juice, lemon juice, sugar syrup, and cream. Shake well and strain into a chilled martini glass.

SODA COOLER

2 oz (60 ml) lemon soda

2 oz (60 ml) orange soda

2 oz (60 ml) soda water

$1/2$ oz (15 ml) freshly squeezed lemon juice

Half fill a collins glass with ice cubes. Add the lemon soda, orange soda, soda water, and lemon juice. Stir well.

VIRGIN ORANGE

2 oz (60 ml) freshly squeezed orange juice

1 oz (30 ml) freshly squeezed lime juice

1 oz (30 ml) grenadine

Fill a shaker two-thirds full with ice. Add the orange juice, lime juice, and grenadine. Shake well and strain into a chilled wine glass.

CINDERELLA

Fill a shaker two-thirds full with ice. Add the orange juice, pineapple juice, sweet-and-sour mix, and grenadine. Shake well and strain into a collins glass. Garnish with the apple.

- **2 oz (60 ml) freshly squeezed orange juice**
- **2 oz (60 ml) pineapple juice**
- **Splash of sweet-and-sour mix**
- **2 dashes grenadine**
- **Soda water**
- **Slice of green apple, to garnish**

YELLOW COOLER

2 oz (60 ml) pineapple juice
2 oz (60 ml) freshly squeezed orange juice
1^1/$_2$ oz (45 ml) freshly squeezed lemon juice

Fill a shaker two-thirds full with ice. Add the pineapple juice, orange juice, and lemon juice. Shake well and strain into an old-fashioned glass over 4–6 ice cubes.

LEMON SQUASH

4 oz (120 ml) freshly squeezed lemon juice
3 teaspoons sugar syrup
Tonic water, to fill

Fill a shaker two-thirds full with ice. Add the lemon juice and sugar syrup. Shake well and strain into a collins glass over 4–6 ice cubes. Top up with tonic water.

LEMON DAISY

1 oz (30 ml) freshly squeezed lemon juice
^{1}/$_2$ oz (15 ml) grenadine
^{1}/$_2$ oz (15 ml) sugar syrup
White soda, such as 7-Up or Sprite, to fill

Half fill a wine glass with ice cubes. Add the lemon juice, grenadine, and sugar syrup and stir well. Top up with white soda.

ORANGE SMOOTHIE

Place milk, orange juice, ice cream, and honey in a blender and blend until smooth. Pour into a highball glass. Garnish with nutmeg.

- **4 oz (120 ml) cold milk**
- **4 oz (120 ml) freshly squeezed orange juice**
- **2 scoops vanilla ice cream**
- **1 tablespoon honey**
- **Grated nutmeg, to garnish**

654

MANGO SLUSHY

3 oz (90 g) fresh mango, cleaned and cubed
3 oz (90 ml) freshly squeezed orange juice
1 tablespoon honey
1/2 cup (125 ml) crushed ice

Place the mango, orange juice, honey, and ice in a blender and blend until smooth. Pour into a hurricane glass.

ORANGE MILK SLUSHY

6 oz (180 ml) frozen orange juice
6 oz (180 ml) cold milk
4 oz (120 ml) iced water
1 tablespoon sugar
1/2 teaspoon vanilla extract (essence)

Place the orange juice, milk, water, sugar, and vanilla in a blender and blend until smooth. Pour into a collins glass.

PAPAYA SMOOTHIE

4 oz (120 g) fresh papaya, cleaned and cubed
4 oz (120 ml) cold milk
2 tablespoons sugar
1/2 cup (125 ml) crushed ice

Place the papaya, milk, sugar, and ice in a blender and blend until just slushy. Pour into a collins glass.

STRAWBERRY YOGURT SMOOTHIE

Place strawberries, yogurt, milk, and honey in a blender and blend until smooth. Pour into a highball glass. Garnish with lemon or strawberry, as liked.

- **1/2 cup sliced fresh strawberries**
- **1 tablespoon honey**
- **3 oz (90 ml) lemon yogurt**
- **2 oz (60 ml) milk**
- **Slice of lemon and/or strawberry, to garnish**

STRAWBERRY SMOOTHIE

10 frozen strawberries
8 oz (250 ml) iced water
4 oz (120 ml) cold soy milk
1 tablespoon sugar

Place the strawberries, water, soy milk, and sugar in a blender and blend until smooth. Pour into a hurricane glass.

FRUIT SODA

2 oz (60 ml) strawberry purée
1 oz (30 ml) apple juice
1 oz (30 ml) papaya juice
1 oz (30 ml) pineapple juice
2 oz (60 ml) soda water

Fill a shaker two-thirds full with ice. Add the strawberry purée, apple juice, papaya juice, and pineapple. Shake well and strain into an old-fashioned glass almost full of crushed ice. Pour in the soda water and stir well.

STRAWBERRY SPLIT

2 oz (60 ml) strawberry purée
1 oz (30 ml) apple juice
1 oz (30 ml) pineapple juice
1/2 oz (15 ml) freshly squeezed lime juice
1/3 oz (10 ml) strawberry syrup
1/2 cup (125 ml) crushed ice
2 oz (60 ml) lemonade

Place the strawberry purée, apple juice, pineapple juice, lime juice, strawberry syrup, and ice in a blender and blend until smooth. Pour into a hurricane glass and top up with the lemonade.

CHOCOLATE BANANA SMOOTHIE

Place the banana, ice cream, milk, and ice in a blender and blend until smooth. Pour into a highball or collins glass and drizzle with the chocolate syrup.

- 1 ripe banana
- 1 scoop chocolate ice cream
- 4 oz (120 ml) cold milk
- $1/2$ cup (125 ml) crushed ice
- 1 tablespoon chocolate syrup

RICH CHOCO SHAKE

2 scoops vanilla ice cream
5 oz (150 ml) cold milk
1 oz (30 ml) chocolate syrup

Place the ice cream, milk, and chocolate syrup in a blender and blend until smooth. Pour into a hurricane glass.

SUNDAE SHAKE

5 oz (150 ml) cold skim milk
1 ripe banana
1 teaspoon sugar
2 tablespoons unsweetened cocoa powder
Maraschino cherry, to garnish

Place the milk, banana, sugar, and cocoa powder in a blender and blend until smooth. Pour into a hurricane glass and garnish with the cherry.

CINNAMON CHOCOLATE

16 oz (500 ml) milk
4 oz (120 g) bittersweet (dark) chocolate
$1/2$ teaspoon cinnamon

Stir the chocolate, milk, and cinnamon in a double boiler over barely simmering water until melted. Pour into 2 heatproof glass mugs.

SPICED APPLE SMOOTHIE

Wash the apple. Peel and core and chop into cubes. Place the apple, milk, ice cream, cinnamon, allspice, and ice in a blender and blend until smooth. Pour into a highball glass and, if liked, garnish with the zucchini

- 1 small tart-tasting apple (Granny Smith)
- 4 oz (120 ml) cold milk
- 2 scoops vanilla ice cream
- $1/2$ teaspoon ground cinnamon
- $1/8$ teaspoon allspice
- $1/4$ cup (60 ml) crushed ice
- Julienne slice of sweet young zucchini, to garnish (optional)

GRAPE SMOOTHIE

1 cup seedless white grapes
1 lemon, peeled and chopped
1 cup pineapple pieces

Place the grapes, lemon, and pineapple in a blender and blend until smooth. Pour into a collins glass half filled with crushed ice. Stir well.

TERRY'S COCKTAIL

2 oz (60 ml) light (single) cream
1 oz (30 ml) pineapple juice
$1/2$ oz (15 ml) grenadine
$1/2$ oz (15 ml) freshly squeezed orange juice

Fill a shaker two-thirds full with ice. Add the cream, pineapple, grenadine, and orange juice. Shake well and strain into a wine goblet.

FRUIT FRISBEE

1 cup (250 ml) plain or fruit yogurt
1 cup mixed fresh fruit, chopped

Place the yogurt and fruit in a blender and blend until smooth. Pour into a collins glass over 2–3 ice cubes.

BLACK AND WHITE COW

Place the ice cream in an old-fashioned glass soda dish and slowly pour the root beer over the top. It will foam as you pour, so go slowly. Top with whipped cream and serve with a long-handled soda spoon.

- **1 scoop chocolate ice cream**
- **1 scoop vanilla ice cream**
- **Root beer**
- **Whipped cream**

■ ■ ■ *This is a variation on the classic Black Cow made with vanilla ice cream.*

BLACK COW

2 scoops vanilla ice-cream
8 oz (250 ml) cold root beer
1 tablespoon chocolate syrup
Whipped cream
Maraschino cherry, to garnish

Place the ice cream in a glass soda dish. Slowly pour the root beer over the top. Finish with the chocolate syrup. Top with whipped cream and the cherry.

COLA SODA

12 oz (350 ml) cola, such as Pepsi or Coca-Cola
3 scoops vanilla ice cream

Place the ice cream in a soda glass and slowly pour the cola over the top.

CHOCOLATE BROWNIE

8 oz (250 ml) cold milk
2 scoops ice cream
1 chocolate fudge brownie
Whipped cream
Grated chocolate

Place the milk, ice cream, and brownie in a blender and blend until smooth. Pour into a collins glass and top with the cream and chocolate.

PONY'S NECK

Use a sharp knife to carefully peel the lemon or orange so that you get a long, unbroken spiral of zest (colored outer layer only). Place the zest in a chilled collins glass, with the end hanging over the edge of the glass. Add the ice cubes and lime juice and top up with ginger ale.

- **1 lemon or orange**
- **1 tablespoon freshly squeezed lime juice**
- **5–6 ice cubes**
- **Ginger ale, to fill**

PELICAN

4 oz (120 ml) freshly squeezed grapefruit juice
1/2 oz (15 ml) lime cordial
Dash of grenadine
Dash of freshly squeezed lemon juice

Fill a shaker two-thirds full with ice. Add the grapefruit juice, lime cordial, grenadine, and lemon juice. Shake well and strain into an old-fashioned glass over 2–3 ice cubes.

RASPBERRY ROSE

1 oz (30 ml) pineapple juice
2 teaspoons raspberry syrup
2 oz (60 ml) light (single) cream

Fill a shaker two-thirds full with ice. Add the pineapple juice, raspberry syrup, and cream. Shake well and strain into a chilled martini glass.

BORA BORA

4 oz (120 ml) pineapple juice
2 oz (60 ml) passion fruit juice
1/3 oz (10 ml) freshly squeezed lemon juice
1/3 oz (10 ml) grenadine

Fill a shaker two-thirds full with ice. Add the pineapple juice, passion fruit juice, lemon juice, and grenadine. Shake well and strain into an old-fashioned glass half-filled with ice cubes.

TRANSFUSION

Half fill a chilled highball glass with ice cubes. Pour in the grape juice and lime juice. Top up with the ginger ale and garnish with the lime.

- **4 oz (120 ml) grape juice**
- **$1/2$ oz (15 ml) freshly squeezed lime juice**
- **Ginger ale, to fill**
- **Slice of lime, to garnish**

VIRGIN PUNCH CUP

1 oz (30 ml) raspberry syrup
1 oz (30 ml) cherry juice
1 oz (30 ml) freshly squeezed orange juice
1 oz (30 ml) freshly squeezed lemon juice
1 oz (30 ml) pineapple juice
1 oz (30 ml) grape juice
2 oz (60 ml) white soda, such as 7-Up or Sprite

Fill a shaker two-thirds full with ice. Add all the ingredients except the white soda. Shake well and strain into a highball glass half-filled with ice cubes. Top up with soda.

ORANGE TONIC

4 oz (120 ml) freshly squeezed orange juice
4 oz (120 ml) tonic water

Half fill a collins glass with orange juice. Top up with tonic water.

GRAPEAPPLE COLLINS

2 oz (60 ml) grape juice
1 oz (30 ml) apple juice
1 oz (30 ml) grenadine
1 oz (30 ml) freshly squeezed lemon juice
1 teaspoon sugar syrup

Half fill a collins glass with ice cubes. Pour in the grape juice, apple juice, grenadine, lemon juice, and sugar syrup and stir well.

FRUIT SMOOTHIE

Place the mixed fruit, banana, orange juice, and ice in a blender. Blend for a few seconds until just slushy. Pour into two chilled hurricane glasses.

- **1 cup mixed fresh fruit (peaches, apricots, strawberries, pineapple, passion fruit, mango, or whatever you have on hand)**
- **1 ripe banana**
- **5 oz (150 ml) freshly squeezed orange juice**
- **1 cup (250 ml) crushed ice**

668

BANANA GRAPE SMOOTHIE

1 large ripe banana
4 oz (120 g) red seedless grapes
2 oz (60 ml) cold milk
1/2 cup (120 ml) crushed ice

Place the banana, grapes, milk, and ice in a blender and blend until just slushy. Pour into 2 hurricane glasses.

FRUIT DAYDREAM

1 large ripe banana
8 strawberries
1 sliced peach
3 oz (90 ml) apple juice
3 oz (90 ml) freshly squeezed orange juice
1 scoop vanilla ice cream

Place the banana, strawberries, peach, apple juice, orange juice, and ice cream in a blender and blend until smooth. Pour into 2 hurricane glasses.

JUNGLE JUICE

1 sliced banana
12 oz (350 ml) freshly squeezed orange juice
Dash of ground ginger

Place the banana, orange juice, and ginger in a blender and blend until smooth. Pour into a collins glass half filled with ice.

CARDAMOM ICED COFFEE

Place the espresso, sweetened condensed milk, boiling water, and cardamom in a small bowl and mix well. Let cool. Serve over ice in an old-fashioned glass or small glass mug.

- 2 oz (60 ml) espresso coffee
- 1 tablespoon sweetened condensed milk
- 1 oz (30 ml) boiling water
- Dash of cardamom

THAI COFFEE

6 teaspoons fine ground whole, rich coffee
1/4 teaspoon ground coriander
5 whole green cardamom pods, ground
2 teaspoons sugar
Whipped cream

Place the coffee and spices in the filter cone of a coffee maker. Brew the coffee as usual and let it cool. In a collins glass, dissolve the sugar in 1 oz (30 ml) of the coffee. Add 5-6 ice cubes and top up with coffee. Top with whipped cream.

ICED THAI COFFEE

8 oz (250 ml) strong black coffee
1–2 teaspoons sugar
Whipped cream
Cardamom pods

Prepare the coffee and sweeten with the sugar. Let cool completely. Place in a collins glass half full with ice. Top with the whipped cream and cardamom.

SPIKED COFFEE

8 oz (250 ml) strong black coffee
Pinch of ground cinnamon

Serve the hot coffee in a mug with a pinch of cinnamon.

CHOCOLATE ALMOND COFFEE

Divide the chocolate between two heatproof glasses. Pour in the hot coffee and stir until the chocolate has almost melted. Add the almond extract and the hot milk. Stir well. Top with whipped cream and chocolate.

- 2 oz (60 g) semisweet (dark) chocolate, finely chopped
- 8 oz (250 ml) hot coffee
- 1/2 teaspoon almond extract
- 4 oz (120 ml) hot milk
- Whipped cream
- Chocolate shavings

ALMOND COFFEE

5 oz (150 ml) hot milk
2 oz (60 ml) hot espresso coffee
1/2 teaspoon almond extract
Whipped cream
Coffee beans

Pour the milk into a heatproof glass mug. Pour in the coffee and almond extract and stir gently. Top with whipped cream and coffee beans.

HOT CHOCOLATE

5 oz (150 g) semisweet (dark) chocolate
12 oz (350 ml) milk
Whipped cream (optional)

Place the chocolate and milk in a double boiler over barely simmering water. Stir until the chocolate is melted. Pour into 2 heatproof glass mugs. Top with whipped cream, if liked.

VIENNA COFFEE

6 oz (180 ml) hot, strong black coffee
Whipped cream
Chocolate shavings

Pour the coffee into a heatproof glass mug. Top with cream and chocolate.

SPICY SANGRITA

Place orange juice, tomato juice, lime juice, and grenadine in a large glass pitcher (jug) half filled with ice. Season with Tabasco, salt, and pepper to taste and stir gently. Pour into collins glasses.

- **24 oz (750 ml) freshly squeezed orange juice**
- **4 oz (120 ml) tomato juice**
- **3 oz (90 ml) freshly squeezed lime juice**
- **1/2 oz (15 ml) grenadine**
- **Tabasco**
- **Salt**
- **Freshly ground black pepper**

TOMATO LASSI

2 oz (60 ml) plain yogurt
2 oz (60 ml) tomato juice
4 oz (120 ml) iced water
Celery salt

Place the yogurt, tomato juice, water, and salt in a blender. Blend for a few seconds until smooth. Pour into a collins glass half filled with ice cubes. Season with celery salt to taste and stir gently.

MANGO LASSI

4 oz (120 ml) plain yogurt
4 oz (120 g) mango, peeled and cubed
1 teaspoon sugar
8 oz (250 ml) iced water

Place the yogurt, mango, water, and sugar in a blender. Blend for a few seconds until smooth. Pour into a collins glass half filled with ice cubes.

SWEET LASSI

8 oz (250 ml) yogurt
4 oz (120 ml) iced water
1 oz (30 ml) freshly squeezed lemon juice
1–2 tablespoons sugar

Place the yogurt, water, lemon juice, and sugar in a blender. Blend for a few seconds until smooth. Pour into a collins glass half filled with ice cubes.

BLACKCURRANT COOLER

Bring the blackcurrant juice, orange juice, ginger, cinnamon stick, and sugar to a gentle boil stirring all the time until the sugar dissolves. Simmer for 2 minutes then remove from the heat and let cool. Transfer to a punch bowl or large pitcher (jug) and chill in the refrigerator for at least 2 hours. Prepare the garnish by lightly beating the egg white. Dip the blackcurrants in the egg white, letting the excess drain off. Roll in the sugar and place on a plate. Just before serving, add the ice cubes and soda water to taste. Pour into glasses and garnish each one with 3–4 frosted blackcurrants (suspend them over the drink on a toothpick).

- 16 oz (500 ml) blackcurrant juice
- 16 oz (500 ml) freshly squeezed orange juice
- $1/2$ teaspoon finely grated ginger
- 1 cinnamon stick
- 2 tablespoons sugar
- Soda water, well chilled, to fill
- 1 cup (250 ml) ice cubes
- About 20 fresh blackcurrants, to garnish
- 1 egg white, to garnish
- Sugar, to garnish

CARROT AND CILANTRO COOLER

Fill an old-fashioned glass three-quarters full with cracked ice cubes. Pour in the carrot juice, orange juice, and lemon or lime juice. Add the cilantro and stir well. Twist the orange peel over the drink to release the fragrant oils then drop it into the drink.

- **4 oz (120 ml) freshly made carrot juice**
- **4 oz (120 ml) freshly squeezed orange juice**
- **1 oz (30 ml) freshly squeezed lemon or lime juice**
- **Fresh cilantro (coriander), chopped**
- **Orange peel**

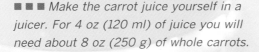

■ ■ ■ *Make the carrot juice yourself in a juicer. For 4 oz (120 ml) of juice you will need about 8 oz (250 g) of whole carrots.*

CHOCOLATE MINT DELIGHT

Place the milk, chocolate syrup, and ice cream in a blender. Blend for a few seconds until smooth. Pour into a chilled wine goblet. Dust with cocoa powder and garnish with 2–3 mint sticks.

- 5 oz (150 ml) cold milk
- 1$\frac{1}{2}$ oz (45 ml) chocolate syrup
- 1 scoop mint ice cream
- Unsweetened cocoa powder, to dust
- Chocolate mint sticks, to garnish

ORANGE MILK CRUSH

8 oz (250 ml) cold milk
8 oz (250 ml) freshly squeezed orange juice
1 cup (250 ml) crushed ice
2 teaspoons sugar

Put the milk, orange juice, and ice in a blender. Blend for a few seconds until just slushy. Pour into 2 collins glasses.

MINTY MILK CRUSH

16 oz (500 ml) cold milk
1 oz (30 ml) chocolate syrup
$\frac{1}{2}$ teaspoon mint syrup
1 cup (250 ml) crushed ice

Place the milk, chocolate syrup, mint syrup, and ice in a blender. Blend for a few seconds until just slushy. Pour into 2 collins glasses.

PINK MILK SLUSH

2–3 teaspoons grenadine
16 oz (500 ml) cold milk
1 cup (250 ml) crushed ice

Place the grenadine, milk, and ice in a blender. Blend for a few seconds until just slushy. Pour into 2 collins glasses.

INDEX

691